"Wise and subtle. *Going Sane* has some superbly suggestive things to say about childhood, depression, autism, and schizophrenia." —*Irish Times*

"Well-argued and stunningly thought-provoking. Phillips has tackled a 'big idea' in a sophisticated yet spirited way." —*Library Journal*

"Probing. . . . Challenges the reader to reconsider the taken-for-granted notion that sanity is just another word for mental health."
—*Kirkus Reviews*

"Phillips radiates infectious charm. The brew of gaiety, compassion, exuberance, and idealism is heady and disarming." —Roy Porter

"Phillips offers a detailed description of what sanity can mean today."
—*Los Angeles Times*

"In classic psychoanalytic style, Phillips strips our lives down to the fundamentals to illustrate the delicate balance between sanity and insanity. His arguments, both thought-provoking and provocative, may affect future definitions of sanity and madness." —*Publishers Weekly*

"Erudite and absorbing, oozes intelligence—and charm. [Phillips is] adept at making the complex comprehensible." —*The Independent* (UK)

"[Phillips] is the closest thing we have to a philosopher of happiness."
—*The Observer* (UK)

"Challenging and inspiring. . . . *Going Sane* is an indispensable guide to what wisdom means today."
—John Gray, professor of political thought
at the London School of Economics

"Beautifully written . . . clever and funny, and properly profound. . . . A lovely addition to Phillips's guides to living a happier life." —*GQ*

"Adam Phillips has written an extraordinarily generous and subtle book . . . beautiful, unfussily important, and emotionally brilliant."
—Jorie Graham, Pulitzer Prize–winning author
of *The Dream of the Unified Field*

© Toby Glanville

About the Author

ADAM PHILLIPS is a psychoanalyst and the author of eleven previous books, including *Going Sane*; *On Kissing, Tickling, and Being Bored*; *On Flirtation*; *Darwin's Worms*; and *Houdini's Box*. He writes regularly for the *New York Times*, the *London Review of Books*, and *The Observer*, and he is general editor of the new Penguin Modern Classics translations of Freud. He lives in London.

Side Effects

ADAM PHILLIPS

HARPER PERENNIAL

NEW YORK • LONDON • TORONTO • SYDNEY

For Alex Coren and Peter Wilson

HARPER ● PERENNIAL

First published in Great Britain in 2006 by Hamish Hamilton, an imprint of Penguin Books.

FIRST U.S. EDITION

Library of Congress Cataloging-in-Publication Data
Phillips, Adam.
          Side effects / Adam Phillips.
               p. cm.
          Originally published: London : Hamish Hamilton, 2006.
          ISBN: 978-0-00-715538-5
          ISBN-10: 0-00-715538-7
          1. Psychoanalysis and literature. I. Title.
     PN56.P92 P52 2007
     801/.92 22   2006051917

07 08 09 10 11 RRD 10 9 8 7 6 5 4 3 2 1

Act so that there is no use in a centre.

Gertrude Stein, *Tender Buttons*

Like us, Achilles has many values, which don't all fit together tidily. Under the influence of powerful feelings based on some of what he cares about, he forgets that he cares about other things too. Like us, he has much to be true to, which means that he is sometimes false to his very greatest loves. This would be a flaw, I suppose, if there were a better alternative . . .

C. D. C. Reeve, *Love's Confusions*

Of course, it is impossible to generalize about people whose main characteristic was their eccentricity.

Boyd Hilton, *A Mad, Bad and Dangerous People?*

Contents

Preface

'Even as a grown-up,' his biographer John Haffenden tells us, the writer William Empson 'would not forget the secrets of a happy childhood: one day, for instance, to the great glee of a friend's son, he stood on his hands and said the boy could have anything that fell out of his pockets.' Psychoanalysis can also be a way of not forgetting the secrets of a happy childhood. Indeed the game Empson played is more often than not what happens in a psychoanalysis; the so-called patient does the difficult thing – talks of the things that trouble him – and the so-called psychoanalyst takes the fallout. Both the patient and the analyst are the recipients of these side effects, of all the things said and implied and unintended and alluded to as the patient speaks as freely as he is able, and begins to understand the ingenuities of the censorship he imposes on himself. Free association, what is said by the way, what is said as aside from the matter in hand, what is said 'off topic', is where the action of meaning and feeling is. In this picture digression is secular revelation, keeping to the subject is the best way we have of keeping off the subject; of speaking up without speaking out. 'Obscurity in a writer,' Empson once wrote, 'may be due not to concentration, but to a refusal to speak out.' Psychoanalysis, essentially, is an attempt to redescribe the whole notion of concentration.

Psychoanalysis as a form of therapy works by attending to the patient's side effects, what falls out of his pockets once he starts speaking. It is customary that before new drugs are put on the market they are tested for their side effects. If someone were to invent a drug – say, in this context, a psychotropic drug, one that is designed to improve people's mental health – and to say that the point of this drug, the whole value of it, was its unpredictable side effects, there would be a public outcry. It would be the ultimate in potentially pernicious irresponsibility. We would wonder about the motives of the drug designers, and anyone who sponsored them; and indeed about the rationality of anyone tempted to take such a drug. Unexpected side effects are not what 'we' want; we prefer things (and people) that do only what they say they are going to do, because then, at least so the argument goes, we can decide whether we want them. It is not surprising then that people become unusually exercised by discrediting psychoanalysis, because this drug I am describing is akin to psychoanalysis. Undergoing psychoanalytic treatment, entering into what the French psychoanalyst Lacan called 'the psychoanalytic opportunity', is, rather like reading a powerful work of literature, a leap into the relative dark. No one can ever know beforehand the effect it will, or indeed won't, have (reading Goethe – perhaps unsurprisingly despite George Steiner's famous astonishment – didn't make the Nazis kinder). The only difference, though one worth remarking on, between psychoanalysis and the arts on the one hand, and this enigmatic drug designed for its side effects on the other hand, is that psychoanalysis and the arts are not drugs. They are, however, both risky and addictive. The owners of psychoanalysis, partly under the pressure of the market, have traditionally been unforthcoming about the risks involved. At its best it is not a treatment for those who prefer their calculations rational, or their investments – emotional and financial – guaranteed. As with reading or talking or listening or looking, the effects of psychoanalysis cannot be known in advance. We can only jump, but we can't jump to conclusions. All we can do – as the essays in this book try to suggest – is see where the side effects take us.

In much modern writing it is the things said in passing, when the writer takes his eye off the point he is trying to make, that are most striking. Concentration, argument, persuasion, deduction can convince us, but being convinced is not only or always the thing we most want to be; changing how people feel is rarely just a matter of amassing evidence. In fact, in many areas of modern people's lives what changes people, what makes a difference to them that matters, cannot be calculated in advance. And more often than we notice, perhaps more often than we can afford to notice, the things that change us are surprising. They are often side effects, things that happen inadvertently (what is traumatic about the official trauma is often eccentric). What the writer writes while he is writing something else, what the patient happens to say when he is saying what he wants to say, what we dream when we are wanting to sleep, how we fail when we are determined to succeed; this is what psychoanalysis, and not of course only psychoanalysis, wants us to attend to. The literary essay as a form – at least from the early nineteenth century onwards – has not only allowed for the artfulness, the interest of digression, but has also positively encouraged it. The essays of Lamb or Hazlitt or Emerson create the conditions, not unlike a psychoanalytic session, for concentrations and me-anderings, for changes of tone and changes of heart over a very short space of time.

For the contemporary writer who finds psychoanalysis illuminating but would betray her own sense of things by believing in it, psychoanalysis can serve as a useful 'regulative fiction', in Nietzsche's phrase; a secular equivalent, if there can be such a thing, of the non-Catholic Christianity of Lamb, Hazlitt and Emerson, in whose writings you can never be quite sure what, if anything, they are trying to convert themselves and their readers to. And yet one is left with an unmistakable sense of the strength of their opinions. They are like dogmatists, but their dogma is a work in progress and can never be formulated like conventional religion or morality. Their enthusiasm for digression, for telling all sorts of stories and non-stories, for telling almost whatever occurs to them while they are writing, tempers their fanaticism. It is as though in their writing, whatever the topic, they want to be distracted, they want to be waylaid. The essays in this book do this where they can. Concentration, as Empson suggested, is the willingness not to speak out.

The anxiety of psychoanalysis about its own status today is reflected in its eagerness to entomb itself in definitives – *the* Standard Edition of Freud's works, *the* Institute of Psychoanalysis, *The Interpretation of Dreams*, and so on; and in its desire for purifications, its desire to define itself by endlessly declaring what it is not – not suggestion, not teaching, not medicine, not anti-science, not a betrayal of Freud, not racist, not homophobic, and so on. In actuality psychoanalysis is everything that is said about it, and not merely the preserve of its critics and devotees. It is only ever going to be as useful as anybody finds it to be. And any individual, or indeed any culture, that wholeheartedly endorsed it – that treated it as a myth rather than a fiction, as a religion rather than a set of tools, as a consolation rather than an affront – would not really have recognized what it was. Psychoanalysis asks us to reconsider the unacceptable, in ourselves and in others; in our personal and cultural histories, in our desires and thoughts and feelings and beliefs. And at the same time it asks us to wonder why we should want to do this; whether it can get us the lives we would rather live. And it has to acknowledge that asking oneself such questions – which can be done only in conversation with others – is not, and never has been, high on most people's list of pleasures. And there could be no self-evident reason why it should be. As a form of moral enquiry psychoanalysis asks what, if any, alternatives there are to scapegoating; and what our lives would be like if there were.

Now that psychoanalysis has really and truly got over its honeymoon period – its belief in itself as a universal panacea, and the more recent, rather more modest, belief that it could reinvigorate a few flagging university disciplines – it can begin to see its very real limitations; and, by the same token, it can begin to enjoy its advantages (its pleasure in people's complexity, its relish of sexuality and amusement, its commitment to the straddling rather than the resolution of conflict, to coexistence rather than consensus; its fascination with reality rather than with magic, and with language rather than visuals, and so on). Hopefully, in the future people will say that just as some people have an ear for music, or a talent for juggling, so some people have an ear for psychoanalysis both as a therapy and as a kind of folk wisdom, a speaking-and-listening talent. It may then be able to be the only thing that it has ever really been able to be, even by its own lights: a pleasure worth having rather than the terrible and absurd institutionalized seriousness it has become. If these writings are, perhaps inevitably, caught in this crossfire, between the earnest and the intrigued, they are at least trying to get to the other side.

The Master-Mind Lectures[*]

There are many things the good life is not. But no one thing
it is bound to be.

John Gray, *Two Faces of Liberalism*

There is a nasty, perhaps Freudian, moment in Ford Madox
Ford's novel of 1924, *Some Do Not*, in which something suddenly occurs to the hero, Tietjens, in the middle of a conversation: 'Suddenly he thought that he didn't know for certain
that he was the father of his child, and he groaned . . .' Tietjens,
Ford continues, 'proved his reputation for sanity' by carrying
on the conversation he is ostensively having, but without
reference to his daunting thought. As though sanity for this
Englishman is about being apparently undisturbed by one's
most disturbing thoughts. It is exactly and exactingly about
what one is able not to say. Keeping to the topic, keeping the
conversation going is the kind of sanity for which one could
have a reputation. 'But it gave him a nasty turn,' Ford writes:
'He hadn't been able to pigeon-hole and padlock his disagreeable reflections. He had been as good as talking to himself.'

This is perhaps a Freudian moment not because Ford was
in any sense a Freudian – whatever that is; and, as we shall
see, that is something that Freud himself made it impossible

[*] This was originally a lecture on Freud given in the Master-Mind series at the
British Academy.

for anyone to be. But rather because Freud gave us a language to redescribe these moments of stray thought, these spots of distraught time, in which we are unable to 'pigeon-hole and padlock' our more disagreeable reflections; in which, in Ford's extraordinary phrase, we are as good as talking to ourselves because, for some reason, we can't speak these thoughts to others. And also because, as Ford intimates, the 'we' is ambiguous; at such moments I am being addressed, but who is addressing me? I am talking to myself, but who exactly is doing the talking, the strangely silent talking we call thinking; and who, perhaps more perplexingly, is the listener when we are talking to ourselves? And it is paternity, as it happens, that is at issue. Tietjens may not be the father of his son, but is he the father of his own thoughts? Something that belongs to you, something as intimate as one's own thoughts, could be illegitimate; could come from someone or somewhere else. A lot turns on these nasty turns we have.

But Freud didn't merely draw our attention to such nasty moments, or redescribe the provenance of our more nomadic thoughts. He invented a therapeutic method that encouraged, that traded in such nasty turns. And the aim of this method – called, as everyone now knows, free association – is that people should be able to have their disagreeable reflections without feeling the need to pigeon-hole or padlock them. The people Freud saw were suffering, in his view, not only from the insistent, inherited forms of anguish that everyone is prone to, but also from their forms of classification, and the confinement of their narrow-mindedness. What do we imagine these disagreeable reflections – these unflattering mirrors that our thoughts can provide – are like? What is it that is being clichéd and criminalized (pigeon-holed and padlocked), and why is this what we are inclined to do with the thoughts we have but can't agree with? Tietjens didn't know for certain that he was the father of his child, and he didn't know for certain what to do about this horrible thought. So he carried on talking about the thing he was supposed to be talking about, but 'he had been as good as talking to himself'. Freud says that these moments of not knowing for certain – these nasty turns that we are prone to – are akin to secular epiphanies. It is when our thoughts throw us, when, however fleetingly, we have lost the plot – when, in short, we can bear to lose our reputations for sanity – that we begin to get some news. But to hear the news we need to do what Tietjens would never do: we have to tell our nasty turns to another person: we have to fall through the holes in the conversation when and if they occur. In the therapeutic conversation that Freud invented, and called psychoanalysis, the so-called patient has to be as good as talking to himself, but aloud, in the presence of another person. He is persuaded to make known the interruptions and disruptions he is heir to. What used to be called, in the secular and sacred traditions that Freud was heir to, self-examination, self-questioning, self-doubt could now be called making a Freudian slip. And being able to make something of that particular making that happens in spite of ourselves, inadvertently. That we think of ourselves as making rather than having Freudian slips is something I shall come back to. Where once, in the service of self-knowledge or religious instruction or medical examination, questions were asked of the self, now, in psychoanalysis, all that was asked of the patient was that he should, in so far as he was able, say whatever came into his head. He is invited to speak as freely as possible; as though reporting back from somewhere that he usually calls himself. 'The treatment is begun,' Freud writes in his 'Two Encyclopaedia Articles', by the patient being required to put himself in the position of an attentive and dispassionate self-observer, merely to read off all the time the surface of his consciousness, and on the one hand to make a duty of the most complete honesty while on the other hand not to hold back any idea from communication, even if (1) he feels that it is too disagreeable or if (2) he judges that it is nonsensical or (3) too unimportant or (4) irrelevant to what is being looked for. It is uniformly found that precisely those ideas which provoke these last-mentioned reactions are of particular value in discovering the forgotten material.

Questions are always a queer species of prediction. And it is noticeable in what Freud refers to in this article as 'Psycho-analysis as an Interpretative Art' that questions are not being asked. It is a matter, as Freud says, of reading off the surfaces; of abrogating our conventional criteria. The disagreeable (also Ford's word), the nonsensical, the trivial and the irrelevant are all to be included. Indeed, the thoughts that provoke precisely these reactions are, Freud insists, 'of particular value in dis-covering the forgotten material'. All the moral and aesthetic criteria we use have to be set aside in order to recover what Freud calls 'the forgotten material', as though these criteria were themselves forms of forgetting; that what we pride ourselves on – our judgements of the appropriate and the pertinent, our aesthetic standards, our selection of the good – are cover stories, disappearing acts. Freud is interested in what we exclude by our inclusions. He and his patients are fascinated by the aesthetics of memory; and so by the choices made in every moment of speech.

All the psychoanalyst has to do, Freud proposes, is suggest to the patient that he speaks as freely as possible – as though, attentively and dispassionately, like a scrupulous empirical scientist, reading off the surface of his consciousness – and then attend to the difficulties people always get into in the telling of themselves. We don't need questions (or authoritative information) to interrupt us, Freud says, because we will interrupt ourselves given half a chance; because there's something about what we have to say that we can't bear. And this is called, as everyone now knows – or as everyone now knows that Freud knows – sexuality. Sexuality, or what Freud more interestingly refers to as 'the forgotten material'. Memory, Freud asserts, is of desire; the thing we keep needing to forget is sexuality, what Lacan calls 'the impossible knowledge of sexuality'. Sex, Freud says, is infinitely forgettable. Indeed, we talk about it so much *because we have forgotten about it*. The forbidden is not something you can chat about. If, in its provenance, our sexuality is incestuous – if the object of desire is by definition a forbidden object – no one is going to be easygoing. Everyone is going to be anxious all the time. If what we seek is what we must not find, our sense of purpose is askew; wholeheartedness, passion, authenticity, integrity all begin to look rather different if we are so radically averse to what we so radically desire. Irony is the religion of the incestuously minded.

Freud – and he was not alone in this – thought that sexuality had become especially traumatic for modern people; not just that some people had been sexually traumatized as children, which many of his patients had been; but that there was something intrinsically traumatic about sexuality. Decadence is when the forbidden becomes the impossible; and it was the impossibility of a satisfying erotic life that Freud was hearing about in the form of symptoms (the patient's symptoms are his sexual life, as Freud remarked). A normal sexual life was a disturbing sexual life. This was Freud's paradoxical conclusion (and this, as I shall come back to, is the opening Freud offers us). It is not, in Ford's language, easy to pigeon-hole and padlock what we think of as our sexual inclinations. There are nasty turns at every turn of our erotic life. A reputation for sanity is always going to be a mixed blessing.

The continual discrediting of Freud, and the endlessly announced death, disproof and fraudulence of psychoanalysis, is not merely the sport of bigots. When psychoanalysis is being wholeheartedly valued it is not being taken seriously; because the understanding of psychoanalysis involves a continual resistance to it. To accept psychoanalysis, to believe in psycho-analysis is to miss the point. A French psychoanalyst once said to me that Judaism is the only religion in which you are not allowed to believe in God. In the same way, you cannot believe in the unconscious, you cannot believe in sexuality, as Freud describes them. Believing in incest is not like believing in God. Your resistance is the only form your acknowledgement could possibly take (there's no such thing as a free love). And even this isn't quite right because the whole notion of resistance implies that there could be acceptance; and psycho-analysis is, among other things, a redescription of the question: what would it be to accept ourselves and others? It is Freud's view that we are ineluctably averse to ourselves (and others) because our desire is fundamentally transgressive. If what we want is what we must not have we are going to be, to put it as mildly as possible, divided against ourselves. If what we once wanted was to live a good life, or to be redeemed by God's grace, what we now want – or what we actually want – in Freud's view, is an object that is by definition forbidden. And this is going to make our relationship to our so-called selves at best ironic and at worst horrified. People, of course, are only ever ironic about the things that they don't feel ironic about. So what then would be a good life for incestuous animals like ourselves? What would be the values, what would be the moral aspirations of a creature whose desire, whose life-force is utterly transgressive, for whom the taboos are in place as a continual reminder of his most intractable needs?

Freud, let us say by way of a beginning, had a genius for describing the impossibility of our lives. He master-minded a story about how and why we are not the masters of what we have been taught to call our minds. By privileging the obstacle over the way forward, what can't be done over what is to be done; by seeing the drama in the interruption, the attention released in the lapse of attention, Freud was encouraging us to prize our incompetence; to be amazed and not merely dismayed by the persistent error of our ways. Freud wants to tell us the success story of failure. So Freud's genius was to describe to us just how and why it is a good and necessary thing – a good thing because a necessary thing – for us to live in conflict with ourselves and others (there is no peace for the Freudian); and, of course, if we are so-minded, to live in conflict with Freud. If psychoanalysis is the kind of common sense that common sense doesn't want to hear about; if it addresses the recognitions involved in refusal, Freud is someone with whom we will feel uneasy. Enthusiasm is a wonderful thing, but one should be wary of the enthusiasts of psychoanalysis. Admiring Freud is not part of the solution to the problem he poses, it is part of the problem. And the problem is: since we are ineluctably unacceptable to ourselves, what kind of relationship is it possible for us to have with the unacceptable?

Adorno once famously remarked that in psychoanalysis only the exaggerations are true. It is also true that Freud was interested in the uses of exaggeration; in the ways in which a culture that forces people to downplay certain of their feelings makes them play up – both the feelings and the people. A Freudian slip exaggerates the difference between an intention and its result. In 'a good many cases' of these slips, Freud writes in *The Psychopathology of Everyday Life*,

the disruptive ideas can be shown to originate in suppressed emotions in mental life. In normal people selfish, jealous and hostile feelings and impulses, upon which the pressure of moral teaching weighs very heavily, quite often make use of slips in order to find some way of expressing their forces, forces that are undeniably present but are not recognized by the higher authorities in our minds. Permitting these slips and fortuitous actions to occur reflects, to a considerable extent, a useful toleration of amorality. Sexual currents of many kinds figure prominently among these suppressed emotions.

It is worth noting, as I mentioned earlier, that in Freud's view we are, however unwittingly, the active makers of our slips. Reputedly normal people quite often 'make use' of slips, Freud writes, in order to find some way of expressing these unacceptable feelings, 'these amoral forces'. As though a slip were an opportunity or a genre, like the sonnet or a linguistic medium; as though we have to be the artists of our amorality – the artists, but also the pragmatists. We make use of slips as though they were one of our tools to get us from A to B, to realize one of our projects, to get us something we want. In replication of the external world Freud suggests that the internal world too has its higher, forbidding authorities – the mind too is a society – who, he says, won't recognize certain feelings. But if we can make use of these secret messages called slips then there can be what Freud calls, pragmatically, a 'useful toleration of amorality'. And these moments of linguistic carnival perform this amorality, they don't merely tolerate it (when I say 'it was just a mistake' I'm hoping for tolerance). What might once have been called bad manners, a lack of self-discipline or, indeed, a mistake is now being referred to by Freud as both a 'useful' tool and a moment of artfulness, a way of 'expressing' powerful feeling. How does the modern individual deal with unacceptable sexual feelings, with 'self-ish, jealous and hostile feelings'? He makes what he needs to call mistakes, Freud says, so the 'disruptive ideas', the amoral, finds the expression it is seeking (in talking about slips in this way, Freud makes us wonder, what does saying what you want feel like you are doing?). So to answer my earlier questions – what would be a good life for incestuous animals like ourselves? What would be the moral aspirations of a creature whose desire was utterly transgressive? – to answer these essentially Freudian questions: a good life would be one in which mistakes were continually sought by someone equipped with a rhetoric to discredit their significance. We are the kind of animal that can say 'I was only joking.'

But Freud, it should be noted, is not exactly satirizing our hypocrisy. This would hardly be news; or evidence of a master-mind at work. He is encouraging us to be connoisseurs of the cover story. For Freud our lives literally depend upon the aesthetics of duplicity. If we are not the artists of our own pleasure there will be no pleasure (and no art). Where once there was the moral authority of satire, the moral high ground of mockery, there can now be a more straightforward, apparently scientific, account of the necessities of pleasure-seeking, and of the necessary difficulties, the ruses, of pleasure-seeking. After Freud people can be accused of being consistent.

But why, in Freud's view, does the amoral seek, indeed

require, expression? Why has Freud replaced the language of will power and self-control with the language of pragmatic artistry? Why can't we behave ourselves instead of expressing ourselves, or behave ourselves *by* expressing ourselves? And Freud's answer is that we are the animals who live in a continual state of temptation. Even though we love safety and self-preservation it is as though something in us likes something else more (the most interesting art is never about safety but about what threatens safety). Darwin virtually says we want to preserve ourselves in order to reproduce our genes; Freud says there is something, which he wants to call sexuality, that is always threatening to destroy us. Our sexuality endangers us – endangers our sense of ourselves, our ego – because it is transgressive. We are, in Freud's view, a continual risk to ourselves. So when he writes to his absent collaborator Fleiss in 1897 (in *The Origins of Psychoanalysis*) of his 'surge of guesses' – that he is 'about to discover the source of morality' – it is because interest in the forbidden, in the unacceptable, is by definition guess-work. 'Only one idea of general value has occurred to me,' he writes:

I have found love of the mother and jealousy of the father in my own case, too, and now believe it to be a general phenomenon of early childhood . . . If that is the case, the gripping power of Oedipus Rex, in spite of all the rational objections to the inexorable fate that the story presupposes, becomes intelligible . . . the Greek myth seizes on a compulsion which everyone recognizes because he has felt traces of it in himself. Every member of the audience was once a budding Oedipus in fantasy, and this dream-fulfilment played out in reality causes everyone to recoil in horror, with the full measure of repression which separates his infantile from his present state.

This is not the place to try to establish the truth or otherwise of the Oedipus complex, its apparent universality or its possible significance. It has to be conceded though that the incest issue doesn't tend to leave people feeling indifferent. What is noteworthy is Freud wanting to account for people's horror of sexuality. Leo Bersani remarked in his great essay 'Is the Rectum a Grave?' that the big secret about sex was that most people don't like it. The big secret about sex isn't quite that most people don't like it, it's that most people don't like it because they are with people they are either not excited by or are too excited by. And if they are with people they are not sufficiently excited by, Freud would say, it is because they are terrified by their own desire. As budding Oedipuses their desire is either incestuous or it is nothing. Real desire is always a reminder of something at once overwhelming and forbidden. When it comes to the choice of sexual partner, better safe than sorry: from the ego's point of view, it's always better not to get too excited. When it comes to sexuality it is what Freud refers to as 'the recoil of horror' that is the sign of desire. This, one might say, goes against the grain of our common-sense assumptions about pleasure-seeking. Isn't pleasure supposed to be at least a pleasure as well? If sex is that Darwinian project why is it so much trouble for us? Freud shows us how if we are not in trouble we are not having sex.

Freud links so-called normal sexuality with a recoil of horror. And we may remember the blander instance of this as the Freudian slip in which we and/or our audience can recoil in surprise at what has been said inadvertently. Whatever this is – call it 'love of the mother and jealousy of the father'; call it 'selfish, jealous and hostile feelings . . . Sexual currents of many kinds' – Freud is describing himself, his patients, among others, as suffering from it. It puts us at odds with ourselves, but in secular terms. It is still a world of forbidden desires, but it is an Enlightenment world in which it is acknowledged that the higher authorities that are doing the forbidding are human and not divine in origin.

For Freud, as he works out his own mythology – and his works should be read, I think, as Harold Bloom intimates, as more akin to William Blake's 'Prophetic Books' than to William James's *Principles of Psychology* – the question becomes: what are the higher authorities higher than in a secular society? Or, rather, what is there to be higher than, what is it that requires this kind of distance in order to be believed, and what is it deemed to be distant from? And Freud's answer is, perhaps unsurprisingly, that it is the parents, and particularly the father, who are the higher authorities for the child. But, perhaps more surprisingly, what there is to be higher than, what there is to distance oneself from and create the illusion of mastery over, is what Freud calls 'infantile sexuality', and that is alive in the adult as unconscious desire. The unconscious, which is Freud's word for the desire of childhood, and the history of its formations – a desire so enduring, so prodigal in its ingenuity, and so extravagant in its claims – is the stumbling-block that is Freud's most wonderful invention. The act alone of describing that which is at once irresistible and that one most resists – whether or not 'it' exists – is a great folly, an act of linguistic heroism. But it is in Freud's desire to describe how what he calls the unconscious works – both its provenance and its wayward logic – that his special claim on us makes itself felt. Our desire, Freud suggests, is always a work in progress, unfinishing and unfinished; and so is Freud's lifelong account of the unconscious. And if you want a picture of the kind of thing the unconscious does – the kind of thing it makes, and makes known – think of a dream, Freud says, or a joke or a slip; or of something you more patently suffer from, like a phobia or an inhibition or an intrusive thought (like the one Tietjens suffered from suddenly in the middle of a perfectly sensible conversation). It is an unusual, perhaps unprecedented, category Freud has created; a category that links, that connects up the dream, the joke, the slip, the symptom. It is a category of unconsciously inspired performance, in which the identity of the performer is obscure. And in which the performance is deemed to be a communication, however enigmatic, to the interested parties. This communication, which is in some sense baffling to both the performer of it and its recipients, is an allusion, a referring back, to the desires of childhood. For Freud, childhood is the forbidden, and memory is always at best a guilty pleasure. There is nothing more transgressive than talking about one's childhood. Except, that is, like a budding Oedipus, to re-create it in adult life. It isn't, in other words, that Freud destroyed the innocence of childhood; it is that Freud showed us that the idea of innocence was invented to destroy the truth of childhood. Our childhood, he wants us to believe, is most akin to a Greek tragedy. We call Oedipus a tragic hero because he is the most ordinary man in the world.

Oedipus, of course, had never seen the play. Just like ourselves as children, he is going through it all for the first time. By the time we get to see or read or even hear about the play, it is far too late. We are already confounded by our fate. Psychoanalysis – and this is another paradox at the heart of Freud's work – is always after the event. It doesn't cure people so much as show them what it is about themselves that is incurable. Or, rather, it shows them the areas of their lives in which 'cure' would be the wrong word; in which we have to come up with something else to do other than get better. And one thing we can do, Freud – irrepressible as ever – suggests, is track the unconsciousness of our lives. We can, he occasionally intimates, learn to enjoy just how unwitting we are. There is nothing more entertaining – nothing more daunting and amusing and horrifying – than the ways in which our intentions and attentions misfire. There is nothing more poignant and absurd than our forlorn and sincere attempts not to wreak havoc. So when Auden writes in his great poem 'In Memory of Sigmund Freud' that Freud 'would have us remember most of all/to be enthusiastic over the night' he was also reminding us that for Freud it was night all day as well. And that enthusiasm, too, is something that has to be remembered. Children are nothing if not enthusiastic given half a chance and an object of desire. But enthusiasm is always going to be counter-phobic, the rushing of a resistance. Freud offers us a way of noticing the ways in which we don't notice; he wants us to reconsider whatever it is about ourselves that we are so tempted to ignore. He invites us to be unselectively attentive. And then to see what happens. Because the problem modern people have is that things keep occurring to them that they don't know what to do with. Without a sense of sin, they don't know what to make of what they are so troubled by.

There is a nasty, perhaps Freudian moment in Dostoevsky's novel of 1868, *The Idiot*, in which something suddenly occurs to the hero, Prince Myshkin, as he wanders the streets of Moscow:

Occasionally he would start peering at passers-by with great curiosity; but most often he did not notice either the passers-by or precisely where he was going. He was tormentingly tense and uneasy, and at the same time felt an extraordinary need for solitude.

He wanted to be alone and to give himself over to all this suffering tension completely passively, without looking for the least way out. He was loath to resolve the questions that overflowed his soul and heart. 'What, then, am I to blame for it all?' he murmured to himself, almost unaware of his words.

The prince oscillates between a state of vigilance and a state of inner preoccupation; at once holding on to external reality – peering at passers-by – and being quite elsewhere, not knowing where he is going, and surrendering to his thoughts and feelings (to try to 'resolve the questions that overflowed his soul and heart' would have been to wrench himself out of those very questions). And suddenly he finds himself as good as talking to himself: ' "What, then, am I to blame for it all?" he murmured to himself, almost unaware of his words.' On the one hand the 'all' for which he feels, momentarily, responsible is the fate of Rogozhin and Nastasya Filippovna; but it is also everything else, all the suffering and confusion in the world that Prince Myshkin confoundingly believes, as he says it to himself, is his fault. This is clearly an extraordinary thing to find oneself suddenly saying to oneself; though, of course, it is not rare for people to suffer revelations of chronic over-responsibility for the terribleness of things. And it is consoling to believe that someone is to blame, that somewhere there is a responsible agent. But Prince Myshkin murmurs this to himself, 'almost unaware of his words'. One can be aware of one's words, the narrator implies; but what is it to be aware of one's words?

To be almost unaware of one's words is as good a description as any of telling one's dream. All the words one uses probably have known referents, and yet what one is actually recounting makes no sense. We are describing something that we have seen, though not with our eyes. But to speak and to be almost unaware of one's words sounds more like a trance state, a being possessed by the words; as though at that moment the prince, rather like the dreamer, is the medium rather than the instigator of what he has to say. He is struck, as we say, because he doesn't quite recognize himself in his sentence. 'Something,' the narrator writes, 'was certainly pursuing him.' This, in Freud's sense, is the individual unconsciously at work; the self as a discrepancy. The self as real – or at its most real – in its unfamiliarity with itself. The unconscious is the fictive source of news, in Freud's mythology; it is where the surprises come from, the surprises whose moral status is always ambiguous. It is the home of trauma and desire, and of the trauma that is desire. The individual never quite knows what to think of what he has thought. Thoughts and feelings that come from the unconscious part of the self have indeterminate consequences. They are the stuff of dreams, not of routines.

But why did Dostoevsky describe the prince as murmuring this sentence to himself, rather than describing it as simply a thought that crossed his mind? And why did Ford describe Tietjen's sudden thought as one in which 'He had been as good as talking to himself'? What both instances are drawing our attention to – and the reason I describe them both as perhaps Freudian moments – is the difference between something occurring to someone, someone having a shocking thought, and this thought being spoken, if only to oneself. Freud's invention of psychoanalysis as a therapy – or as a new kind of conversation – turns, after all, on this difference. Freud invited his patients to 'as good as talk to themselves', but aloud, in his presence; to be almost unaware of their words, that is to free associate, to speak without censorious vigilance whatever happened to, in both senses, cross their minds. There is nothing more defensive, Freud implies, than understanding what one is saying. Psychoanalysis, in short, is based on the idea that talking is different to thinking; and also that surprising or shocking oneself in the presence of another person is of value. Indeed, the point is that such nourishing surprise, such productive shock, may be possible only, is made possible only, by the very presence of the other person. The project of the unacceptable in oneself is to make itself known. The forbidden, the transgressive, is always an annunciation. It is a demand made on at least one other person. Freud invented a therapeutic setting, called psychoanalysis, in which this self could be overheard. The experiment, of course, was what followed from that overhearing. Unlike confession, psychoanalysis offers a person, at best, an essentially unpredictable redescription – an unpredictable consequence – of what they have said.

The psychoanalyst – the new figure that Freud invented; the other protagonist in his epic poem, his never-ending story called *The Unconscious* – is a person with an unusual conversational manner. He responds to what his so-called patients say to him not quite like anyone else. And this is because he has two aims, which are actually more at odds with each other than Freud was ever prepared to acknowledge, or perhaps even to mention. On the one hand he aims to cure, to relieve suffering, to help to make a life more worth living. But on the other hand he aims for what is technically called 'maximal symbolization'. He wants, that is to say, to respond only in ways which will facilitate the expression of unconscious desire. He wants to 'let the unconscious speak'; to modify the person's defences against what he has to say, and what he has to hear himself saying. The question is – and it is, of course, a political question – does freer speech, does the frankest possible articulation of wants, give people a life they prefer, or make a better world? By inventing psychoanalysis, Freud invented what he might have called a laboratory for the evaluation of the effects of free speech and free listening. And, perhaps unsurprisingly, not everyone liked, or likes, the sound of it. People want to speak freely only about what they must not speak about.

In Freud's view the question the modern individual seems to be asking herself is whether she can make her wanting compatible with her (psychic) survival. For Freud, to speak is to articulate one's wants, to make known to oneself what is absent, what of significance is lacking in one's life. And the performance of wanting – in mood, in language, in action – puts one's life in danger. There is the danger of punishment for desiring the forbidden, which Freud infamously (and accurately) referred to as castration; and there is the danger of acknowledged dependence, and the potential for loss. One cannot live, one could not have survived, without wanting; and without having achieved some success at it. But the wanting that is our lifeline throws us into interminable conflict: it involves us ineluctably with others and ourselves. 'Originally,' Freud writes in *Civilization and Its Discontents*, 'renunciation of instinct was the result of fear of an external authority: one renounced one's satisfactions in order not to lose its love.' There is the urgency, the emergency of instinctual desire, and there is the fear of loss of love as a ruling passion. A person begins, Freud tells us, in fear of losing his parents' love; and then, having internalized their authority, he ends up fearing (and courting) losing his love for himself. And this self-hatred, that can be so obscene in its voraciousness, is called guilt. We cannot help but be harmed by what we cannot help but want. We have morality that we may not perish from the truth. We are the animals that need to be protected from themselves.

Good, now, means safe and satisfied, or satisfied safely enough; bad means deprived beyond measure of one's need. Good means, as it always has done, desirable; but desirable now also means forbidden. What is good is against the law. Bad now means traumatic, but traumatic is not simply or solely the things that happen to oneself; or, rather, one's desire can feel like something that happens to oneself, like having an attack of one's own nature. So 'trauma' becomes another word for living a life. For Freud, in other words, we are in shock; in shock, but wishing our way through. It is as though there is a design flaw in the human animal; our childhood is more than our development can cope with. We are all in recovery from having been children.

As Freud tracked, in his clinical work, the ways in which the old-fashioned solutions of childhood became the repetitions of adulthood; and how repetition was a refusal to remember, and how memory was full of hiding-places, he was struck by a peculiar fact: that suffering can sometimes be transformed by applying words to wounds, by being seen as meaningful. In the nonsense that we talk there is the spectacle of happiness; in and of itself the appeal to another person to listen and reply is fraught with hope. Freud shows us just how extravagant it is to speak. The task of the modern person, as Freud sees her, is to find the new ways of wanting that keep wanting alive; but in the full knowledge that wanting is a species of risk. What became known, after Freud, as psychoanalytic theory is nothing but an encyclopaedia of modern risks. And desire is usually the contemporary word for the risk not taken, for the missed opportunity; the unlived life that seems the only life worth living.

So Freud, I want to suggest, leaves us with one overriding question: what is a good life for incestuously minded people like ourselves, people who must not have what they really want? People whose fraught, doomed love for their parents has made love a hopeless passion; and who fear the loss of love they know to be their birthright and their fate? It is always going to be difficult for us, Freud says, to be excited and kind, to be fair and satisfied. Because, in reality, we can never be or have the object of our desire, we are always the left-out ones. And because the object of our desire is forbidden, it is imperative for our (psychic) survival that we *are* left out. Oedipus was the man who couldn't bear being left out.

Freud, then, has given us a lot to be going on with. We must start, he seems to be saying, by ironizing the masteries of the mind. We must not hide ourselves away for safe-keeping, because safety only keeps us safe. We must learn to desire with guile and without hope; to love in conflict, rather than betraying our desire in fantasies of harmony. We must, in short, take our pleasures where we may. And speak as well as we can of what we want. People have not been keen to recognize that the Reality Principle was Freud's most exciting idea.

Talking Nonsense
and Knowing When to Stop

Tyrants always want language and literature that is
easily understood.

Theodor Hacker, *Notes*

I want to start with two propositions and entangle them with
a view to saying something about the vexed question of
endings in psychoanalysis, and about what, if anything, the
issue of endings in psychoanalysis has to tell us about endings elsewhere. The first proposition is that it is impossible
to know the consequences of one's words – the spoken, the
heard and the overheard. The analyst can never predict the
effect that his words will have on the so-called patient, and
vice versa. So, for example, whatever psychoanalytic training is, it can never train people to know what to say when,
if knowing what to say means knowing what one's words
can do for the patient. By the same token, one can be taught
what to listen out for, but, by definition, one could never be
prepared for the surprising, for whatever it is about someone
else's words that is peculiarly evocative. Lacan was referring
to this when he said that if the analyst has been properly
analysed, he is more not less likely to fall in love with the
patient. However well educated one is about one's unpro-
tectedness, the words used are unpredictable in their effect.
Language is to the speaker and listener what the dream-day is

to the dreamer, idiosyncratically enlivening. Learning to speak, learning to interpret, is never merely learning what to say. Learning to listen can only be learning – if that is the right word – to bear what listening calls up in you. It would have been better if Freud had said: speaking and listening is like dreaming in language. What is called interpretation is the dream evoked by a dream. It is impossible to know the consequences of one's words, the spoken, the heard and the overheard.

The second proposition is – to adapt Valéry's famous remark about completing a poem – that an analysis is never finished, it is only abandoned. And in this, despite suggestions to the contrary, the so-called analytic relationship is like, or at least similar to, every other so-called relationship. The language of completion is unsuitable for what goes on between people. It is possible to know that one no longer sees someone, no longer has sex with someone; it is less possible to know whether one no longer thinks of someone. Indeed, one of the things psychoanalysis reveals is just how haunted we are, in spite of ourselves, by other selves, by bits and pieces of others. It is impossible, though, to know when or whether a relation-ship has ended. Or what it is for a relationship to end, rather than change. And yet the idea that a psychoanalysis must end – or, indeed, that one of the things that makes it so-called real analysis is that it is undertaken with a view to its ending by consent or decision rather than death – is more or less taken for granted (though perhaps in different ways) by both the prac-titioners and the recipients of the psychoanalytic opportun-ity. The opportunity of the psychoanalytic relationship is, for some people, precisely the opportunity of working through, as they would say, the ending of a relationship – something that rarely happens, and never happens in this special way, in ordinary life. 'Cure' is the psychoanalytic word for the happy ending.

The assumption that a psychoanalysis must end – and, ideally, that it must end in a particular way that can be described and taught to the aspiring practitioner – is itself an assumption worth analysing and is something that both Freud and Winnicott were exercised by. If, say, there is a sense in which what we call relationships never end, then there is a sense in which what we call mourning may be, for want of a better word, unrealistic. (If it was a how-to book, it would be called *How To Go On Having a Relationship with Someone Who Isn't There*.) If, as Freud suggests, pleasure-seeking or unconscious desire is unceasing, if the unconscious is timeless and without contradiction, then a capacity to bear frustration settles nothing. It is not about something ending but about something stopping. That wanting is endless, and that we have to have a sense of an ending; that desire is transgressive; that we fear loss of love, loss of the object and castration – these are the preoccupations at the heart of psychoanalysis. Endings in the plural – endings as experiences that go on happening – are what psychoanalysis is about: frustration and taboo, murderousness and the limits of one's life encompassed by the word 'death'. Endings are to psychoanalysis what full stops are to punctuation: they refer to, they arrange, a transition. Whether they are formal periods of hesitation – a resistance to going on that looks like a satisfactory place to end – always remains to be seen. One of the best things Winnicott did for psychoanalysis was to add the word 'transition' to its vocabulary. And this is because of what it does to the idea of endings, to the strange notion of knowing when to stop. An analysis is never finished, it is only abandoned.

I want to suggest that what are loosely called endings in

analysis should often be called something else, but that a capacity for abandon, and the abandon that is abandonment, could be one of the things we might hope to get from a psychoanalysis. Giving up, or giving up on, is better than finishing because it acknowledges limitation in a way that the sense of a good ending never can. Endings are not there to be engineered by us; they (and we) are not that kind of thing. If a good ending is other than a great piece of luck, it can only be a contrived (that is, defensive) calculation. Endings, like so-called beginnings, are risks; there is nothing to tide us over except what happens next. If an analyst was described as being good at endings, we might wonder exactly what it was that he or she was so good at.

It may be useful to think of at least some endings in psychoanalysis in terms of knowing when to stop. And, to be more specific, knowing when to stop talking and knowing when to stop turning up. But what, from a psychoanalytic point of view, does knowing when to stop mean? If knowing and acting upon one's so-called knowledge are often so at odds with each other; if psychoanalysis makes us wonder, to put it mildly, who the knowing subject is; if the human subject is constituted by something unstoppable called, variously, unconscious desire, instinctual drives, lack – then how is the stopping going to happen? And even if we don't take psychoanalysis on its own terms, or at its word, the knowing-when-to-stop question turns up as one among many telling critiques of the psychoanalytic method. Is the analyst, for example, trained to know when to stop the patient associating, when to interrupt, given that association is both unpredictable in its rhythm and pace and uncircumscribable in its reach? Wittgenstein was famously struck by this in his discussion of Freud's method of dream interpretation. Freud, Wittgenstein is reported to have said in *Lectures and Conversations on Aesthetics, Psychology and Religious Belief,*

wants to say that whatever happens in a dream will be found to be connected with some wish which analysis can bring to light. But this procedure of free association and so on is queer, because Freud never shows how we know where to stop – where is the right solution. Sometimes he says that the right solution, or the right analysis, is the one which satisfies the patient. Sometimes he says that the doctor knows what the right solution or analysis of the dream is, whereas the patient doesn't: the doctor can say that the patient is wrong. The reason why he calls one sort of analysis the right one does not seem to be a matter of evidence.

What Wittgenstein calls, wittily, Freud's 'procedure of free association and so on' is, of course, a matter of putting a stop to the 'and so on' of the patient's associations. How many associations are enough, and how could the analyst or the patient know whether the more telling, decisive associations lay up ahead, after the intervention that interrupted them? Clearly the phrase 'an associative chain' itself jumps to conclusions about pertinence. It is likely, after all, that knowing where to stop – at least from the patient's point of view – means knowing how to keep at bay the forgotten, the forbidden, the altogether unsettling material. Knowing and stopping can too easily be redescribed in psychoanalytic language as resisting. Knowing when to stop the flow (or otherwise) of associations can be, for both the analyst and the so-called patient, a mechanism of defence. A mechanism because it can have an automatic, seemingly inevitable quality; it feels right at that moment.

The queer things that Wittgenstein is picking up on are the puzzles and paradoxes associated with free association, and the resistances to it, as a procedure of truth-telling, of finding the right solution. 'Freud never shows how we know where to stop,' Wittgenstein says. But how could such a thing ever be shown? Where to stop cannot be known; it can only be tried out. And it will have been right not because the analyst could predict the effect of his intervention – that is, predict what the patient might say next – but because more valuable words will accrue from it. Knowing when to stop the associating makes no more sense than knowing when to stop dreaming, or knowing when to stop making slips.

The idea of knowing when to stop implies, perhaps, more coherence, more narrative structure than is always available. We say that novels and pieces of music and films end, but not paintings; the painter finishes her painting, but that is not what the viewer does. The viewer walks away, abandons the picture, and may return to it. Winnicott suggests in *Playing and Reality* that for some people, sometimes, 'free association that reveals a coherent theme is already affected by anxiety, and the cohesion of ideas is a defence organization'. The patient's presenting or revealing a coherent theme, and, presumably, the analyst interpreting a coherent theme in the associations, is a defence. The analyst's need to find, to articulate, a coherent theme, Winnicott intimates, may also be a defence organization. Psychoanalytic theory, we should remember, is always the presentation of a coherent theme. Knowing when to stop, in this context, means not allowing the nonsense to happen.

Perhaps it is to be accepted that there are patients who at times need the therapist to note the nonsense that belongs to the mental state of the individual at rest without the need even for the patient to communicate this nonsense, that is to say, without the need even for the patient to communicate this nonsense, that is to say, without the need for the patient to organize nonsense. Organized nonsense is already a defence, just as organized chaos is a denial of chaos. The therapist who cannot take this communication becomes engaged in a futile attempt to find some organization in the nonsense, as a result of which the patient leaves the nonsense area because of hopelessness about communicating nonsense. An opportunity for rest has been missed because of the therapist's need to find sense where nonsense is.

'An opportunity for rest has been missed,' Winnicott says; and it is rest from the vigilant self-holding that coherence involves. It should not be missed that in this passage (and elsewhere), Winnicott is describing both a new need of the individual, the need to speak the nonsense that he is, the need for his incoherence to be accepted as such by another person; with the implication that, sometimes at least, our coherence is a front (and an affront to ourselves), including, of course, theories of psychoanalysis, such as Winnicott's. He is also describing a new kind of person. Winnicott is always careful on these writing occasions to stress that he is talking about a certain kind of patient or a patient at a certain kind of time in the treatment.

For him, it is the environmental deprivation that neces-sitates the vigilant self-holding of coherent narrative. The patient, let us say, as a child had recurring experiences of having to know when to stop forgetting himself; he was absorbed in whatever he was doing, and this was interrupted, periodically, by a bout of need, either his own need (the need for the object) or the object's need for him. The problem of need, the problem of demand, for Winnicott is that in his view it over-organizes the individual. There is the chaos born of need that misfires because the object is unable to respond adequately. Ideally, in what Winnicott calls 'the full course of the experience', the appetite experience has a more or less coherent narrative. There is dawning appetite, the breast is hallucinated, the hallucination fails to work and the baby cries, at which point a good-enough mother turns up, hungry to be eaten. For Winnicott, it is not about knowing when to stop, because, if all goes well, the process, as he calls it, has an inbuilt conclusion. Knowing when to stop in this picture could only equal inhibition about damaging the mother through appetite, or using the mind to control the process. Here, the individual has to make himself coherent against the problem of appetite; appetite is only chaotic, is only made chaotic, in Winnicott's view, by the object's insufficiency. Appetite will be a good story for you if you are lucky enough to have the right mother.

But what Winnicott is most interestingly attentive to is the ways in which the demand of the object over-organizes the individual by organizing at all. Winnicott is, I think, the first analyst who wanted to let the nonsense speak, as opposed to letting unconscious desire speak through free association. There are, Winnicott seems to be saying, very good psycho-analytic stories – Oedipal and pre-Oedipal – about the hazards of desire, and the consequent necessities of conflict, defence and symptomatology. There is clearly, he acknowledges, a desiring subject as described by Freud and Klein. But there is also an incoherent, chaotic, nonsensical, eccentric subject, described by no one in psychoanalysis but suggested by the idea, the method, of free association, but free association listened to in a certain way. This is the person Winnicott wants to introduce us to. The chaotic person who needs, however temporarily, to speak nothing but his own nonsense. Winnicott finds it extremely difficult to marry, or even link, the nonsensical person with the desiring person. (His useful distinction between disintegration and unintegration is an attempt at this.) The desiring person, as he develops, is always involved, one way or another, in having to know when to stop. But knowing when to stop is the enemy of chaos, or it is the omnipotent delusion that chaos can be under control. Perhaps, Winnicott intimates, what we most need to defend ourselves against, what we most believe needs to be stopped, is not the appetite – or only the appetite – but the nonsense. And nonsense can only be stopped by making sense. Why, he asks us to wonder – but in a psychoanalytic context and language – can't we let the nonsense be? Why couldn't an aim of analysis be to enable the patient to speak and bear, and even enjoy, his nonsense? And, indeed, to be able to hear the nonsense of others?

Winnicott, it should be noted, refers very infrequently to free association. He quotes with approval, indeed italicizes, in his 'Child Analysis in the Latency Period', Berta Bornstein's comment in her 1951 paper 'On Latency': *'Free association is experienced by the child as a particular threat to his ego organization.'* Indeed, it seems as if for Winnicott 'play' is the word for the kind of free association that need not be a threat to ego organization. And play, of course, is not exclusively verbal. In a paper dated 1954 (but not published until 1989), 'Play in the Analytic Situation', Winnicott reports on a supervision:

After the interpretation given by the student the patient leaned over and rearranged the mat and gave associations to this bit of play. In the circumstances it is understandable that the student neglected to continue on the subject of play and became bogged down in the material of the free associations which indeed were important on their own account.

Clearly, getting 'bogged down in the material of the free associations' is to be doing psychoanalysis as traditionally taught, but for Winnicott, in this example, that is to miss the point, which is the play. So there is free association, which, in latency, and not only in latency, is a threat to ego organization, and there is play, which for Winnicott is famously the aim, the means and the definition of psychotherapy:

Psychotherapy takes place in the overlap of two areas of playing, that of the patient and that of the therapist. Psychotherapy has to do with two people playing together. The corollary of this is that where playing is not possible then the work done by the therapist is directed towards bringing the patient from a state of not being able to play into a state of being able to play.

Winnicott here, in 'Playing, a Theoretical Statement', has redescribed the so-called golden rule of free association in terms of play, thereby de-emphasizing, in practice and through analogy, Freud's privileging of the verbal and the necessity of teasing out the unconscious desire being kept at bay. And somewhere between free association and play there is non-sense, which is verbal, but not exactly to be played with so much as to be accepted as such. If free association is supposed to reveal the unconscious logic of desire, playing, for Winnicott, is something quite different. 'Bodily excitement in eroto-genic zones,' he writes, 'constantly threatens playing, and therefore threatens the child's sense of existing as a person. The instincts are the main threat to play as to the ego.' The instincts, in Winnicott's counter-Freudian story, are a threat, a word used three times in the sentence; and what they threaten is the child's 'sense of existing as a person'. Once again it is about sense, and once again Winnicott's phrasing might make us wonder what, if the child no longer exists as a person, he will have a sense of existing as. This takes us straight to the nonsense question and to whether, or in what sense, talking nonsense threatens a person's sense of existing as a person.

Instinct, in Winnicott's view, puts a stop to playing – and so, presumably, to psychotherapy, which is supposed to be a form of playing. Free association, in Freud's view, can lead to the wording of desire. Do we want to be able to play or to seek sexual satisfaction or to talk nonsense? Of course, we don't necessarily have to choose; but if we want to play or be free to talk nonsense, our psychotherapy need never end. If we are seeking sexual satisfaction, the analyst's couch won't, beyond a certain point, do the trick.

If you look up 'free association' in the Index of Marion Milner's book *The Suppressed Madness of Sane Men* you find: 'free association – *see* absent-mindedness in art'. This is, I think, instructive. Free associating, playing, nonsense and states of sexual desire are all, at their best, states of absent-mindedness, of self-forgetting, of abandon. The psychoanalytic question becomes – and this is bound up, as we shall see, with the notion of knowing when to stop – what might make someone stop something as potentially pleasurable as two people playing together? If you end up getting on, and the conversation is good, why stop? This is a question any child would be radically puzzled by. (Freud, in his correspondence with Binswanger, refers to 'one of my closest women friends, formerly a patient'.) Winnicott, it should be noted, does not say that psychotherapy is two people playing together: he says that 'it has to do with two people playing together', and that the psychotherapy, as such, cannot begin until the patient is able to play. If psychoanalysis, in the Winnicott way, is somehow like playing – has at least, something to do with playing

– then what makes playing stop? What must be acknowledged, as Winnicott does, is the difference between a set game – which has a defined beginning, middle and end – and open-ended play. Open-ended play is open-ended play or a defence against open-endedness. This chapter is about whether the phrase 'open-ended' could possibly mean anything, and in particular could mean anything in a psychoanalytic context.

Winnicott is quite explicit that it is 'bodily excitement in erotogenic zones' that 'constantly threatens' play, and 'there-fore threatens the child's sense of existing as a person'. In other words, it is play that gives the child a sense of existing as a person, whereas it is instinct, which constantly threatens play, that gives the child a sense of existing as something other than a person, or as not existing at all. So it is time to drop the idea that in some sense Winnicott wasn't interested in sex, or has nothing to tell us about what Freud wanted to tell us about. Winnicott is acutely mindful of 'bodily excitement in eroto-genic zones' as that which is disruptive. It is defined by him as that which interrupts, that which waylays and disfigures play. Sex, to put it as crudely, as Winnicottianly as possible, is what threatens play, what constantly threatens to put a stop to it – and, of course, to put a stop to the playing that is psychotherapy. If you want to know what sexuality is, see what you are up against when you start playing. Or, indeed, notice what stops you playing. Play is sexuality in abeyance. At a certain point, one might say, the artist loses her absorption and finds herself all too mindful that she needs something, needs someone else, something the activity of painting cannot supply. And by the same token, as it were, the point of analysis, the making and breaking point, is that the analyst and the so-called patient do not have sex with each other. The analyst, in the traditional story, is the one who is supposed to know when to stop.

Just as the Freudian analyst traditionally analyses the resistances to free association, the Winnicottian analyst, in his project of enabling the patient to play, is going to analyse the obstacles to such playing as is possible; and the obstacles are 'bodily excitement in erotogenic zones'. But is the aim a capacity for such excitement, or a capacity for play? How is the excited, desiring self linked, if at all, to the self that plays? And what of the version of the self that needs the 'rest', as Winnicott calls it, of talking nonsense? It is essential to the whole idea of playing, Winnicott intimates, to acknowledge what playing cannot do for the self. You can't eat art. When appetite starts, playing stops. 'The pleasurable element in playing carries with it,' he writes in 'Playing, a Theoretical Statement', 'the implication that the instinctual arousal is not excessive . . . Playing is inherently exciting and precarious. This characteristic derives *not* from instinctual arousal . . .' There is a hint of equivocation here, but it is at the moments when Winnicott's language is at odds with Freud's that the text can wake us up. Playing is pleasurable because instinctual arousal is not excessive; but – or and – the pleasure in playing is that it does not derive from instinctual arousal. The threat for Winnicott is the instinctual arousal that waylays development by over-disturbing the individual's ego organization. Playing, for him, either has no instinctual pressure, or just the right amount. In one reading of Freud, that is precisely what instinctual arousal is: the threatening of ego organization, what Laplanche refers to as 'the attack of the drives on the ego'. For Winnicott, where instinctual arousal was, there play should be. Or, to put it another way, the best form our instinctual life can take is in play.

And yet what playing, in Winnicott's version, cannot contain – excessive arousal – might be more exactly what psychoanalysis is about. Knowing when to stop playing might be as important as knowing what stops playing. It is, perhaps, the transitions that count: how the child moves from and through playing towards appetite and satisfaction; how the adult goes from absorption to arousal and gratification (from the vertical to the horizontal). The transition, I want to suggest, involves – is through – incoherence. One kind of chaos occurs when absorption, or preoccupation, begins turning into appetite and the hope of satisfaction. The no-nonsense self cannot make that move. Wanting comes out of an incredible muddle. Life's nonsense pierces us with strange relation.

'When we scrutinize the personalities who, by self-selection, became the first generation of psychoanalysts,' Anna Freud wrote in 1968, in her Freud Anniversary Lecture 'Difficulties in the Path of Psychoanalysis',

we are left in no doubt about their characteristics. They were the unconventional ones, the doubters, those who were dissatisfied with the limitations imposed on knowledge; also among them were the odd ones, the dreamers, and those who knew neurotic suffering from their own experience. This type of intake has altered decisively since psychoanalytic training has become institutionalized and appeals in this stricter form to a different type of personality. Moreover, self-selection has given way to the careful scrutiny of applicants, resulting in the exclusion of the mentally endangered, the eccentrics, the self-made, those with excessive flights of imagination, and favouring the acceptance of the sober, well-prepared ones, who are hard-working enough to wish to better their professional efficiency.

There is a poignant nostalgia in these words, delivered in New York in that fateful year, 1968. It is, as it were, a plea for the incoherent, for the self-contradictory, for the nonsensical; for what the critic Naomi Lebowitz calls 'styles that slum in an avid adoption of amateurism'. We are now fairly and squarely in the age of the sober professionalized ones, the people who know all too well when to stop. Psychoanalysis as the art and science of the indeterminate is what Winnicott and what Anna Freud, in her quite different way here, are speaking up for. The unconscious and professional efficiency are uneasy bedfellows. Which brings me back to my initial propositions: the coherence and incoherence of my theme, the connection between knowing when to stop and talking nonsense. Something about which Anna Freud's wonderful repertory company of the unconventional – the doubters, the dissatisfied, the odd ones, the dreamers, the neurotics, the mentally endangered, the eccentrics, the self-made – would know a lot about.

My two propositions were that it is impossible to know the consequences of one's words – the spoken, the heard and the overheard – and that an analysis is never finished, it is only abandoned. Both formulations are sceptical in Stanley Cavell's sense: 'Our relation to the world as a whole, or to others in general, is not one of knowing, where knowing construes itself as being certain.' 'Scepticism,' he continues in *Must We Mean What We Say?*, 'is a function of our now illimitable desire.' In other words, there would be a kind of madness, a kind of omniscience, in believing that it was possible to know the consequences of one's words, or to finish – in the sense of complete with any kind of certainty – an analysis. Our illimitable desire, Cavell intimates, can be displaced into an illimitable desire for certainty.

But how are we then to define, to publicize, the professional competence of the psychoanalyst – especially in the present technologically driven economic climate – if we can never be quite sure what to say or what we are saying, and if we can't know when and whether a psychoanalysis should end? How, to take up Anna Freud's late challenge, are psychoanalysts going to be selected, let alone trained? If hard work and bettering one's professional efficiency, to use her terms, are not going to be the ambition or even the aim of the aspiring psychoanalyst; if self-selecting dreamers, eccentrics and the mentally endangered are the preferred candidates for a psycho-analytic training – what is this training going to be like? To be acceptable to such a group of people, the training would have to be unusual, as indeed the trainings of the first analysts inevitably were. More of a circus school, or a singing school.

When Winnicott is speaking up for nonsense – 'organized nonsense is already a defence' – and Anna Freud is promoting the 'mentally endangered, the eccentrics, the self-made', they are both, in different ways and in quite different contexts, telling us that there is something valuable, from a psychoana-lytic point of view, in not being impressively coherent, some-thing about not being wholly plausible, or, in a conventional sense, intelligible, that psychoanalysis might ignore to its cost. It is as though they are asking us to wonder what we are doing when we are making sense; when, for example, we are being, or wanting to be, strong theorists or persuasive interpreters – as though we might be at our most defensive when we are at our most plausible.

Of course, the idea that we should be suspicious of intelligib-ility is itself paradoxical. As an aesthetic principle, it is perhaps best captured in the poet John Ashbery's remark that 'the worse your art is the easier it is to talk about'. This might translate as: 'The more defensive you are the more plausible you will seem to yourself (and other people).' This, of course, has implications for the practice and theorizing of psychoanalysis. Making the case for nonsense, like making the case against 'the sober, well-prepared ones', at least in a psychoanalytic context, allows us our dismay about making sense, while making us wonder where in psychoanalysis we can find now the intoxicated and the unprepared. It would be silly to take this too literally, but it would be sillier to ignore what was at stake for both Winnicott and Anna Freud in taking the positions that they did. They bear witness to the fact that, after Freud, we are awkward about our reasonableness. And our reasonableness seems to depend on our talking sense, and knowing when to stop.

If psychoanalysis has made us reconsider our beginnings – indeed, the whole notion of our origins as human subjects and objects – it has also revised our sense of endings. When I suggested at the beginning of this chapter that an analysis is never finished, it is only abandoned, I wanted to draw attention to relationships as by definition incomplete, and uncompletable. Another way of saying this would be that the ways we talk about finishing things, or about things coming to an end in other areas of our lives, are peculiarly unsuited to the ways we talk about so-called relationships ending. As readers we know where the poem on the page ends, and we know when the ironing is finished, when we have done our homework, when the football stops at the final whistle. Of course, the poem may linger in our minds after we have read it; we may find ourselves thinking or talking about the football afterwards. But there has been an official, an agreed-upon end that is recognizable. I think the formal ending of relationships bears only a superficial resemblance to these examples. A psychoanalysis ends, officially, when either the analyst or the patient decides, for whatever reason, to stop, or when the two parties agree to stop. But the question is, what is knowing when to stop knowing about? Knowing when to stop a football match means knowing about the rules of football; knowing when to stop reading a poem means knowing about the conventions of poetry; knowing when you've finished the ironing means seeing what's in front of your eyes.

There are no comparable conventions or perceptions available in knowing when to stop a relationship, unless, of course, you have prepared criteria for what it is for a relationship to end. And yet, relationships do end, in the sense that people stop doing certain things together. In professional relationships at their most pragmatic, the relationship ends when the problem is solved. And this is clearly one reason why the concept of cure has been so important, and so contentious, in psychoanalysis. It makes perfect sense, using a quasi-medical analogy, that the patient and the analyst stop seeing each other when the patient is cured. Knowing when to stop means feeling cured; knowing about people in a cured state, so to speak. But what of the afterlife of relationships, which is as real in its own way as is the life of relationships? And yet, as everyone knows who likes the sound of psychoanalysis, it is not solely or simply a problem-solving exercise. For some people, the relationship can end when the presenting problem has been solved. It is a kind of common sense that if you go to a psychoanalyst with claustrophobia, your involvement with the analyst will finish either when you are no longer claustrophobic or when you have finally given up hope of ever being changed by this kind of therapy. But you may also find, given a psychoanalytic opportunity, that whether or not you get symptom relief, you may want to go on; you may even come to believe that symptom relief may not be the be-all and end-all of the process. Not suffering matters, but not living as well as you can may matter more, and that is likely to involve suffering. Indeed, when Freud was offering us the prospect of transforming hysterical misery into ordinary human unhappiness, he was offering us a better life in terms of a better form of suffering. In other words, knowing when to stop should mean knowing what's good for you; and so, by the same token, the analyst knowing when the patient should stop means that the analyst knows what's best for the patient. My knowing what's good for me, and someone else's knowing what's good for me, can be the difference that makes all the difference.

Everything we do in psychoanalysis is a version of knowing what's good for someone; agreeing to begin the therapy, intervening (or not) in the patient's associative flow, not giving advice or giving it, and, of course, finishing the analysis. There are the generalizations of theory – in Winnicott's view, say, being able to play is good for people; in Freud and Ferenczi's view, being able to free associate is good for people – and there is the singularity of the individual analyst and the individual patient. And, as everyone knows, singularity and theory are uneasy bedfellows. There is, as it were, the order, the coherence, the no-nonsense of theory, and the uniqueness, the idiosyncratic singularity of the individual. 'Only a true theory,' the Lacanian analyst Serge Leclaire writes in *Psychoanalysing*, 'can advance a formalization that maintains, without reducing it, the domain of singularity; the always recurring difficulty of psychoanalysis, which no institution will ever be able to resolve, derives from the fact that it is vulnerable on the one hand to the degradation of a closed systematization and, on the other, to the anarchy of intuitive processes.' What Leclaire is drawing our attention to is the senses in which theory, systematization, is supposed to protect us from what he calls the 'anarchy of intuitive processes'. But the countervailing risk is that singularity, the individual in his personal delirium, is abandoned. In the 'degradation of a closed systematization', there is no place for the individual's nonsense; and it may be, as Winnicott only intimates, that his singularity resides in his nonsense. I think we should consider the possibility that Winnicott also believed that a person is at his most compliant when he is at his most coherent, that making sense, the wish to make sense, can be a species of conformism. In promoting the potential value of incoherence Winnicott is part of an honourable and perhaps fading tradition in psychoanalysis. There have always been nonsense and no-nonsense schools of psychoanalysis.

Singularity begins where a person's intelligibility to him/herself and others breaks down. This would be one possibility. Or, we might say, a person's singularity is his or her own idiosyncratic way of being coherent. Of course, how it has come about that singularity matters to people like us is a larger question with a contentious history. But psychoanalysis, if it is to be anything other than indoctrination, has to pay attention to the connections and otherwise, between the ambitions of theory and the (unconscious) projects of singularity. This chapter wants to offer up, as case studies for this particular issue, the related and unrelated notions of talking nonsense and knowing when to stop in psychoanalysis. In what sense can there be a psychoanalytic theory about knowing when to stop – that is, knowing when to stop the patient's associations to interpret, or clarify, or comment, and knowing when to stop the treatment? Could there be, for example, exemplary instances of these things, vignettes that illustrate a general point? Are there individual examples that could serve as general guidelines? If there were, could they be anything other than a consensual agreement among a group of people about what constitutes an excellent finish? We could, for example, formulate a list of the aims of psychoanalysis and see whether or not they have been achieved; we could look at all the sentences in the professional literature about interpretation, and about endings, and see what, if anything, they have in common. We could do some research into outcomes – but where would it end? How would we know, other than by agreement, when to stop our enquiries? Some things finish; some things are brought to an end; and some things finish or are brought to an end, but are discovered to be neither finished nor to have ended. Having the last word is never going to be the last word. What makes the last line of a nonsense poem the last line could never make sense. It is part of the ambition of theory to be coherent, plausible and persuasive; knowing when to stop the associations, the analysis, the nonsense is more like what the religious would call a 'species of prophecy' and the secular might call 'guess-work'. In psychoanalysis there is, then, the dream-work, the death-work and the guess-work.

Knowing when to stop, whatever else it is, is always guess-work. Psychoanalytic theory about clinical technique, whatever else it is, is a more or less coherent, plausible and persuasive account of guess-work; of why the guess-work worked, when it seemed to, and why it didn't when it didn't seem to. Whatever the analyst's decisions are informed by, whatever their prehistory, their preconditions, whatever their training, to speak or not to speak, to end the analysis or not to end the analysis, is a guessing game. Indeed, these moments of decision may be anybody's guess; they are certainly, judging by the controversy that surrounds these issues, undecided and undecidable. Psychoanalysis, at its best, tells the individual that he or she does not need a consensus in order to speak and that that sometimes involves talking nonsense and not knowing when to stop. 'Life's nonsense,' Wallace Stevens wrote, 'pierces us with strange relation.'

Making the Case:
Freud's Literary Engagements

The New Perseus, I also wrote, had to draw a mediating
mirror out of the very elements that threatened him.

Geoffrey Hartman, *Scars of the Spirit*

The literary engagements of psychoanalysts are legion. Indeed,
the question of whether psychoanalysis was itself a form of
literary engagement – of whether the writing of psychoanalysis
was more akin to what used to be called literature than to the
languages of science – began to occur to Freud once he started
writing (and publishing) case histories: story-telling created
uncertainty about the kind of story being told. In 'Discussion
of the Case of Fräulein Elisabeth von R.', from his *Studies in
Hysteria* of 1895, Freud famously wrote:

I have not always been a psychotherapist. Like other neuropathologists, I was trained to employ local diagnoses and electro-prognosis,
and it still strikes me myself as strange that the case histories I write
should read like short stories and that, as one might say, they
lack the serious stamp of science. I must console myself with the
reflection that the nature of the subject is evidently responsible for
this, rather than any preference of my own. The fact is that local
diagnosis and electrical reactions lead nowhere in the study of
hysteria, whereas a detailed description of mental processes such as
we are accustomed to find in the works of imaginative writers

enables me, with the use of a few psychological formulas, to obtain at least some kind of insight into the course of that affection. Case histories of this kind are intended to be judged like psychiatric ones; they have, however, one advantage over the latter, namely an intimate connection between the story of a patient's sufferings and the symptoms of his illness.

The accumulation of distinctions and disclaimers here are suggestive of a man suffering from genre-confusion. When Judith Butler says in an interview, 'crafting a sexual position . . . always involves becoming haunted by what's excluded. And the more rigid the position, the greater the ghost, and the more threatening it is in some way' (*Radical Philosophy*), she could also be taken to be saying that any genre is also ghost-written by the genres it excludes. Freud wants to be writing, and to be writing with, 'the serious stamp of science': and his case histories, he insists, are at least 'intended to be judged like psychiatric ones'. And yet they 'read like short stories'; and this is because, Freud says, attempting an explanation, the subject matter itself dictated the form the writing took. Freud – who clearly needs consoling for this – consoled himself 'with the reflection that the nature of the subject is evidently responsible for this, rather than any preference of my own'; as though the subject matter itself was an agent, indeed a writer, that chose its genre: or as though Freud experienced the subject matter as a form of temptation: call it the temptation of the literary. And indeed the subject matter of psychoanalysis would seem to be 'good material, so to speak, for the modern writer'. And yet, Freud also tells us (and himself), psychiatric case histories – accounts of 'local diagnosis and electrical reactions' – 'lead nowhere in the study of hysteria'. Unlike what he calls 'the works of imaginative writers', these more definitively scientific case histories are not productive of insight; or not of the new kind of insight that Freud is seeking. What distinguishes Freud's new kind of case history is that it assumes 'an intimate connection between the story of a patient's sufferings and the symptoms of his illness'. The patient's story of his suffering is somehow inextricable from his symptomatology. Indeed, the symptom is itself a story; or a story kept at bay.

When Freud writes as a neuropathologist, his case histories threaten to turn into short stories; and this is because – though Freud's causality is clearly askew – in the works of imaginative writers, unlike the works of neuropathologists, we are accustomed to finding what he calls 'a detailed description of mental processes'. There are already in the work of what he calls 'imaginative writers' the kinds of description Freud needs. As though the language of science that Freud aspires to write may itself be a problem; the aspiration itself could even be a version of a sexual conflict. Sexuality, Freud is beginning to realize in the *Studies in Hysteria*, is about choice of words; about how the preferred words tend to be the defensive words; and just how defensive written words may be compared to spoken words. The said cannot be unsaid in the way the written can be revised. For the patient, as for the psychoanalyst – and Freud implies that to all intents and purposes they have effectively invented each other – the story is about a quest for a new kind of story. Both have an (ambivalent) appetite for alternative descriptions; or, rather, the languages at their disposal don't quite work for them. Freud's scientific methods don't give him the language he needs; and his patients' hysterical methods don't give them the language-memories they need. The psychoanalyst, in his position as scientist, has tried to exclude the language of the short story in order not to lack the 'serious stamp of science'; the patient, in her position as hysteric, has tried – in Freud's view – to exclude the memories that are constitutive of her desire. They both suffer, Freud seems to be suggesting, from language failure, from languages that are buried alive inside them; from censored, alternative accounts. Freud is trying to work out, in his case histories, what (or who) his patients are being true to; and what, or who, he is wanting to be true to in his written accounts.

In the new science of psychoanalysis the analyst will enable the patient to remember, and so to desire: will analyse the patient's resistances, the wardings off stage that keep everything in the wings waiting to come on (the repressed is always something that is waiting its turn). And, by the same token, the example of the imaginative writer enables the psychoanalyst to tell the new story of his different kind of therapeutic work. When Freud comes to write his case histories he is remembering himself as a reader of short stories; it is a reading past that informs his work. The so-called hysterical patient is trying not to remember; and the psychoanalyst is trying not to write short stories. So one question here would be: what, for the psychoanalyst as writer, is wanting not to write short stories wanting not to do? To say that there is no such thing as a case history, there are only short stories, might be to acknowledge that there is no such thing as an exemplary instance; that psychoanalysis is a science with no examples, with nothing that can really be replicated; a science of the specific; a science of the special case. As though writing, modern writing, had some allegiance to particularity.

Whatever else is being intimated at this moment in Freud's writing, something haunting is being pointed out: the psychoanalyst is made possible by his prior literary engagements that he thought he needed to exclude. What seems to distinguish a psychoanalytic case history from a psychiatric one is the acknowledgement that it is a case history daunted by the short story it needs to repress. The psychoanalyst as scientist is always under threat of turning into an imaginative writer. A psychoanalyst, in other words, is someone who has found his literary affinities so alluringly unacceptable, such a disarmingly forbidden and forbidding pleasure – threatening, indeed, to deprive him of 'the serious stamp of science' – that he has to guard against them. But he also can't help but incorporate them, whether he likes it or not. And this will be Freud's definition of the repressed: it is that which you cannot help but include; even if, or especially if, you include it by warding it off. Freud discovers that there is a ghost-writer in the machine. He wants to write one kind of thing but it reads like something else. He is writing a psychiatric case history – and wants it to be judged as such – but it reads, in some ways dismayingly to him, like a short story. His writing is a kind of mistake. His literary engagements, as what he calls in 1896 a psychoanalyst, become a problem, a source of conflict. Or, rather, it is when he becomes a reader of his own writing that he first hears of this conflict and has to write about it.

There is a banal, and therefore partially true, explanation of all this in terms of the contemporary prestige of scientific discourse; the economic, the professional necessities of Freud carefully affiliating himself. If psychoanalysis did not acquire the symbolic capitol of science, it might be relegated as a 'Jewish science', or some other kind of disreputable cult. And yet what Freud refers to as 'imaginative writers' were not, in fin de siècle Vienna, merely negative ideals for Freud; the scientist as man of letters was a recognizable late nineteenth-century type. Nor, despite Freud's reiterated remarks that the poets had got there before him, is this simply or solely an anxiety of influence. Indeed, in Freud's work – and in the work of most analysts after Freud – 'imaginative writers' and literary writing itself are usually idealized. What used to be called literature is embraced by analysts of diverse persuasions. And the writer and the text are usually presented as the analyst's accomplices. The patient must, by definition, resist the analyst's interpretation; but the literary text never seems to when an analyst gets to it. It is as though, from a psychoanalytic point of view, the text has nothing to resist with. When Freud reads *Oedipus Rex*, when Klein reads *The Oresteia*, when Lacan and Winnicott read *Hamlet*, it is always a confirmation. The texts do their bidding. The psychoanalysts never seem to say: psychoanalysis led me to believe that X was the case, but then I read, say, *Pride and Prejudice*, and realized the error of my ways. Among the psychoanalysts the literary is that which never revises a psychoanalytic insight. The literary can never falsify the psychoanalytic; at best the literary text is a kind of fashion accessory, used at best merely to further a point. Literature becomes a historical archive for the confirmation of psychoanalysis.

So when Freud at the outset is so worried that his case histories in the *Studies in Hysteria* read like short stories, what could he be so worried about? It is as if it occurs to him that the kind of literary engagement that makes his psychoanalytic case history possible is precisely what threatens to de-legitimate it. It dawns on him at this moment, in other words, that it could be written and read in all sorts of ways, some more prestigious than others. But what exactly does a literary engagement represent such that Freud should at once require it and distrust it? Because this courting and cursing of the literary has been an integral part of Freud's legacy. The writing and the practice of psychoanalysis has been in a continual crisis of appraisal; from its inception psychoanalysis has been the Freud wars. There have been no Shakespeare wars; no one is likely to write a book called *Why Wallace Stevens was Wrong*. The literary engagements, or otherwise, of psychoanalysis – what the literary is to psychoanalysis as opposed to what the literary is to, say, philosophy or history; what you do as a psychoanalyst if you don't do science; what a cure would be for the psychoanalyst as poet as opposed to the psychoanalyst as research scientist – these have been the organizing perplexities that have made up the history of psychoanalysis. If psychoanalysis is not an applied science, perhaps it is an applied literature, the history of psychoanalysis, of course, being contemporary with all the contentions about the applications, the uses of literature. Once the psychoanalyst starts writing – as opposed to just practising psychoanalysis – she finds herself enmeshed in these issues.

The reason that Freud's explicit concern in the *Studies in Hysteria* is so instructive, I think, is that it is voiced, it is staged by Freud as at once a fear and a desire. A more literary form has become the necessity that threatens the credibility of the enterprise. Freud fears that in writing a psychiatric case history that reads more like a short story he has found a language for the transmission of that which cannot be replicated. A scientific case history by definition reports on a method of treatment that can be reproduced, and in being reproduced can be tested. The reason psychiatric case histories are useful is that they can be used to teach people how to do something; in this case a method for treating hysteria. If a case history reads like a short story, lacks the serious stamp of science, it may be because, in Freud's view, it refers to that which cannot be replicated. A psychoanalytic treatment, like a psychoanalytic case history, is an experiment that happens only once.

Of course, this may at first seem absurd. Freud describes in these case histories a method with discernible techniques; we discover what the doctor says and does, how he responds to the patient, what seems to work, and some kind of account of how it works. And yet Freud still thinks something is missing – or something has been represented – that lacks the serious stamp of science. The only difference – what Freud calls the 'one advantage' – of his version of a case history is that it assumes 'an intimate connection between the story of a patient's sufferings and the symptoms of his illness'. To put it crudely: the doctor's therapeutic method may be replicable, the patient's symptoms may be reproduced by many patients, but the story the patient tells of his sufferings will be singular. Patients, may, from the doctor's point of view, tell similar stories, but the story will never be the same. The psychoanalytic case history is the short story that privileges the singularity of the patient's story. A story of accidents transformed by desires. A specific story. It is, in Freud's words, the conflict between 'local diagnosis' and 'detailed description of mental processes'. The question – the scientific question – is does detailed description facilitate or waylay diagnosis? Does detail militate against generalization? Does the psychoanalyst want theory, and what is this a wanting for? Freud was beginning to want more of the patient's words, but in a different order: and fewer of the doctor's words. But he also found, more interestingly, that writing involved him in the allure of specificity.

It is not incidental that it is in the *Studies in Hysteria* that Freud makes, as Strachey notes, possibly the first reference to free association, which was soon to become the 'fundamental rule' of psychoanalytic method. Frau Emmy von N. is described as 'unburdening herself without being asked to. It is as though she had adopted my procedure, and was making use of our conversation, *apparently unconstrained and guided by chance*' (my italics). Free association can never be replicated. Freud will go on to say: if you encourage someone to say whatever comes into their minds they will every so often, more often than not, be unable to do this; and it is where they are unable that the resistance is, that their desire is. Hesitation is secular revelation. And, if you let people say whatever comes into their minds, certain patterns, certain repetitions, will become evident; that free association discloses the repetitions – the freeze-frames – that make free association impossible. Freud is preoccupied, in other words, with the pathologies of repetition; and, at its most extreme, with repetition as pathology. In the scientific method that Freud was trained in, that which could be repeated as experiment could be true.

The experimental method was based on replication; the psychiatric case history as exemplary instance. After all, what use is a so-called clinical vignette if it is in no way applicable? It is offered as a clinical vignette only because it is deemed not to be unique. It is not a curiosity but a tool. When is a case history not a case history? When it is a short story. When is a short story not a case history? When it is of no obvious use to the psychiatric profession. And yet why, in Freud's view, does Sophocles's *Oedipus Rex* work on the audience? Because, as he wrote to Fleiss in 1897: 'Every member of the audience was once a budding Oedipus in fantasy, and this dream-fulfilment played out in reality causes everyone to recoil in horror, with the full measure of repression which separates his infantile from his present state' (*The Origins of Psychoanalysis*). The literary work repeats, re-presents, everyone's early experience. And yet there is, to put it mildly, a certain singularity in Oedipus's story. It may be like our experience, there may be overlaps, but this is unequivocally Oedipus's own story. Freud is trying to explain something to himself here about the love of likenesses, the craving for identification. About how repetition makes identification possible; and about how identification is always a repressed acknowledgement of difference (it is only because I am not Oedipus, say, that I can be like him). That there is an appetite to be unlike the self one takes oneself to be; and that this appetite is so specific, so picky, fascinates Freud (like all avid hero-worshippers he was a hero to himself). Freud's theory of transference – his invention of a treatment organized around our need to reinvent figures from the past – was a way of wondering what people would be like if a cure for identification was found. But it was the writing of psychoanalysis that both revealed and forged likenesses to different traditions of writing.

Oedipus Rex, by the imaginative writer Sophocles, is sufficiently like our experience of our own lives, in Freud's view, to have a powerful effect; something about it breaks down our capacity to resist it. We can't estrange ourselves from its drama. And Freud's new kind of case history is too similar to imaginative writing, and not similar enough to a conventional psychiatric case history. In Freud's case history, one might say, as in *Oedipus Rex*, there is sufficient singularity; the people are more like people than cases (or allegorical figures); they are sufficiently unlike other people to be like other people. Freud fears that the patients – and possibly even the doctors – in his case histories are not types. In psychiatric case histories the patient has to be a type, or is too much of a type; in short stories people are not too much like types, they are just the right amount. Free association as a method threatens to undo the patient as type; the patient's resistance to free association is a resistance to unfathomable singularity, to the delirium of idiosyncracy. As a method it is Freud's antidote to the typecasting of everyday modern life, which psychiatric diagnosis may be complicit with.

In Freud's therapeutic method, and in his re-presentation of it in his case histories, the singularities of an individual's history come up against – and are enmeshed with – the reassuring generalities of theory. Psychoanalysis as theory is about the provenance of the unprecedented. In Freud's language it is about the compatibility of detailed description and diagnosis. It is as though, clinically, knowing when to stop the associations – through interpretation – is knowing when the theory starts, and when, perhaps, the writing starts. It is, in other words, the destiny of the details, the destination of the patient's associations, that exercises Freud. What makes you, as the doctor, stop someone talking and start talking yourself? (And this question could, of course, be applied to so-called ordinary conversation in which interruption is a form of desire, the form desire takes.) And what makes the psychoanalyst interrupt his clinical work by writing about it? The literariness that troubles Freud about his own writing – the sense in which it shows up his literary instincts, and might require a more literary engagement by his readers – is to do with the anxiety of uniqueness linked to Freud's anxiety about becoming a writer; and about what kinds of claims a person might be making for himself – a late nineteenth-century Jewish psychiatrist in Vienna – as one who privileges the unique, the accidental and the specific. 'Science,' David Lodge writes in *Consciousness and the Novel*,

tries to formulate general explanatory laws which apply universally, which were in operation before they were discovered, and which would have been discovered sooner or later by somebody. Works of literature describe in the guise of fiction the dense specificity of personal experience, which is always unique, because each of us has a slightly or very different personal history, modifying every new experience we have; and the creation of literary texts recapitulates this uniqueness, that is to say, Jane Austen's *Emma*, for example, could not have been written by anybody else, and never will be written by anyone else again, but an experiment demonstrating the second law of thermodynamics is and must be repeatable by any competent scientist.

This is not news, but it is pertinent, and succinctly put. What may be old news – at once both absurd and banal – is that for Freud, and for most psychoanalysts after him, the literary was at once both a refuge from the generalities of theory and a confirmation of them. And a psychoanalytic session, a psychoanalytic treatment, was supposed to straddle the contradiction that Lodge refers to; it could not have been spoken by anybody else, and never will be, but it had to be repeatable by any competent analyst. So, to rescript Judith Butler's remark, if crafting a position – in this case a therapeutic position, a writing position – always involves becoming haunted by what's excluded; and the more rigid the position, the greater the ghost, and the more threatening it is; then what happens when you find yourself in a position – as Freud does in his position as psychoanalyst of so-called hysterical patients – in which it is no longer clear what is being excluded: when one writes and perhaps practises psychoanalysis as a short-story writer *and* a scientific psychiatrist? Of course, any position can be described in terms of its exclusions, in terms of its presiding ghosts. (Butler's formulation could not be more psychoanalytic.) And Freud implies that his literary engagement with the short story shows him, against his wishes, what scientific writing can't do for him. In that familiar nineteenth-century way, the literary is there to describe the limits and the limitations of the languages of science. Freud wanted, consciously, to exclude the short-story writer in himself, but he couldn't. It would be worth wondering, historically, when and why a short-story writer would fear sounding like a scientist.

And yet, through the return of the repressed – by finding the short-story writer included in his case history – what is perhaps revealed to Freud is that the short-story writer and the scientific psychiatrist share an assumption: they both take for granted, in their very acts of exclusion, that we can describe only the unique and the repeatable, the singular and that which can be replicated. Freud's literary commitment, which he discloses to himself in the writing of his case histories, draws to his attention not merely the literary as opposed to the scientific, but to the position they share. That there are only two kinds of stories: how-to stories and just-so stories. And, indeed, the idea that one can describe only the specific and the replicate, the accidental and the patterned, is a rigid position, and one can't help but wonder what great ghosts may be threatening it. Freud would go on to show us the ways in which our descriptions are always in search of further descriptions; that we speak with a conflicted appetite to have our words redescribed to us; that there is a hunger for the misunderstanding called conversation.

The psychoanalyst as case-history writer may be a short-story writer masquerading as a psychiatrist, or vice versa, but the psychoanalyst as clinician was to use a therapeutic technique that was neither one thing nor the other. The case history may sound like a short story but the patient is encouraged to tell their story in a way that makes story-telling virtually impossible: to sound very unlike a story-teller. In free association the patient is encouraged to renounce the satisfactions of conventional narrative coherence in the service of truth-telling. And if the patient, encouraged to free associate, began to sound as inductively coherent, as evidentially and empirically persuasive as the psychiatrist did in his case report, his informing coherence would be analysed in terms of its defensive operations. In telling the truth about his psychoanalytic clinical work – about his recent professional past – Freud needed to have something of the short-story writer about him. In telling the truth about his predicament the patient, needless to say, must not sound like a scientist; but Freud now needs him not to sound like a nineteenth-century short-story writer either. He invites the patient, to all intents and purposes, to exclude their literary engagements. They are not there to tell the doctor a good story. Free association, as a therapeutic tool, is a renunciation of the literary: it is suspicious of rhetorical skill. It requires the suspension of artfulness.

In his 'Two Encyclopaedia Articles' of 1923, Freud describes 'The fundamental technical rule of this procedure of "free association"'. 'The treatment is begun,' he writes,

by the patient being required to put himself in the position of an attentive and dispassionate self-observer, merely to read off all the time the surface of his consciousness, and on the one hand to make a duty of the most complete honesty while on the other hand not to hold back any idea from communication, even if (1) he feels that it is too disagreeable or if (2) he judges that it is nonsensical or (3) too unimportant or (4) irrelevant to what is being looked for. It is uniformly found that precisely those ideas which provoke these last-mentioned reactions are of particular value in discovering the forgotten material.

Freud asks the patient to do precisely what the short-story or any other literary writer cannot do; that is, be unselective in his linguistic attention. The free-associating, speaking patient must not be in search of the right word; indeed, getting it right, finding the words for what he has to say, is the problem not the solution. A kind of anti- or counter-aesthetic of speaking is proposed. It would surely be part of any writer's or orator's gift or technique to reject any word or phrase that seemed, in the context, to be nonsensical, too unimportant or irrelevant. Even the surrealists, for whom Freud had so little time, were calculating their lack of calculation. The patient is encouraged to have a quasi-scientific method – he must be a 'dispassionate self-observer' – but he must be rigorously unliterary in his speech, an anti-artist. It is his moral and aesthetic criteria that he must suspend, if not actually abjure. What we might call, for want of a better word, the literary – judgements about the acceptable, the appropriate or the beautiful – is to be excluded. The paradox is that the forms of exclusion are themselves to be excluded.

It is the analyst who is to do the phrasing and the formulating; in the traditional psychoanalytic model, the patient's coherence will return from outside, in the form of the analyst's interpretations. It was not entirely clear, though, whether the aim of the psychoanalytic method was to release the patient into their delirium of association or, ultimately, to release him from it. There was, of course, a logic to the appeal of free association, a method, not incidentally, that Freud confessed to having got from a writer, Ludwig Borne. The so-called ego seemed to be, by definition, a taker of strong positions; for whom the name of the game was exclusion, which in turn leads to the creation of ghosts. Sustained by its own hauntings, the ego's method was paranoid. Paranoid was another word for coherent or organized or boundaried. If the ego was continually haunted – threatened and persecuted from outside – it was, by the same token, reassured that the bad things were outside. If one was living in fear one knew one was safe. The ordering of words – ordering words about – is the form defensiveness takes. Unconscious desire is at odds with arguments about it. Freud was becoming interested in disposable coherences.

But writing, of course, even when it isn't scientific, has its own coherence, its own necessary plausibility. As a writer, at least of case histories, Freud is tempted by what he thinks of as the literary; as a clinician he adopts the literary technique of a writer as the 'fundamental technical rule' of his new therapy, which is, of course, a talking and listening cure, not a writing cure. What is distinctive about psychoanalysis, Freud tells us, is that it assumes that there is 'an intimate connection between the story of a patient's sufferings and the symptoms of his illness'. And what is distinctive about the practice of psychoanalysis is that the patient is encouraged to tell the story of his sufferings in a way that makes it impossible to tell a story. The literary engagements informing the work of psychoanalysis in its beginnings – Freud's uses of the literary as point and counterpoint to the sciences he allies himself with, and from which he seeks his sureties – seem to function as both obstacles and instruments. It is as if Freud's more literary engagements are integral to the writing and practice of psychoanalysis, but are not to be wholeheartedly endorsed. At best, for Freud and for many of the psychoanalysts that followed him, psychoanalysis was to be the science that could legitimate the literary. It is the literary engagements, not the scientific ones, that are the sources of unease; that are confessed to and resisted by Freud. Clearly there was nothing remotely shameful about scientific method, or the ambitions of science; but there was something furtive, something undeclared, about the literary. Where literature was, there science should be. It is the literary, and suspicions of the literary, that is the source of conflict.

Freud, Ferenczi, Klein, Lacan and Winnicott are all convinced by, and explicit about, their scientific allegiances and aspirations. But for the strongest voices in psychoanalysis, psychoanalysis as a literary engagement has been something to shy away from. The literariness of psychoanalysis is to be resisted. For psychoanalysts, at least, the literary represents something. This is what the psychoanalyst faces if she thinks of herself as a writer. Because in writing the psychoanalyst threatens to stray from something or other.

Doing It Alone

Leo Bersani once said in an interview that the reason most
people feel guilty about masturbation is because they fear that
masturbation is the truth about sex; that the truth about sex
is that we would rather do it on our own or that, indeed, we
are doing it on our own even when we seem to all intents and
purposes to be doing it with other people. The desire that
apparently leads us towards other people can lead us away
from them. Or we might feel that what we call desire is evoked
by details, by signs, by gestures; that we fall for a smile or a
tone of voice or a way of walking or a lifestyle, and not exactly
for what we have learned to call a whole person; and that this
evocation, this stirring of desire, releases us rather more into
our own deliriums of fear and longing than into realistic
apprehension of the supposed object of desire. There is nothing
at once more isolating and oceanic than falling for someone.
Lacan formulated the 'objet petit a' to show us that the
promise of satisfaction always reminds us of a lack – that to
desire is to remember the one thing we are trying to forget –
and that this lack, disclosed by our longing, sends a depth-
charge into our histories. It is as though to desire someone is

to be sent back into yourself; it reopens the issues that have made us who we are. In other words, it may not be cynical – at least from one point of view – to think of desiring as something we do by ourselves; even if the phrase 'by oneself' needs now to be redescribed. The object of desire – as some psychoanalytic theory suggests, though it is mostly not British or American – may be rather more of a hint, a suggestion, a clue, than we are willing to acknowledge. And the subject of desire may not be interested in other people in quite the way we are encouraged to believe.

There is a puzzle here that is worth wondering about, and which is far more difficult to talk about than a secret. It is not so much that there is something which is hidden or concealed, but that there is something which is very difficult to describe. And this is that sexualities that are not linked to sociability make us uneasy; but sexualities too exclusively linked to sociability can leave us unappeased (if watching pornography is bad, watching pornography with your partner is marginally better). It is the more isolated and isolating sexualities that give us pause; the sexualities of sharing, of exchange, of connection – of what Keats called 'mutual delight' – that reassure and inspire us. At one end of our spectrum of descriptions there is bullying sexuality, in which it is as though one person is enraged that the other person is not part and parcel of their omnipotent fantasy, and forces them to fit; at the other end it is as though the desire – that what is exciting – is that the object of desire is outside one's omnipotence. Or, to put it in another language, one project is to find an object that by virtue of being everything to oneself forever conceals one's own vacancies; and another project is to find an object that keeps one's appetite alive by not being just what one wants. Either way, and there are other ways, what is being struggled with is whether the question of how to keep appetite alive is the same as the question of how to keep relationships alive.

Something of this is reflected in the history of psychoanalysis; where Freud often more starkly put sexuality, some of his revisionary followers put relationship. Where, for Freud's desiring subject in the *Three Essays on the Theory of Sexuality*, the object was 'soldered' on to the instinct, for some of Freud's followers the object was integral to the instinct; pleasure-seeking could look like a degraded form of intimacy-seeking. And development was essentially the humanizing of the instincts in the service of sociability. Instinctual life may be resistant to acculturation, but we could get this very description of instinctual life only from our culture. After Freud, to put it as crudely as possible, it seemed that people were no longer suffering from sexual frustration, they were suffering from loneliness and isolation. Either modern people were suffering because they were having the wrong kind of sex, or sexuality should be regarded as a kind of privileged – and perhaps over-privileged – metaphor for what goes on between people. Either there were secrets we needed to know about our sexuality in order to get it right, or our sexuality was part of the larger exchange called a relationship. It could be made to sound like a war between the cosy and the cruisers, between those who sought continuity and comfort and those who wanted risk and release; but unfortunately it was more complicated than that. It hinges on what, if anything, people want to exchange with each other; and whether 'exchange' is the best word for what people want to do together. The whole notion of exchange is at the heart of psychoanalysis, as of so much else in what we now think of as the modern world. We are most frightened now of those people who refuse to exchange anything with us. And psychoanalysis tells us that exchange –

that becoming subjects who see themselves as part of an exchange – is a developmental achievement.

And yet virtually everyone in psychoanalysis agrees that desiring often begins in the absence of the object; in the aftermath of the object, as it were. We all begin desiring by ourselves; after what looks like an exchange from the outside and from the mother's point of view, and before a further exchange. Desire begins in the interval. The object becomes a presence by being at first absent, by making the baby wait. Some people would say – people like Winnicott – that if all goes well this desiring that begins prompted by hunger in the absence of an object will precipitate the baby towards reunion; is indeed the vital and vitalizing bond; because I am innately a sociable creature – a dependent creature, an attached creature – I desire. It's not just that desire gives us an excuse to be together, it's that we are together because we desire. It is what we all have in common, even if what we have in common is a desire for different things.

This, of course, is not a new question: do we take sociability for granted, as in some sense innate, and then track its failures and defeats; or is sociability something that we learn, that we acquire, but not something inevitable? And what follows on from this is whether what we call our sexuality is part, is the medium, of our sociability, or whether there is something about sexuality that is averse to the consensual and the shared. We are likely to want to have it both ways: to think of our sexuality as culturally constructed on the culture-goes-all-the-way-down model; and to want to think of our desire as in some mysterious way outside or beyond or supplementary to culture, as the outlaw and outlawed part of ourselves, as where we are most abject and heroic. It is likely that we have constructed our sexuality as that part of ourselves that outdoes our constructions; and that there is something about our sexuality that makes us drift in this direction. We are probably the only animals that want to be the only animals that are unpredictable. But perhaps we need to take seriously, to follow through on, our psychoanalytic picture of desire beginning in the absence of the object; of desiring and being by ourselves as in some sense going together. Desiring being what we do on our own. There is, as we shall see, a tradition of philosophy that believes that what we do on our own is begin to doubt our own existence.

And we need to remember, of course, that this is the pre-Oedipal picture, if pre-Oedipal is still a word; in the pre-Oedipal world of so-called mothers and babies, the infant begins desiring by herself, on her own. In the Oedipal world she desires most fervently what is forbidden; what is against the law. And to desire what is against the law is its own kind of solitude, even if you can get fellow sufferers to join you. One begins desiring on one's own, and then one discovers that the object of desire is not on her (or his) own. I was on my own desiring someone or something that I took to be on their own; and then I discovered that I was on my own desiring but my object of desire had other options. The primal scene is our set-piece, our emblem for the solitariness of the desiring subject. To desire is to be doubly left out; left out from the presence of the object of desire, and left out of the desiring of one's objects of desire. Wanting and a certain kind of aloneness are inextricable; as Barthes wrote, in one's mind it is never the other who waits.

So against this, or alongside this, I want to put two clinical propositions; and by clinical I mean the kinds of things we hear ourselves and our patients say in one way or another all the time – though they don't of course put it in quite the way

I am going to put it for the purposes of this essay. First, everyone finds it difficult to join up the solitude of desiring with the actuality of possible consummation. There is, to put it mildly, a gap between our solitary longings and lusts (in fantasy) and the real people we meet in our everyday life. That our wishes are unmarried to the world. And, second, that many people feel unusually free in the absence of the object – providing it is known to be somewhere present – and get their most intensely exciting sexual pleasure in that solitary experience of desiring in fantasy; as though anticipating the object, or knowing it is there to anticipate, is somehow better than being in the real presence of the object. As though the actual object were a problem in a way that the fantasy, the remembered and expected object, is not. There is clearly something about the reality of the actual object that is off-putting, in a sense counter-erotic. At least this is the case for some people, or for all people some of the time. We do most of our desiring by ourselves, and we learned how to desire, we discovered what desiring was for us, when we were on our own.

Anna Freud once said, in your dreams you can have your eggs cooked the way you want them, but you can't eat them. The implication is clear: magic is satisfying but reality is nourishing. The question is – and it is a question that has haunted psychoanalysis – are the appetites analogous? Is hunger a good picture for sexuality? Because if it isn't, if sexuality isn't akin to, isn't a form of feeding, then the consequences are serious. Indeed, we could reverse Anna Freud's formulation and say that when it comes to sexuality it is the fact that you can't eat the eggs that makes them so satisfying. The fact that, as Freud remarked, desire is always in excess of the object's capacity to satisfy it is the point not the problem;

it is the tribute the solitary desiring individual pays to reality. This is a problem only if you are the literalist rather than the ironist of your own desire. It's not that reality is disappointing, it's that desire is excessive. It's not that we lack things, it's just that there are things that we want. We have never properly realized that we desire by ourselves, that we desire in and of ourselves; we have been misled into believing that we should either get reality to conform to our fantasy (tell people in no uncertain terms what to do); or submit to reality and sacrifice some of our desire. You will notice that both these solutions share a relish for sacrifice; either reality or desire has to be somehow given up. The psychoanalytic setting is the place where these illusory and, indeed, all too traditional alternatives are suspended; it is a space invented, I think, both to persuade us of the value of these traditional renunciations, and to persuade us that we may now need extricating from both our supposed solipsism and our supposed sociability; and from the idea that we are locked in this banal battle between our selfishness and our concern for others; and, indeed, that our sexuality is the site for this mythic contest. Desiring by myself might mean that my desire is not my own, and that it is not, by the same token, a desire for other people, as conventionally described.

In a section unfortunately entitled 'An Experience of Extimacy', Jacques Alain-Miller writes in his paper 'The Analytic Session':

This is why, in what the analytic session disposes, thoughts – these inputs that differ from what the subject receives in his [usual] activity – appear as messages received from within, as if the subject was inhabited by an emitter of thought messages.

If one were to give a phenomenological description of the experience of the analysand, one would end up formulating what Lacan enunciates at one point in his 'Instance of the Letter'; namely that there is the experience of an other 'that moves me at the heart of my utmost self-identity'. I am there, nothing of what I perceive can hold me back, there is only me, and yet there are thoughts which occur to me, thoughts of which I am the seat, the transmitter, and which are motivated solely by this psychical reality itself.

The analytic session, when it is considered in this very basic way, induces an experience of extimacy. In other words, within what is most interior to me, there appear elements that I cannot answer for and which are there, they sometimes link up [are lacking to me], or on the contrary flood in, and dispossess me of my initiative.

It is this experience, which is in a way primary, of extimacy, that led Freud to resort to Fechner's metaphor, 'the other scene'.

What Alain-Miller is calling extimacy here – the experience of our most intimately alien thoughts – is a version of that desiring by oneself that is picked up in Freud's method of free association. What is revealed is that these thoughts – as Blake famously said of his poems – are at once mine and not mine. And what indeed could be more mine and not mine than my own desire, and the so-called objects of that desire? One desires by oneself in the sense that one sits by a fire, and not in one. We often cannot answer for these thoughts, and they dispossess us of our initiative; it is like creating the conditions for the acknowledgement that one is possessed. The analytic project here, it is worth noting, is to bear being possessed – by this emitter of thought messages, this desiring source – and not to recover self-possession. Where id was id shall be. Desire, in this picture, is more like being told a secret about oneself that someone else had made. It could never be a confession, because the confessor always already knows his secrets. For

Lacan, following Freud, one's desire is like someone else's secret; but it is not one's own.

When people are by themselves they can have very strange thoughts. Descartes, in an inaugural moment of Western philosophy, doubted his own existence and had the strange thought that the fact that he was thinking proved his existence. In his *Treatise* David Hume, after being 'first affrighted and confounded with that forelorn solitude, in which I am placed in my philosophy', found that the only cure for this scepticism induced by solitude was company. When, in the relative isolation of his study, he began to doubt in a way that might make it impossible to live, what he called 'common life' was the cure for the scepticism that he called 'a malady which can never be radically cured'. 'If we are sufficiently reflective,' the philosopher Michael Williams writes in a commentary on the Cartesian tradition, 'Rorty on Knowledge and Truth', in *Richard Rorty*:

we will be sceptics in the study but, as a matter of psychological necessity, believers everywhere else . . . just as commonsense certainty is the standing condition of everyday life, scepticism is the natural outcome of philosophical reflection pursued to the limit [by oneself] . . . The business of the study is the pursuit of truth about the most fundamental matters. This pursuit demands that we withdraw from all social interaction, set aside all practical concerns, turn our attention away from our surroundings, and suppress all emotions. Life in the study is thus solitary, theoretically oriented, reflective and detached. Common life is the exact opposite. It is socially practical, perceptually responsive and emotionally engaged. Thus every aspect of common life works against taking scepticism seriously.

In this philosophical tradition the strange thoughts you have in solitude, in the study, are at once the most profound and the most disabling. Common life distracts you from the scepticism that is deemed to be truth about the most fundamental matters. For these philosophers solitude makes you doubt what common life distracts you from; for Lacan the unique solitude of the analytic situation makes you think and desire in a way that common life outside the consulting room will never let you. There is clearly a link to be made between philosophical doubt – beginning to fear for one's own foundations – and the emergence (and emergency) of desire. Sex becomes the word we use to refer to our not knowing where (or who) we are. And self-doubt becomes, say, the best cultural device we have come up with for tempering our aggression. The extimacy that Alain-Miller refers to is not, or not exclusively, a scepticism; on the contrary, it is evidence, so to speak, of the other scene, of unconscious desire. The suggestion in both this philosophical tradition and the psychoanalytic tradition is that the effect of the presence of other people – other people apart from a psychoanalyst – is either to stop one having one's most profound thoughts or to persuade one from taking them seriously. In both traditions, linked as they are by their intriguing similarities and their palpable difference, other people are the saboteurs of either self-knowledge or desire, or both.

When Freud invented the psychoanalyst he invented someone who valued, who listened out for, who perhaps even encouraged, these strange thoughts. Freud, as it were, put someone in the study with the suffering self-doubter and discovered unheard-of forms of sexual aliveness going on. But sexuality, paradoxically, turned up in the form of defences against sexuality. The individual can only desire by himself again, Freud's method suggests, in the presence of another person; but they must be in search of an extimacy not an intimacy otherwise they will replicate the distraction of common life the way common life conspires to waylay desire. Freud tried to invent a person, or a way of being, called a psychoanalyst, that would not distract a fellow human being from their own thoughts and desires. As though there was a growing realization of the extent to which common life, other people – and the parts of the self that were over-identified with this common life – were recruited as a kind of buffer against what Alain-Miller called the 'messages received from within'. Psychoanalysis was the new refuge for that extimate realm, that other scene, in its secular version. A place where people can hear what they happen to think and want.

It is clearly not incidental that Freud is developing the analytic setting – exploring what Lacan calls the 'analytic opportunity' – against the rise of fascism. 'Fascist regimes,' the historian Robert Paxton writes in his *The Anatomy of Fascism*,

tried to redraw so radically the boundaries between private and public that the private sphere almost disappeared. Robert Ley, head of the Nazi Labour Office, said that in the Nazi state the only private individual was someone asleep. For some observers this effort to have the public sphere swallow up the private sphere entirely is indeed the very essence of fascism ... Although authoritarian regimes often trample civil liberties and are capable of murderous brutality, they do not share fascism's urge to reduce the private sphere to nothing.

The private sphere retreats under pressure until it is called the other scene; and it requires a new form of privacy, called psychoanalysis, to let it speak. And it speaks in the least publicly accessible form, called free association. If language represents our ineluctable publicness, then language as free association is the closest we can get to speaking that contradiction in terms, a private language, a language of desire. Psychoanalysis has been consistently attentive to the public swallowing up the private; it is, for example, what Winnicott called the false self, and Lacan called adaptation. And there is nowhere in which we are more eager for the public to swallow up the private than in our sexuality.

It is very difficult not to talk of sexuality in terms of pre-scriptive generalities; and one might have hoped that, while everyone else was prone to do this, psychoanalysis, with its commitment to the idiosyncracies of personal history, and the unconsciousness of desire – not to mention its strong acknowledgement of our resistances to sexuality – would have assumed a sceptical but curious position faced with the sexual theories of adults, who were once children, even those adults who are called psychoanalysts, even though they were once children too. Musings on desire are more promising; when it comes to sexuality, theory is too explicit, it is like pornography. Desiring by oneself could never, by definition, be theorized; we can offer nothing more grandiose than our musings and our impressions, our hopes and our fears. Indeed, the need to rhetorically privilege these musings as theory we should take with a pinch of salt. Just as what is exciting for people who are excited by pornography is that in pornography everything is hidden, so too what is exciting for people who are excited by sexual theories is that in sexual theories a great deal seems to be known, understood and revealed. Sex, psychoanalysis once showed us, is that which it is virtually impossible to talk about. One's desire is not something about which one can be fluent. We desire by ourselves and it doesn't translate; the real questions are why we are so bothered by this? And what do we propose as an alternative?

For the Family

If this is a lesson in love, what's it for?

John Hiatt, 'Cry Love'

Ideally, families are groups of people of more than one generation who have a passion for living together. No child growing up in a family, of course, has anything to compare it with for some time; nor is the child in a position to leave. To begin with, whatever the actual arrangements, the family from the child's point of view is just the way the world is. The child in the family is, in this sense, like Sartre's rebel, the person who keeps the world the same so he can go on rebelling against it; he is not the revolutionary who wants to change the world. However discontented we are at the beginning of our lives we are not, for many years, critics of the family. And when we first become critics of the family we are critics of our own families, not of what we might later call *the family*. It is worth wondering what has to happen to someone, or what someone has to make of what happens to them, to make them begin to wonder not what was wrong with *their* family but what might be wrong with *the* family as a way of doing things. Families being primarily now ways of bringing up children and regulating sexual relations.

If the family, at its very best, inspires and is inspired by a passion for living together, this passion, like all so-called passions, involves frustration. Because the thing the family exposes, perhaps more intensely than any of our other social arrangements, is each individual member's capacity to bear frustration. What is revealed in every family is the way each person deals with frustration, their attitude to it; their 'relationship' to not getting what they want. However good the family is it is the place where we learn not to get what we want, and how to do this. Before you have children, the novelist Fay Weldon once said, you can believe you are a nice person; after you have children you understand how wars start. All critiques of *the family* that are not simply or solely grievances against one's own are grand narratives about possibilities for satisfaction. At their best they are stories about new ways of bearing frustration, at their worst – at their least promising and most utopian – they are about abolishing at least some of our frustrations. If, as Wittgenstein proposed, the way to solve the problem you see in life is to live in a way that makes the problem disappear, then the family would seem to be the place to start.

And yet, in so far as people want to have children and regulate their sexual desire, it has been very difficult to live in a way that makes the problem, and the problems, of the family disappear. Modern critics of the family have been unable to provide compelling or even plausible alternatives to it; alternatives that have caught on. Of course, families come in more configurations, more unprecedented varieties now than ever before. But they are all variations on a theme; and the theme seems to be the link between having children and the organizing of desire. The question is: what, if anything, does the raising of children require us to be faithful to? In our erotic lives we abandon our children, and in our familial lives we abandon our desire. It is not that couples with children don't desire each other, even though the having of children radically refigures desire in the couple; it's that their erotic connection, in the moments of enacted desire, excludes the children. In the family, of whatever configuration, what cannot be hidden is the fact that two people's pleasure in each other is always someone else's exclusion. That in our pleasure, whatever else we are doing, we are frustrating someone; and this is one of the things that makes our pleasure-seeking so difficult, so guilty, so confounding. Couples, of whatever kind, can be partners in crime. Once they have children they are the criminals.

Most people feel far worse about betraying their children than about betraying their partner. And children can be used far more effectively for the policing of desire than partners; at its most extreme it is as though the thing we can't do to our children is live our desire outside the family. Given that we can't always live our desire that intensely inside the family, it might seem sometimes as though a strange sacrifice is being made. In so far as we have become the animals who have to choose between having children or having sex we have made a terrible pact that must be to everyone's detriment, particularly the children's. It casts them as both the objects and the saboteurs of their parents' desire. This could make someone at once both a critic of the family and unable to conceive of anything better.

On Not Making It Up:
The Varieties of Creative Experience

The one thing which we seek with insatiable desire is to
forget ourselves, to be surprised out of our propriety, to lose
our sempiternal memory, and to do something without
knowing how or why . . . Nothing great was ever achieved
without enthusiasm. The way of life is wonderful: it is
by abandonment.

Emerson, 'Circles'

I

The Varieties of Religious Experience is a quite different proposition from the varieties of religious belief. By concentrating
on experience rather than belief William James was asking
himself, in his remarkable book: what happens, what does it
feel like, to have a religious experience? And what is it about
these experiences that makes us want to call them religious
rather than, say, political or artistic? What James puts his
modern pragmatic faith in – at least what he prefers to put his
faith in – are people's descriptions rather than their explanations. Or, rather, James is interested in how people's descriptions of what happens are entangled with explanations. The
title of his book makes us wonder, which comes first: the cart
or the horse? Are people's experiences the consequences of
their beliefs, or vice versa? Are beliefs foisted on experiences

or constitutive of them? Or is belief, as Wittgenstein asked, an experience? These, James acknowledges at the outset, have traditionally been questions for theologians and philosophers, and more recently – James was writing in 1902 – for anthropologists. And James confesses that he is none of these things. He is, he says, that relatively new professional thing, a psychologist. As a psychologist, he writes, 'the natural thing for me would be to invite you to a descriptive survey of [those] religious propensities'. Psychology, he suggests, is a kind of secular protestantism. It craves the singular account. 'If the enquiry be psychological,' he writes, 'not religious institutions but rather religious feelings and religious impulses must be its subject, and I must confine myself to those more developed subjective phenomena recorded in literature produced by articulate and fully self-conscious men in works of piety and autobiography.' It is as though, James intimates, institutions formalize (as belief) what individuals can't help but informalize (as experience).

That there were *varieties* of religious experience, and that we needed to take the variety of experience as seriously as the variety (or otherwise) of belief; and that the way through to this was a 'descriptive survey of religious propensities', of feelings and impulses and the 'more developed subjective phenomena recorded in literature produced by the articulate'; all this – which smacks for us of the varieties of creative experience – was a pretext, among other things, for James to develop a theory about theories. That is, a theory about why our theories matter. And theories matter for James according to their use. They are not destinations, they are our means of transport. For James the question about a belief is not whether it is true but, rather, how would my life be better if I believed it? So a belief can never be an idol or a fetish (or a resting-place), it can only be a tool or an instrument (we don't believe in violins, we play them). Our experiences may seem more various than our beliefs; but beliefs are things we use to get ourselves certain experiences. The only thing that matters for James about our theories is that they have consequences. He wants to know not how we have come by our theories, but where they can take us.

What we believe about God – like what we believe about the differences between the sexes, or about creativity – will above all affect what James calls our conduct. 'Every difference,' he writes in *The Varieties of Religious Experience*,

must make a difference, every theoretical difference somewhere issue in a practical difference, and the best method for discussing points of theory is to begin by ascertaining what practical difference would result from one alternative or the other being true. What is the particular truth in question known as? In what facts does it result? What is its cash-value in terms of particular experience?

What is creative about theory-making is that it creates consequences; our theories 'somewhere issue in a practical difference'; 'somewhere' because there isn't always a simple causal connection in play. However subtly, however difficult to discern, what we believe issues in what we do. Our theories are compasses, if not maps.

All this has been a roundabout way of saying that, from James's point of view, our theories about creativity are somewhere of a piece with our experience of creativity. What we believe about creativity affects our creative conduct. And if so-called creativity implies a creator then histories of religious experience must inform our modern ideas about creativity. If, for example, at its crudest, it is part of our post-romantic legacy to think of artistic work as akin to divine creation, and also to sometimes think of artists as mad, does that mean that we have a theory that the Judeo-Christian God was mad, or mad to create the world? Or mad to create the world like this?

What we believe – wittingly or unwittingly, consciously or unconsciously – creators and creativity are like will, as James puts it, result in certain facts, buy us certain experiences. When he asks of any particular truth, 'What is its cash-value in terms of particular experience?' he is asking us to imagine what this particular truth, this particular belief, can buy us, what experiences it can provide us with. If I believe that, at least potentially, I have something inside me called creativity; whether I describe it as a gift, or a skill; whether I think of it as coming from God or my childhood or my genes; if it feels somehow akin to sexual desire or is robotic; whether it is automatic, like a machine, or inspired, like grace. Each assumed likeness takes me down a different path. If writing poetry is a skill, like carpentry, or a game, like tennis, then I must practise regularly; if it is a gift, an epiphany, I must learn to wait, if not actually prepare my waiting, so that I am sufficiently receptive at the given moment, should it occur. James asks us to be attentive to these differences. Our truths are not out there, like new planets, waiting for us to discover them; they are made by us (and for us) like uniforms. In the service of our needs, they equip us for our particular tasks. James's pragmatism, in short, is itself a theory of creativity, among the varieties of creative experience.

The truth of your beliefs is what they can do for you, James says. Truth is the name you will give to whatever turns out to have been good to believe. So what then, James obviously prompts us to wonder, is good to believe about what we call – perhaps for want of a better word – creativity? And that means, in this context, what are the consequences of our beliefs about creative experience, and what do these useful beliefs reveal about what we want? If there really are varieties of creative experience then we can't hope – or shouldn't want – to come up with some essential definition that covers all our examples. Our wants can be as various, as idiosyncratic, as the facts resulting from our beliefs. And yet there is an emblematic dilemma that often turns up when modern people begin to discuss what modern people call creativity. Though it comes, as we shall see, in various forms, the dilemma itself can be simply stated: is creativity the imposition of something or the discovery of something? Is the creative act an assertion or a disclosure? We talk of people discovering the laws of nature, but not discovering poems in the language. We talk of someone making up a story, but not, at least not in the same way, making up how the brain works. It is as though there are things that are always already there which we may or may not find; and there are things which we make, which we put there, and by doing so we add something to the world that wasn't previously there. Gravity was always there, but the *Mona Lisa* wasn't. And yet, of course, we think of both so-called artists and scientists as creative. Are we making additions to the world as we find it, or are we revealing more and more of what's already there?

There is always a temptation to think too deeply about things. Indeed, William James is keen to keep us practical, to stop us being waylaid by our own profundity. But without being unduly portentous it is worth noting the recurrence of this particular dilemma in what are otherwise quite disparate modern writers. Denis Donoghue, in *Thieves of Fire*, used Adrian Stokes's distinction between carving and modelling to illustrate what he called the Promethean imagination; which, he says, 'starts with an incorrigible sense of its own power, and seeks in nature only the means of its own fulfilment'. 'In carving,' he writes,

the artist assumes that the block of stone contains within itself the form invented for it by nature; the artist's desire is merely to liberate that form, to disclose its hidden face . . . In modelling, on the other hand, the artist gives the stone his own truth, or what he insists is his own truth; the truth of the stone as a different truth is not acknowledged.

The great American critic R. P. Blackmur makes, in a similar spirit, a distinction between the erotic and the sacramental poet who, respectively, foist themselves upon their objects in an act of virtual ravishment or indeed cannibalism, or reveal and revere an object by definition other than themselves. When the poet Charles Tomlinson praises Marianne Moore in *American Essays* it is to this issue that he refers: 'In an age when major poets such as Eliot and Yeats have treated nature with an imperiousness that, at times, recalls their symbolist forebears, Miss Moore is ready to accord to objects and to animals a life of their own.' When he celebrates George Oppen for having 'his mind on what he is making and not on the coruscations of self-presentation', a similar point is being made. In one kind of creative experience the artist uses his art to elaborate, to expose, to fashion himself. In the other kind of experience the animating intention of the artist is to reveal something other, something separate, something aside or apart from the self; not, in Tomlinson's word, to 'fuse' with the object, but to differentiate it. The sacramental poet, the carver, forgets himself; the erotic poet, the Promethean, the modeller, endorses himself. In one version the self is the instrument, in the other it is the obstacle. In one version the so-called self is privileged, in the other versions something beyond the self is revealed. At one extreme of this strange dualistic vision there is the cult of personality, the artist as the emperor of egotism; and at the other extreme there is a cult of the object, of a world whose virtue and substance resides in the fact that it resists manipulation. Creative experience is either self-promotion or self-surrender. The moral and aesthetic question becomes: do I value something because I can make it mine, or because I can't? Whether we are talking about the individual's relationship with God, or the relationship between parents and children, or between lovers or friends, or simply our involvement with the so-called external world, the creative experience, whatever else it is, is our sorting out our making from our finding. In the language of psychology, this would mean wondering about the difference between perception and projection.

It would be tedious to catalogue the modern instances of this essential perplexity. When, for example, the political philosopher Jerry Cohen wanted to illustrate a point in his recent Gifford Lectures about utopian socialists, he suggested that they 'prescribe a new form to reality. Contrast midwives, who deliver the form that develops within reality' ('If You're an Egalitarian, How Come You're So Rich?'). Put like this the gender distinction seems most vivid; but the familiar thing is once again at stake. Prescription of something new, or facilitation of something there already, and ready to happen. 'The artist,' according to Adrian Stokes in his *Critical Writings*, 'has seized upon a pose and almost painted the object out.' Whereas the artist as midwife allows the object its own shape. Like all such contrasts the differences blur in the middle. When Ted Hughes writes about a pike the poem is at once startlingly real and has Ted Hughes written all over it. But the distinction I have been labouring over catches something of our sense of what selves might be like; and particularly creative selves, reminiscent as they often are of earlier representations of deities. There is the imperial (and imperious) self who colonizes the world, or replaces the world with a world of his own: the artist who makes the world in his own image. And then there is the self as midwife, creating the optimal conditions for something other than the self to come to life; the artist as servant of a process. For the imperial self, the world needs to be improved. For the midwife self, the world needs to be seen as it is.

This way of categorizing the varieties of creative experience is clearly more applicable to some arts than to others. It doesn't, for example, tell us very much about music. And it seems to make slightly more sense of the visual arts than the verbal arts. But it is most instructively confounding, I think, when it is applied to one thing that psychoanalysis as a treatment has in common with at least some of the literary arts; that is, the narration of personal history. What if the creative experience is the telling of a life story, or the writing of an autobiography? What if the object to be creatively transformed is what we quaintly call the past? For Rousseau, for Wordsworth, for Freud – indeed for William James in *The Varieties of Religious Experience* – to tell one's life stories was a paradigmatic creative experience. It was the creative experience that accounted for one's creative experience. But is the patient in psychoanalysis, or the romantic (and post-romantic) autobiographer, a carver or a modeller? A Promethean or a midwife? What would it be, in other words, to tell the story of one's life but not to make it up? An autobiography without a self in it, or a self without a past in it, would seem like a contradiction in terms. We couldn't help but wonder whose life story it was. Unless, that is, the past has a life of its own that the self – or what we call the self – can get in the way of. What Freud is saying, as we shall see, is that the past does have a kind of life of its own inside us; and that what he calls the ego is always trying to make it a life of our own. The ego is a modeller, the part of ourselves that imposes form and meaning on our lives. But the past – our desire, and our memory that is of desire – insists, like a carver, on liberating its own forms. It keeps releasing versions of itself, called repetitions, and quite un-expected, expectant desires. It keeps disrupting our plans. We break our resolutions. The ego is a utopian, but the past keeps giving birth to itself. What Freud calls the return of the repressed, we might call the carver's triumph over the model-ler. Prometheus enflamed.

If, for some people now, God is neither the source of nor the model for our creative experience; and if, for some people, the rumoured death of God prefigured the death of the subject, of the self as agent, then the whole notion of creativity – of creators and their creations – looses its moorings. There is no privileged analogy, no model, no agreement about origins or aims. Just as William James asked, what makes people want to call an experience religious? We might want to ask now what is it about an experience that makes us want to call it creative? And, of course, the antonyms in play make a differ-ence, affect the cash value of our experience; secular is not the same as destructive. Towards the end of his life – as a kind of theoretical valediction, an elegy for one world war and a foreshadowing of another – Freud described the individual as a war between creative and destructive forces; as constituted by this conflict between what he called, in his own mythology, Eros and Thanatos. But psychoanalysis, from its inception, was always a story about the varieties of destructive experience. And the first word in psychoanalysis for destructive experience was 'trauma'. The second word was 'instinct'.

II

In a sense, the issue of trauma can be stated quite simply: is a life interrupted by events, or are the interruptions the life? Do we, as organisms, have an aim, a teleology, a true life story from which we can be deflected, or is what we call a life – and the telling of a life story – a series of more or less productive and satisfying adaptations and transformations of what happens to happen? Just as acorns become oak trees people could be described as having essential selves, organic destinies, which are either distorted or realized – depending on one's point of view – in the haphazard of circumstance. We are, alas, back in the world of carvers and modellers; of midwives and Prometheans. If what we call the self is already there it just has to be delivered; optimal conditions must be created for its birth and development. Events are assessed according to whether they nurture or thwart this intimate, innate, unfolding form. Events like wars, epidemics, economic slumps can be the ultimate bad luck, the ultimate affront to this self. Indeed, the problem of having such a self – of having such a preferred life story – is that it can be sabotaged. If you are very lucky – and with this kind of self you have to be very lucky, for you are prone to bitterness and disappointment, to not having been given a chance (your chance) – the world will be your midwife. But the onus, so to speak, is on the midwife. Or perhaps it is more accurate to say that the project depends upon the midwife.

For the Promethean, of course, circumstances are there to be used; contingent events – and the not so contingent event of who is in charge – are the point not the problem. They are, indeed, an opportunity – the only opportunity available – to make the self. Whatever happens to be there is potentially material to fashion the self with; any occasion that presents itself is an opportunity to make the self in performance. The only thing the Promethean has to complain about is how the world resists him: how recalcitrant the medium can be in which he needs to exhibit himself. The Promethean makes himself by persuading others of the value of the self he is making. The Promethean self hopes he can be threatened, or at least challenged; the midwived self hopes he can go on growing. The Promethean self thrives on trauma; for the midwived self trauma is dismaying.

The midwived self is prone to feel that the world has let him down; the Promethean self is prone to feel that he has let himself down (the depressed are disappointed Protheans). I could go on, though the distinction, clearly, is not endlessly resilient, or endlessly fascinating. But what it does show, I think, is a modern conceptual configuration – a field of terms – that we can use to describe so-called creative experience. A surrender, a yielding, a giving oneself up (or over) to something not exactly (or remotely) oneself; or an imposition, a foisting, a fashioning of something of one's own. 'It is the difference,' Richard Rorty writes in *Consequences of Pragmatism*, in another context, 'between regarding truth, goodness and beauty as eternal objects which we try to locate and reveal, and regarding them as artefacts whose fundamental design we often have to alter.' Each of these two versions involves us in telling a different kind of story about the self; about its gifts and talents, its purposes and functions, its presence and absence. There are muddles to be had here, as well as perplexities to be considered. It is not clear, for example, in these terms whether what we call our selves are the obstacle to or the instrument of creativity; whether what we call creative experience is the unmaking or the making of the self.

What Freud adds to the conversation (apart from a change of terms: he drops the self and uses the word 'ego' for the way we want to represent ourselves to ourselves and others) is a question about therapy, about life aims. Is the aim of psycho-analysis to strengthen the ego or to weaken it? Should we be strengthening our characters, or putting a stop to them? Is Prometheanism the problem or the solution? What Freud uses psychoanalysis to describe is what might be called an alternative to egotism; and this is both a new variety of creative experience and a new story about creative experience itself. Freud invents a technique which reveals – despite his wish to use it as a cure for symptoms – what happens, what turns up, when a person chooses to relinquish his egotism, his sense of himself as a, as *the*, creator. When, that is to say, he says whatever comes into his mind in the presence of another person; when he free associates. What is said (and thought and felt) when the person who he thinks of as himself stops thinking about making it up?

What Freud hears, as he listens to his patients – as he listens to himself listening to his patients – is the prodigal vagrancy of modern human appetite. Or, to put it another way, he discovered – even though he resisted the discovery – that there was no such thing as a normal sexual life: no such thing as a normal life story. Freud, in other words, makes us wonder: what would a theory of creativity be if it was a theory of appetite? And what if our appetite, essentially, is for appetite regained? So the paradoxical aim of creativity was to keep creativity alive, just as the point of appetite is to sustain it. There was the creativity of telling one's life story, and the creativity of whatever it was that hampered, that paused, that interrupted the telling of a life story. But the life story itself – whatever else it was – was for Freud a memory of desire. To speak is to remind oneself, to re-create what it is one wants and fears.

Freud can't work out whether the psychoanalyst, not to mention the patient's ego, should be carving or modelling. And this is partly because what is deemed to be there to carve or model is not stone, it is personal history; it is instinctual life, and the strange logic of its unconscious representation. What Freud calls the unconscious is not analogous to the material the sculptor uses; in fact, it is not clear what, if anything, it is analogous to. And therefore it is not clear whether it makes sense, from a psychoanalytic point of view, to think of a person (or a patient) as the artist of his own life. What, exactly, are the materials that he is going to transform? Is the past or our desires – in whatever form they are assumed to be alive inside us – akin to an artistic medium, and therefore available for us to transform? What, if anything, is creative about ourselves; and what or who is doing the creating?

Whatever our analogy for the storage, for the accumulation of past experience – the archive, the museum, the tomb – and however we imagine the instinctual desire inside us – as drives or energies or wild animals – the only way through which the life inside us of which we are unconscious can make itself known is through bodily movement and language. There may not be palpable or observable selves inside us to be carved and modelled, but words can be spoken. The psychoanalyst shows the so-called patient how he stops himself speaking, and what he feels he must not say. In prescribing the method of free association the analyst encourages the patient to become a carver rather than a modeller of his speech flow. The modeller, we may remember Denis Donoghue wrote, 'gives the stone his own truth, or what he insists is his own truth'; whereas the carver 'assumes that the block of stone contains within itself the form invented for it by nature; the artist's desire is merely to liberate that form'. The analyst's desire, one can say, is to liberate the form, the unconscious logic of desire, contained with the patient's words. 'The fundamental technical rule of this procedure of "free association",' Freud writes in his 'Two Encyclopaedia Articles' of 1923,

has been . . . maintained in psychoanalytic work. The treatment is begun by the patient being required to put himself in the position of an attentive and dispassionate self-observer, merely to read off all the time the surface of his consciousness, and on the one hand to make a duty of the most complete honesty while on the other hand not to hold back any idea from communication, even if (1) he feels that it is too disagreeable or if (2) he judges that it is nonsensical or (3) too unimportant or (4) irrelevant to what is being looked for. It is uniformly found that precisely those ideas which provoke these last-mentioned reactions are of particular value in discovering the forgotten material.

If the patient makes 'a duty of the most complete honesty', in the way Freud prescribes, what will come through? What, in Donoghue's words, will be 'liberated' or 'disclosed' will be 'the forgotten material'. If you free associate, Freud says, if you speak freely, what you are speaking about, unbeknown to yourself, is the past. Honesty is simply memory; truth-telling is remembering what it is you want. What the patient is resistant to, what has made the patient a modeller, a Promethean rather than a carver or a midwife, is this horror of the past.

'When conscious purposive ideas are abandoned,' Freud writes in *The Interpretation of Dreams*, 'concealed purposive ideas assume control of the current of ideas.' Something else is liberated, something else called 'concealed purposive ideas' takes over; as though there are hidden counter-intentions awaiting their chance. And yet what Freud describes is a kind of creative struggle; a battle, as it were, between two artists. If we look at the patient's criteria for excluding ideas, for not speaking, they are rather like the standards a writer might use in revising his work; if the words are disagreeable, nonsensical, unimportant or irrelevant they are taken out. The writer, as Promethean modeller, is a master of relevance, a maker of his own preferred sense. He lives by his own criteria, whether or not he is ever able or willing to articulate them. For someone – a carver-analyst, or a carver version of himself – to suggest that he should abandon his way of doing things would be a form of character assassination. What, after all, the ego as Promethean modeller might wonder, would he be abandoning himself to? And to what end? Is there something else, something better, that the Promethean, by being a Promethean, has been warding off, which would give him a better life? Is creative experience a warding off or a surrendering; or, as Freud intimates, an essential and irresolvable conflict between the two? But there is, we can see, a version of creativity that is essentially a conflict between two kinds of creative experience: between two kinds of creative selves. Freud seems to believe that our life has a life of its own – has lives of its own – going on inside us. And that when the patient who is suffering from his own Prometheanism (his infernal self-fashioning) meets the analyst as midwife, as carver, something vital will be liberated; and that is called, variously, the re-pressed, 'the forgotten material', the memory that is desire.

What is creative, Freud intimates – though this would not necessarily be his word – is the sustaining of the relationship between these two figures, these two versions of oneself. There is the creativity, the inventiveness of defence and resistance; Harold Bloom, and Lionel Trilling before him, refer to the Freudian defences as poetical tropes. And one of the more insidious implications here is that we are at our most creative in the ways in which we frustrate ourselves. That creative experience is the art of turning renunciation into its own kind of pleasure. And then there is the creativity involved in releasing or disclosing or acknowledging – it is difficult to know what the right word is here – whatever is disowned or estranged within ourselves. Or, indeed, what is quite other to ourselves as we know them; whatever has been hitherto out of reach of the human (the non-human human environment). And all this creative struggle that is deemed to be going on both within the individual and between the analyst and the patient has a simple aim: to prevent the future from being merely a repetition of the sufferings of the past. To make the future unheard of. It is creative to produce variations on a theme or to change the theme.

And yet it is clear in this modern, secular, virtually Darwinian story of creativity – that is to say, a story about creativity that is a story about appetite, pleasure-seeking and psychic survival – that there is a tension between conservation and renovation. The rebel, Sartre says in his book on Baudelaire, 'is careful to preserve the abuses from which he suffers so that he can go on rebelling against them'. The revolutionary changes the world. The rebel, in other words, is the person who fears the future. What is creative about the rebel, one might say, are the ways he finds to keep the world the same so that he can go on rebelling against it. If you hate change you have to be clever at conservation. Sartre pits the nostalgia of the rebel – his passion for repetition, for sameness – against the innovation, the improvisation of the revolutionary. There is the making new, and there is the keeping fresh.

The point about a God is that he always already exists; the point about a secular future as an object of desire is that it doesn't. It is as though – when we think about the varieties of creative experience – either everything is already here and all we have to do is find it and let it be as it is; or that the point about what is already here is that it is here to be transformed into something else that has never been here before. William James, as a pragmatist, would favour the second view; Freud as a psychoanalyst hovers between them, sensing that if there is a mind it can't make up its mind. And especially not about this. It is the conflict between conservation and improvisation, between the rebel and the revolutionary, that bewitches him ('given the divergent temporality', Arnold Davidson remarks in *The Emergence of Sexuality* of the emergence of new concepts and the formation of new mentalities, 'it is no surprise that Freud's mental habits never quite caught up with his conceptual articulations'). And it is perhaps the creative and peculiarly modern creative experience of autobiography that bring these particular issues into striking relief. Is the autobiographer – and the autobiographer that is the psychoanalytic patient – a rebel or a revolutionary in Sartre's terms; a carver or a modeller in Stokes's terms? Is the autobiographer – which is a virtual synonym now for the middle-class person – making it up; which means making something new that never previously existed? And if that is what she is doing why does it matter, why should anyone be cross?

III

The psychoanalytic patient as autobiographer is an unusual kind of artist; he is, as he free associates, an artist without standards. The artfulness of the writer is her selection of words; consciously or unconsciously some words are considered to be better than others. Knowingly or not, the creative experience of writing is a series of decisions. Freud defines his patient by requiring something specific of him; that he will become, as it were, the anti-artist of his own life; he will abrogate, in so far as he is able, the choice of words. He must speak as though none of his words are any better than any others; none are more accurate, or more truthful, or more melodious. He must speak as though he is someone who doesn't yet know which of his words are valuable, and in which ways they are valuable. He must become like a medium for the language inside his body. He is not being encouraged to speak as though he didn't know how to speak, but as though he didn't know how to mean what he said, or when he said what he meant. The experience, at its starkest, is of speaking as though one's language had no meaning. Or, rather, that one's language had concealed or indeterminate meanings (like pretending one was bilingual in one's own language). In so far as the patient resists, as he must, saying whatever comes into his mind he is conserving himself; maintaining the status quo of who he wants to be. He tries – against the odds, so to speak – to narrow the range of what he has to say; to stay within orbit of what makes sense to him. He wants to be a recognizable kind of person, primarily to himself. And he can do this, Freud intimates, only if he is sufficiently ingenious, sufficiently artful, one could say, in censoring himself. Rebelling against his own nature – his other nature – this is the creative experience of keeping oneself safe. This is a modelling of the material, the selecting of words, that, one imagines, keeps one acceptable, indeed lovable, to certain others. This account is me as I would prefer to be seen; so anything new, anything surprising, anything at all disruptive, has to meet my already existing criteria of what my self should sound like. And this, one could say, is the bind for the modern poet who has found what we call his or her voice; that having found the voice it then has to be imitated. One has to sound, one should sound, like oneself (the poet of the future may fear sounding like himself). The modeller, the rebel, wants to discover a style, an idiom, a personal voice. He wants to be recognizable, even if no one, including himself, understands what they recognize. The creative experience here is of not being thrown too far off balance; of not loosing one's moorings in the world of shared interests and consensual pleasures. The autobiographer – the psychoanalytic patient as oral autobiographer – may sound eccentric, but we will be able to locate the centre that he is off. We will be able, in short, to call him a person, a character; an extraordinary individual compared with all the ordinary individuals we reassuringly think that we know.

The patient speaks: the analyst helps him recognize and understand his resistances to speaking; and, ideally, the patient can speak a little more freely. This is Freud's more or less traditional account of creative experience, redescribed and adapted for a therapeutic setting. The post-romantic image of the struggling artist – emotionally tormented and economically deprived – becomes the neurotic patient struck dumb, or struck banal, by his forbidden (incestuous) desires. In this version creative experience is a creative overcoming.

The patient may not be able to make sense of what he is saying but it is hoped that the analyst can. The patient free associates not exactly to or at a listener but in the presence of one. There is, that is to say, a modeller somewhere in the room; someone who can make some sense of the verbal proceedings. And yet it might be equally plausible to say that the analyst is a carver and that the patient is the modeller. The patient keeps imposing himself on his own words (keeps performing his egotistical sublime); and the analyst, through analysis, tries to get his own censorious ego/super-ego out of the way so he can speak without impediment; release the words banked up, waiting inside him. But it's clearly more complicated than this; especially if what is there deemed to be seeking some kind of release is unconscious memory and desire. After all, what would it be for all this pastness (in whatever form), all this forbidden desire, to come through? It is, of course, at moments like this that people start using words like 'floodgates' and 'barbarism'; and, indeed, 'family values'. So perhaps it would be better to say that the analyst is helping the patient to be a better modeller, more satisfyingly selective. The patient might become a less restrictive guardian of his vocabulary; he may, at least to some extent, be able to tell people what he seemed to want from them, and be prepared to take the consequences of such desire as he has. But if the analyst helps him with his modelling; frees him, not necessarily to be less censorious, but to be more able to evaluate for himself his own censoriousness, and to see what it is worth to him; then the question arises – when it comes to talking or writing, when it comes to words, when it comes to autobiography – what would it be to be a carver? Is there a life story waiting to be told, awaiting the conditions for disclosure? Can we assume, to adapt Denis Donoghue's words, 'that the person contains within herself a life story invented for her by nature; so the artist's (the analyst's) desire is merely to liberate that

94

story, to disclose its hidden face'? If one's life story, or the life stories that constitute one's life story, are like this – if the analogy with sculpture holds – then, if the carver has done her work, nothing will have been made up. For the carver there is a true story to be told; the creative experience is this struggle for accuracy, for sentences that correspond to what happened. If the autobiographer told us at the outset that she was aiming not to tell the truth we would wonder what she was up to; we would wonder what to call what she was doing.

'This,' Rousseau begins his *Confessions*, 'is the only portrait of a man, painted exactly according to nature and in all its truth, that exists and will probably ever exist'; it is, he writes, 'the only sure monument to my character that has not been disfigured by my enemies'. If this is the 'only' portrait that is strictly mimetic – 'painted exactly according to nature and in all its truth' – it is clear that Rousseau is the first person ever to have told the truth about himself; that there is a truth to be told about oneself, and if one is sufficiently honest it can be told. Enemies, he intimates, are those people who disfigure this truth. That is how you recognize an enemy: he distorts your account; he defaces your monument to yourself.

   In this creative experience there is a creator, and he knows what he is doing. Like a God he seems to know where he stands in relation to himself and his creation. 'I have told the truth,' Rousseau concludes his *Confessions*, in a flourish of barely concealed righteous indignation,

If anyone knows things that are contrary to what I have just set out, should they be proved a thousand times over, he knows lies and deceits, and if he refuses to explore and to clarify them with me while I am alive, he loves neither justice nor truth. As for me, I hereby declare publicly and without fear: that anyone who, without even having read my writings, examines with his own eyes my nature, my character, my morals, my inclinations, my pleasures, my habits, and can think me a dishonourable man, is himself a man who ought to be choked.

There is, perhaps, a certain bravado in this provocation, a certain amount of self-doubt to be dealt with if sceptics of his account ought to be killed. Correspondence theories of truth can bring with them murderous forms of self-assurance. Is such honesty in itself honourable, or is it the truthfulness of his account that has disclosed just how honourable Rousseau has really been in his life? Rousseau's insistence, one could say portentously, suggests, at least to our more modern ears, that there was a crisis about truth-telling in the air. And a crisis about the nature of the self.

Freud was to redescribe honour as part of the tyranny of self-love; and to redescribe those who are utterly convinced of their own truthfulness as paranoiacs. Rousseau, as we can see, is a man utterly dependent on his enemies for his self-definition. It is of course glib and therefore silly to talk in this kind of reductive shorthand about issues of such (historical) complexity. But it is worth noting some of the ambiguities – the potential for a certain kind of arrogance – in the carver's attitude. In cherishing his truthfulness, in simply delivering his truth in all its apparent integrity and which he could not, by definition, have made up, he renders himself curiously unassailable. He apparently abrogates his egotism only to produce something wholly self-sufficient. We may remember Charles Tomlinson praising Marianne Moore over Yeats and Eliot because she was 'ready to accord to objects and to animals a life of their own'. Rousseau is ready here to accord to his life story a life of its own. What would it be to criticize such integrity; after such honesty, what forgiveness?

The variety of creative experience that Freud adds – and that Sartre elaborates on in his distinction between the rebel and the revolutionary – is that the autobiographer is always a modeller, always a Promethean; is always inventive and self-inventive in his account of himself. And, indeed, may be at his most Promethean, at his most imposing, when he claims to be telling the truth. That we are not, to put it as crudely as possible, trying to get it right, but trying and trying not to get what we want. Truth is the rhetorical compliment we give to our desires to persuade people of the value of gratifying them. The truth-teller, the autobiographer as truth-teller, wants something, wants everything from the people he addresses. This is what the psychoanalyst asks herself; what is the patient wanting, unbeknown to himself, in this telling? What unconscious drama of satisfactions is being staged? The paradox, in other words, of the autobiographer, at least from a Freudian point of view, is that he is always looking forward. 'Psychoanalysis,' Lacan wrote in the *Écrits*, 'is a question of recollection . . . in which conjectures about the past are balanced against promises of the future.' But the future, of course, can promise only what we make it promise. Left to itself the future has nothing to offer. We have to make up the future until we get there.

We are allowed, it seems, to make up the future, because that is all we can do with it; but we are not supposed to make up the past. And yet, as I have said, there is a paradox about that peculiarly modern form of creative experience called autobiography. Since the past, our personal history, has already happened it must always be there awaiting our discovery of it; the lost tribe of oneself is there to be found. And yet the autobiographical account is something new, has never existed before. And, each time you tell it, it will be different. To write or speak one's life story is an experiment that cannot be replicated; it is antithetical to our most rudimentary notions of science because no one else can try telling your autobiography to see if it's true. And even if a biographer can verify or falsify elements of one's life story, it remains true that, for whatever reason, one has chosen to remember, to tell things in a certain way. What might more traditionally, for example, be called lying, Freud would call wanting; the form one's wanting has had to take, in the circumstances. In Freud's view, by talking about the past we are talking about what we want; so talking about the past is one of the best ways we have of talking about the future. When people talk or write about the past we can also describe them as fashioning a future for themselves. Indeed, from a pragmatist point of view, what we call the past is just one of the tools we have for solving our present problems – for getting us from here to there, wherever we want there to be. So it would be part of this modern variety of creative experience called autobiography to wonder what we think we are getting when we are getting it right. We might have to avoid what Wilde famously called falling into careless habits of accuracy (the secular fall of mimesis).

Whether we are making something new or reconstructing something that, in some sense, already exists, can be a useful question in relation to many of the arts. When a poet writes a sonnet, when a concerto is composed – when any kind of artist observes any kind of traditional formal constraint – she is being, as it were, a benign rebel. In Sartre's sense, she keeps the sonnet the same even through her innovations. There is still a world of sonnets. A rebellious autobiographer would be writing (or speaking) something discernibly autobiographical;

it may be 'fictionalized', chronology may be disfigured, but we would recognize what we think of as a person telling us something about what we think of as a life. And in terms of so-called content, the rebellious autobiographer would perhaps be keeping himself the same by sustaining his grievances and admirations; he would be at his most self-assured in his criticism and his praise of himself and others. But a revolutionary autobiographer would change the world. Or, rather, a revolutionary autobiography – if there could be such a thing – would be a radical transformation of the self. Presumably it would be such a transformation that the word 'self' would become redundant. Where once we had described a person, say, we would now be describing drifts of attention. As though what was being censored in internal censorship were alternatives to being a person, a character as traditionally conceived.

Clearly, apocalyptic thinking is nostalgia at its very worst. But if we were to come to no hard and fast conclusions as to what we thought people were like; indeed, began to see the wish to come to such conclusions as in itself a problem; if we could more freely associate with (and to) our own words we may begin to see how the idea of a creator can be the obstacle to the varieties of creative experience. A creator is only ever a rebel. And by that I simply mean that a creator always knows when he has got it right, or has got it as right as he can get it. He may not know how or why he knows – he may not be able to articulate his criteria of rightness – but at a certain point choices will be made. In other words his creation may be new, but his criteria are not. They pre-exist his final creation. The part of the self that is, however intuitively, making decisions in the ongoing work of creation, has standards; and, whatever their provenance, they pre-date the finished work. So when Freud proposes that, as a therapeutic measure, a person should abrogate that judgemental voicing of the self he calls the ego (or the ego/super-ego), he is suggesting that the past exists inside us in its most stultifying form, as judgement itself. As though somebody or something inside us always already knows what it is good (and bad) for us to think and feel and say.

What is most striking about the carver and the modeller, the rebel and the revolutionary, is that, as accounts of creative experience, each of them is committed to an idea of agency; of an abiding and insistent purposive project; of somebody who already knows something. Depending on which kind of artist we are we have either a Promethean or a midwife, a rebellious or a revolutionary homunculus inside us. The midwife believes that, given a chance, the other will give birth; the Promethean believes that, chance or no chance, he will, as far as he can, give birth to himself. In these varieties of creative experience, we have to choose between a religion of self and a religion of otherness. We have to choose between two quite different kinds of creator. Both of whom must have some sense of when they have got it right, when it is as good as they can make it; and of when it is finished. But what would it be – what kind of creative experience would it be – to ablate such continual assessment of what we have learned to call the self; to assume a more assured vagrancy. We have already judged what a person not sitting in judgement on herself would look like. Perhaps that is a judgement too far. 'The way of life is wonderful,' Emerson wrote: 'it is by abandonment.'

Time Pieces

... the critic must resist all the time the temptation to write
as if the discussable things were the most important ones.

Christopher Ricks, *Poems and Critics*

I

Memory is often described as both the object and the instrument of our desire. The capacity to remember, indeed a good memory, is something that we want. As a form of access to the past, to information, and for keeping us successful liars, a good memory makes us more efficient, productive and better problem-solvers, which means better pleasure-seekers. But modern memory, at least in what we might call for shorthand the Freud/Proust version, is also essentially of desire, our recalling of what it is we want. And desire is something that can be forgotten and needs to be remembered because it is at worst forbidden, and at best riddled with conflict. We want memories, and memories remind us of what we want. It is clear, in other words, that what we most want is to want, and that what we are most terrorized by is loss or absence of desire. Memory, at least in its modern versions, has been recruited as the best way we have of talking about the problem that desiring has become.

One of the more obvious things that distinguishes us from

other animals is that we are puzzled by our wants; that what we want, and not merely how to get it, is our abiding question. Pragmatism, the how-to-get-it bit, depends upon our being clear about what it is we want, and about our being clear that wanting has to be practicable in order to be any good (that is, any use). What Freud, among others, adds to this picture is the idea that not only can we forget what we want, but also that we need to forget what we want in order to survive. As incestuously minded animals, forgetting ourselves (that is to say, what we want) becomes second nature, and remembering what we are becomes a virtually unspeakable terror. From Freud's point of view pragmatists are people who don't have an Oedipus complex; people for whom the only problem that their wants present them with is how to satisfy them.

A good memory for Freud is one that forgets properly. In his view the realistic pleasures depend upon a forgetting (of our desire for our parents) and a moving on (to people with whom we can consummate our desires). Progress means memory loss; we may still, as adults, love our parents and long for them but we don't think of them as people we might fall in love with (or, indeed, as people we might start lusting after). We don't forget our parents but there are things about them – feelings we had about them, and that they had about us – that seem to disappear. 'Remembering everything,' a character in Brian Friel's *Translations* says, 'is a form of madness.' To remember everything is to desire everything, and that is a form of madness.

If remembering is the form our desiring takes we are always, to some extent, going to live in fear of our memories; of losing them, of gaining and regaining them, of being surprised by what returns from the past, and how it makes its return. A good memory is one that gives us what we want, and preferably when we want it; a bad memory is surely a more interest-ing prospect. If we want to surprise ourselves – if we want to reveal ourselves – a good memory can only let us down.

II

When Wittgenstein said that death is not an experience in life he was saying that death is something that happens to other people. Because dying is so much an experience in life – whether or not as some philosophers and some biologists tell us it is what the experience of life is, what it effectively amounts to – it is easy to forget that death itself may not be. There are many things in life, and more now than ever before, that we experience only as spectators, and very few of them will inevitably happen to us; nor does it occur to us that they will. Death, and the dying that will go into it, we can anticipate with a certainty, but anticipate it is all we can do. There is no experience so universally vicarious, so infinitely virtual for the secular minded, as death itself. For the secular we are the afterlife. There is death, but not for us.

And yet living in a continual aftermath we are more than capable of saying that we know we are going to die, with all the rhetorical gravity or glibness this seems to bring with it, but less than capable of living as if the people we love are going to die. All deaths are inevitable, but some deaths mustn't happen. As we divide our lives into what we can anticipate and what we can't, deaths, sometimes our own, are always in the worst possible category; the inevitable that we can't bear to anticipate. The precariousness of life has never been news; the prevalence of accident, illness and malevolence, not to mention ageing, is our most certain surprise. And yet we spend so much of our lives discovering what can be taken out of the world that won't stop us wanting to live in it. In the anguish and dismay that is grief we find out what we can afford to lose. The world without the people who matter to us is not the same world, and so not the world at all. Life becomes progressively stranger as we get older – and we become increasingly frantic to keep it familiar, to keep it in order – because people keep changing the world for us by dying out (mourning is better described as orientation, the painful wondering whether it is worth re-placing oneself). There is something about the nature of our attachments that is unrealistic: unrealistic in that we live as if certain people must not die, and so we must live with the strain of willing what cannot be willed. It is obvious why it is comforting to believe that everyone dies at the right time; and why it is reassuring for some people that they can't be late for their own death.

But the exemption Wittgenstein referred to points both ways. Conception and, indeed, preconception are not experiences in life either. And our deaths are inevitable, and to be anticipated, in a way that our conceptions were not. If the fact that we are going to die has been taken by the great religions and their secular counterparts as the most salient fact about us, perhaps we should note the more improbable fact that we were conceived at all (that, in Empson's words, we came out of the nowhere into the somewhere). We are probably over-impressed by anticipation and inevitability – have, in a sense, organized our lives around them – because we have grossly overrated the significance of our own deaths. To the unborn such things could not have occurred. We are what did occur to them, but we have done too much looking forward with a future in mind. The fact of death has made us addicted to prophecy, and to its secular equivalent, predictability; and therefore to a strange relationship to time. The fact of conception could make us more wedded to randomness and accident. Surprise could replace mourning as our preferred depth-charge.

The deaths of others should be the only deaths that matter to us, not because we are altruistic, but because they are the only deaths available to us (death in the abstract, that is, one's own, always makes people portentous and pretentious, that is, sentimental). We can't forget about our own death, because there is nothing to remember; but we can resist being lured into the larger profundities of taking our own deaths at all seriously (my death should only be a 'problem', or whatever, for others, and so it goes on). Grief, even at its most desolate, is at least full of surprises, in a way that people talking of their own 'finitude' tends not to be. When people are alive, for example, they can be a barrier to what we feel about them (my being alive cannot be said to be a barrier to what I feel about myself). When the dead cannot reply we find, occasionally, that we can speak to them; when we know there can be no answers we can ask our questions. Indeed, death often reveals most shockingly not only whether people have mattered to us, and the unexpected ways in which they did and didn't, but also how we shied away from them, how we kept to ourselves. It is easy not to notice people when one is in their presence, and far more difficult to hide from them when they are no longer there.

We suffer more from the promises we could never make than from the promises we could never meet. And the one thing the dead (or the lost) always leave us with is what we might have given them, what we might have been. We are always more puzzled than we want to be by things left unsaid, by inclinations unnoticed. And in this sense the dead leave us stranded with our potential as it once was, intact. It would be terrible if we could be reminded of what we wanted only when we could no longer have it. But the dead can answer us only in our own words. And that too is an experience in life. And should be a surprising one.

The Dream Horizon

I

I don't like to dream (or to recall that I've dreamed); if it was
a bad dream it darkens my awakening; if it was sweet it tears
me to pieces when it stops: I could never imagine a sleep
utopia filled with dreams, with sweet dreams.

Roland Barthes, *The Neutral*

If no one had ever dreamed, if dreaming was something that
nobody had either ever done or ever remembered, the way
we describe prophecy, reality, scepticism, memory, desire,
identity, irrationality and hope – to take the more obvious
examples – would be quite different. And to imagine what
kind of difference the absence or non-existence of the dream
would make to our lives – what effect it might have had, for
example, on the invention of photography, or on the sense
we made of sleeping – seems baffling. So much seems to
depend, so to speak, on the fact of our dreaming; or, rather,
on our capacity to remember and represent our dreams. The
dream as example, the dream as analogy, the dream as material
for interpretation, the dream as vitalizing enigma, the dream
as key to something or other, as clue to something essential
about ourselves and our fate; the sheer usefulness of the dream

as an object in the cultural field, and of dreaming and the telling of dreams as a cultural activity, is striking. How dreaming fits into so-called waking life, what the dream has got to do with the rest of a person's activities, what if any significance should be ascribed; these are issues, it seems, that most if not all cultures have something to say about; and usually something quite forceful. When people speak about dreaming they tend to be speaking about something that somehow matters to them. Dreams, in other words – to adapt Lévi-Strauss's formulation – are good to think with. I want to consider in this essay what talking about dreams is an opportunity to talk about. Or, perhaps more exactly (and exactingly), how talking and writing about dreams gets people talking and writing. If, for example, the figure traditionally referred to as the Dreamer was a character in a novel, what can the novelist, the dream-theorist, use him to do; to give voice to? The Dreamer as hero – the heroism of dreaming – is like a permission or an invitation or even an incitement to say certain things that are otherwise difficult to articulate. The fact that we dream is an opportunity to describe someone we call the Dreamer. The Dreamer, we might say, at its most minimal is a character subject to alternative constraints. In our dreams we can do things and things are done that we can't do and can't be done. It is a familiar elsewhereness, but it is elsewhere nonetheless.

So, to ask the pragmatic question: what do we want to talk about when we talk about dreams? What do dreams help us describe? In the modern period they help us describe our uncertainties, our not knowing who or what to believe or, indeed, what kind of experience believing is. They show us radical disorientation, they make us spectators of the unintelligible. 'Wee owe unto dreames,' Sir Thomas Browne writes in *On Dreames*, that Galen was a physitian, Dion an historian, and that the world hath seene some notable peeces of Cardan, yet hee that should order his affayres by dreames, or make the night a rule unto the day, might bee ridiculously deluded.

Dreams, Browne tells us, force us to speak in contradictions and about contradictions; they make us sound paradoxical to ourselves. Galen, Dion and the Italian physician and mathematician found their true vocations, made their original discoveries, in their dreams; and yet if we were to order our affairs or use the dream as blueprint or guideline for our waking life we might be ridiculously deluded. It's not clear, of course, how we would do this even if we wanted to. But what Browne is intimating – and this is a common intimation in modern writings about dream – is that we may be ridiculously deluded creatures; and that part of our deludedness – or the conundrum of our delusion – is that there is no available reality compared with which we can see ourselves as deluded. Dreams tell us the truth about ourselves, and they could not be more misleading. One of the things we are implicitly seeking reassurance about is that there are two distinct realms, night and day, sleeping and waking, dreaming and . . . what? There is a danger in not seeing the difference. It is as if for some reason we see or want to see that there are two realms – even if they are somehow interwoven – but we are not quite sure how to prove that there are. When Browne asserts that to order our affairs by dreams, to make the rule of the night the rule of the day, might be to ridiculously delude ourselves he is suggesting that Dion, Galen and Cardan might therefore be ridiculously deluded and we doubly so to be impressed by them. If we might be ridiculously deluded we might not be. And why would it matter even if we were ridiculously deluded? Who is ridiculing us? Presumably the figure who is in touch with the reality that makes delusion discernible. This, one could say, is the territory you get into; these are the kinds of sentences that come up when you write and read about dreams. What do dreams provide? What do we owe to them? Are there two orders, two sets of rules: a self by day and a self by night?

It is notable that Browne assumes that the night, the dream life, is rule-governed, is organized, although quite differently to the waking life. What do dreams reveal to us? Or what are we tempted to make of them? Two quite different questions. Browne says that one thing we could make of dreams is a model for waking life. And this, again, becomes a familiar and enigmatic question asked by modern writers: how would we live if we were to live according to our dreams (a question implied, if not asked, by Freud)? What would our lives be like if we lived them as though they were dreams? Why is it better to live undeluded, and hence with the distinction, uppermost in our minds as it were, between truth and reality? Is it better for us to become creatures who seek out and are impressed by people who can tell us the difference between truth and delusion? There is something, maybe several things, that dreamers are not good at; and other things that we are not good at when we are wide awake. If we didn't dream we would have no Galen, and we would have no picture, in Browne's view, of what it might be to be ridiculously deluded. 'That some have never dreamed is as improbable as that some have never laughed,' Browne writes in a conjunction that looks forward to Freud. We are amused, we dream, we can be deluded and subject to ridicule for our delusions. Dreaming is integral to who we are – we can't imagine ourselves without it; it is one of the ingredients with which we essentialize ourselves, even if dreaming is the very thing, according to one view, that undoes our essentializing of ourselves – and it spells, or we spell it out as, a dangerous and/or a benign dividedness. There isn't, Browne leads us to believe, a third realm; the fact that we dream – whether or not dreams are divine or daemonic – doubles us. The fact of the dream invites us to speak of ourselves as divided with and against ourselves; as subject to division, but to uncertain purposes. If the dream represents here our paradoxical obscurity to ourselves, it also exposes something our sentences want to get to grips with, something fascinating that we do, or that is done to us, at night. Something that makes us wonder about the provenance of our images and what they have to do with us; what being interested in dreams is being interested in. One thing being interested in dreams is a way of being interested in is wondering what we see when we are not looking. And what it is – what kind of experience it is – to recognize what we see when we are not looking.

The thing that is most striking to Browne – as I would guess it is to many other dream writers – is the disparity, the incongruity, the gap between what happens, what we see, in dreams and what happens, and what we see and feel, when we are not dreaming. In other words, an alternative to dreaming is being proposed – another scene – and it is the kind of life we have after waking. It is worth noting that the dream experience is often described as a kind of journey, as though dream-telling was a species of travel writing. We live in two worlds, waking and sleeping, and they must be linked because we ourselves are the link; we do both, even though it is as if one is done in our presence and one in our absence (or with our absence). We want to tell stories, for some reason, about these two worlds and the links between them; we are both the makers of these links, in our various cultures, and we are the ones who believe there are links; that there must be senses in which the two worlds are one world. We can reverse our perspective and imagine, for example, a culture for whom dreaming was the norm, so to speak, and waking life was the enigma, the thing we wanted to know more about, the source of endless bafflement. If dreaming was the norm we might not assume, say, that looking was something we did with our eyes, or that language rather than images was second nature, or indeed that more or less intelligible verbal communication was expectable. We would have a quite different sense of what it was to hear things or smell them; and we probably wouldn't describe time as cyclical, or as a medium that connected events together, and so on. All this serves to illustrate is that we tend to describe the dream world as a world of recognizable but not obviously assimilable differences; as an elsewhere to which we are ineluctably joined, but where we are not, in the ordinary sense, at home. 'The idea that we are all strangers to each other,' Adrian Poole writes in a review of A. C. Bradley's *Shakespearean Tragedy*, 'is no more or less of a fiction than the idea that we can reach fair understandings' (*Essays in Criticism*). And, one can say, the idea that we are strangers to ourselves in dreams is no more or less of a fiction than the idea that we can reach fair understandings of ourselves in dreams. Or, to put it slightly differently, in much of the Western writing about dreams – which would include, of course, the writings of Western anthropologists – the supreme fiction tends to be that our dreams are strange; or that in our dreams we, or our more usual life, have been made strange. Dreams, in other words, seem to encourage us to describe waking life as fairly understandable or at least more intelligible than something else: this is the reassurance offered by dreams; we can wake up from them. We may live in two realms but one, supposedly, is more intelligible; or one requires less, or maybe different forms of, interpretation. But dreams show us – which means in my version that we can use them to say – that there is somewhere else, somewhere beyond our sovereignty though, which each individual is nevertheless the sovereign reporter of; and that this somewhere else, this alternative place, which we come to or which comes to us unbidden, is the holder of clues or secrets that can help us live the lives we prefer; if only we can find the right take or the right method or the right person dreams will provide unique access to otherwise unavailable resources. The dream is an opportunity to talk about obscure resources; apparently unheard-of desires, or versions of ourselves, or predictions of the future, or messages about our physiology or our destiny, or our wishes. Paradoxically, for the dream valuers, for the keepers of dreams, in our dreams we are at once most obscurely and most essentially ourselves. Dreams, that is to say, are frequently recruited – and, indeed, are suitably recruitable for – what is now called essentialist discourse. Dreams tend to be described – and Browne intimates this in his reference to his great geniuses Galen, Dion and Cardan – as being closer to, or revealing of, something more true or more real or more necessary than so-called ordinary consciousness is aware of. It is perhaps one of the most interesting things about dreams that when they are valued they are always highly valued. They are taken to be and presented as something or other that matters very much. And it is, of course, assumed that there is some connection between obscurity and value, or that cultures that associate mystery with value are more likely to rate dreaming; that we have to go the distance, that there will be obstacles in our quest for the best resources (as though we use the dream to ask ourselves, what good is strangeness? Or, what do we need or use strangeness for?). Dreaming is always the prime suspect when the conversation is about the dividedness of the individual, as though dreams are used as reminders that we don't know what's going on inside us, as if we needed reminding of this. The stress, the imaginative energy, tends to fall on telling us how different sleeping is from waking, dreaming from consciousness, consciousness from unconsciousness. In these familiar binaries it is the differences, not the similarities, that we are prone to spell out and insist upon. It can often sound as though it isn't so much that our dreams are so different, so bizarre, so wayward, but rather that we want them to be; as though, whatever else is going on, we crave this radical otherness in ourselves that dreams are our favourite picture of.

'When we are awake,' the psychoanalyst W. R. Bion said in a seminar at the Tavistock Clinic,

I don't think we really know much about the state of mind in which we are when asleep. As a psychoanalyst I have been taught a good deal about the interpretation of dreams. The only thing I am not quite clear about is, what was the dream? Because when I am told that the patient has had a dream, it is told me by a person who is in an 'awake' state of mind. I sometimes ask patients, 'Where were you last night? What did you see? Where did you go?' I don't accept the answer that they didn't go anywhere, they simply went to bed and went to sleep. But I still think they went somewhere and saw something. It is possible that if the patient says he had a dream, it is a sort of vestige that is sufficiently robust still to be apparently available when he is awake.

Bion is quite clear – that is, quite insistent – that sleeping is not of a piece with waking, at least epistemologically: 'When we are awake I don't think we really know much about the state of mind in which we are when asleep.' Not much, but perhaps something. The question 'Where were you last night?' alerts us, with its echoes of the jealous partner or the anxious parent of an adolescent, that something must have been going on last night, whether admitted to or not. The intractable assumption is that the patient has been away overnight and, indeed, has seen something. But perhaps the most interesting moment in Bion's account – apart from the tone of indomitable certainty about such definitionally uncertain territory – is his use of the word 'vestige': 'It is possible that if the patient says he had a dream, it is a sort of vestige that is sufficiently robust still to be apparently available when he is awake.' A 'vestige' is something that has survived, though no longer used (the *OED* has 'a surviving memorial or trace . . . serving as an indication of its former existence', though I suspect Bion was using it in its more biological sense as 'a surviving trace of some part formerly existing in the species; a vestigial organ or structure'). If a remembered dream is akin to a vestige then despite Bion's presumably unintended implication that the remembered dream is merely a survival of something redundant he is wanting to say that the dream has to be extremely resilient, 'robust', to survive for so long, to have come such a long way from sleep to waking. The sleeper went a great distance that night, and only if the dream is a robust vestige will it be what Bion calls 'apparently available' on waking. 'Apparently available' makes a compact point; the dream is only apparently available – that is, it's not entirely clear whether it is or it isn't; and it is not clear what this robust vestige is available for (what it avails). There is intimated here the heroism of dreaming, the dreamer has been on a mysterious journey and he has brought back ambiguous treasure; the status, the nature of the dream as an object, is not self-evident. We make dreams, or in Bion's picture we go and see them and bring them back as memories of experience; and then dreams are what we make of them. We experience them whether we want to or not; at night I have no choice but to be in the audience. But how they are described – the genre of dream-telling – and what is done with them, the nature of the redescriptions to which they are subject, are, as we say, culturally constructed. Dreams may be unusual and uncanny but the images in which they proliferate and the languages in which they are told and interpreted come from nowhere but the culture of the dreamer. They are, let us say, an intriguing example of the way culture goes all the way down; it goes all the way down into our unintelligibility to ourselves. Dreams are sometimes apparently available and we have to make what is apparent to us available. Which is to do no more and no less than to see what occurs to us in the hearing of the dream; the told dream, whatever else it is, is a singularly evocative object. The listened-to, the listened-for dream – associated to by the dreamer and the listener – takes us off in expected directions. And this is because, for want of another way of putting it, something in us responds to something in the dream. In the cultural field we have learned that dreams are worth our attention. The dreamer has, in Bion's picture, gone somewhere and seen something, and it may stay with her; and she knows that, for some reason, seeing certain things, and remembering them, matters. If dreams are democratic artefacts – if everyone has access to them irrespective of wealth or status – their value, once we assume they require interpretation of whatever sort, is something we have to make up. Dreams don't speak for themselves; we make them give voice. In this sense dreams – dreams as told stories – are what we might call literary; not simply because they exist in the shared world in language (even if you paint your dream you have to say something, if only, this is my dream), but that they observe conventions (a dream sequence in a film works only if it dawns on us that this is a dream sequence). Culture goes all the way down into our dreams in ways that we can't give an account of, or can give only competing accounts of.

So when the art historian Michael Baxandall says in his book *Patterns of Intention: On the Historical Explanation of Pictures* that 'We do not explain pictures: we explain remarks about pictures – or, rather, we explain pictures only in so far as we have considered them under some verbal description or specification,' this could also be said of dreams. We cannot explain our dreams, we can explain only our descriptions (or explanations) of dreams. We only ever interpret or associate to the story of the dream. And when Baxandall goes on to describe the history of art criticism he touches something peculiarly pertinent to the dream, something that the psychoanalyst Bion is getting at: 'The history of art criticism in the last five hundred years,' Baxandall writes,

has seen an accelerating shift from discourse designed to work with the object unavailable, to discourse assuming at least a reproduced presence of the object. In the sixteenth century Vasari assumes no more than a generic acquaintance with most of the pictures he deals with; in particular his celebrated and strange descriptions are often calculated to evoke the character of works not known to the reader . . . in the nineteenth century [art] books were increasingly illustrated with engravings and eventually half-tones . . . We now assume the presence or availability [through reproduction] of the object, and this has great consequence for the workings of our language.

In talking or writing about dreams there can never be this shift Baxandall describes from 'discourse designed to work with the object unavailable, to discourse assuming at least a reproduced presence of the object'. When it comes to dreams we are all Vasarians whose strange descriptions are always calculated to evoke the character of works not known to the listener. All we can compare our descriptions and explanations of our dreams to are other people's descriptions and explanations. The object of description and explanation will never become available, it will never be reproduced, there will be no progress. We will only ever have words for dreams, the description, never the thing itself. Our dreams will only ever be apparently available in language. This is one of the many reasons why the attempt to give what one might call an accurate account of one's dream is such an interesting experience; by the time you are providing your account the dream is no longer there, and the listener is never in a position to compare the account with its object. This is true, of course, of any recounted memory; the questions are what, if anything, is the teller being true to? And what is this truthfulness deemed to be in the service of? Freud believes the dreamer has to tell himself what is not there in the dream, through the process of free association. The Freudian dreamer is a Vasarian in the sense that he has to provide strange descriptions to evoke the character of a work not known by the listener; but he also has to provide a different kind of strange description, called his freeish associations, to evoke the character of a work not known by the dreamer himself. It is as though he is describing a work that is not as yet there, except in its apparent form. He is a historian of pentimento rather than of a work of seeable art. If the Freudian dreamer was an agent we would say he was an agent that did not want to disclose his work; he, the dream agent, so to speak, wants to pass off a satisfying fake in order to smuggle through the Old Master underneath the surface. In this sense the Freudian dreamer is akin to the listener of his dream in that neither of them has seen the dream; the dreamer has seen what Freud calls a façade, and it is only in words, in his view, that we can get behind or get through the scenes (of unacceptable desire). Without associations, the dreamer's associations mostly, both the dreamer and the analyst or listener are outside the dream. Like Vasari, the dreamer has to describe what he has seen; but after that it is as though a new sense, a sixth sense, is brought into play. Language becomes the lure and the lead. The dreamer neither goes on describing his dream nor does he try to explain it; he just notices and reports the words that occur to him from the verbal descriptions he has already given. When the Lacanian analyst does what she calls 'returning the signifier' she is simply repeating back to the dreamer a word or a phrase from his account of his dream to see what other words it prompts in him. For the Freudian dreamer, like the art critic Vasari, the visual becomes the pretext for the linguistic. The visual object is soon left behind as an opportunity for description, a source of clues and angles and sentences. It is there to stir us into words, to call up language, an appetite to speak; to take the direction of our desire.

II

. . . the text of the last hours of the night is, theoretically speaking, the text the furthest removed from the day that is about to dawn.

Louis Althusser, *For Marx*

For Freud, in a sense it is simple; on the one hand we are Darwinian creatures bent on survival, and on making survival as pleasurable as is possible. We are essentially desiring animals, appetite being the medium through which we survive and, if we are able, reproduce. But we are also in Freud's view possibly the only desiring animals whose desire is forbidden. Desire in the Freud–Lacan account is that without which our lives feel futile, and yet desire is that which puts us in mortal danger. Dreaming is simply one of the ways we manage this conundrum of our being. When Freud famously wrote that dreams were the 'royal road to the unconscious' (and we know that 'royal roads' according to *Chambers English Dictionary* are 'a short and easy way of circumventing difficulties'), then we know that Freud is telling us that dreams – or, rather, dreams under his description of their workings – are the most direct way of getting at our desire. Which in turn is the most direct way of getting at the constitutive conflicts that make us who we are. The unconscious is, in his words, 'the other scene' because it is where our forbidden desire formulates itself, and our forbidden desire is other to, is outside of, what we prefer to think of ourselves as wanting. Freudian people would rather not know what they want – indeed, are likely to devote their lives to this not-knowing, seeking out substitute satisfactions at all cost; and dreams as 'disguised fulfilments of child-hood wishes' are ways of more or less successfully keeping this secret of our desire from ourselves. Freud, that is to say, agrees with Sir Thomas Browne that 'hee that should order his affayres by dreames, or make the night a rule unto the day, might bee ridiculously deluded'. In the infantile part of the mind that in Freud's view is of a piece with the dreaming mind, a desire always prompts a picture of its satisfaction, and we always believe the picture. Our desiring selves are indeed ridiculously deluded, that is, excessively wishful. Desire is always in excess of any object's capacity to satisfy it, in the Freudian universe, and this is what we get to hear about if we can bear it, through the interpretation of our dreams. Whether we would prefer to or not we do order our affairs by dreams – or, rather, dreams show us how our affairs are ordered – we do make the night the rule of the day and we are therefore essentially ridiculously deluded. Freudian dreams expose that we prefer wishes to reality, that we instinctively replace a negative hallucination with a positive hallucination – that is, we have tricks for hiding our essential frustrations from ourselves – and that in order to survive psychically we believe that above all we must not know ourselves. Dreams tell us that our delusions and illusions are our preferred truths, and that truth means to us just whatever gives us enough pleasure to bear our lives. Perception is distorted by wish and this is what we are seeing night after night in our dreams. According to Freud, Charles Rycroft writes in his sober *A Critical Dictionary of Psychoanalysis*, 'the function of dreams is to preserve sleep by representing wishes as fulfilled which would otherwise awaken the dreamer' and that they are 'normal processes, with which everyone is familiar, but which none the less exemplify the processes at work in the formation of neurotic symptoms'. But the implication is that the dream, described like this, is a literalization, a stark picture of a permanent state. Awake or asleep we do not want to be awakened to, or by, our wishes, the wishes that represent our unconscious forbidden desire. Dreams just help us to stay asleep when we are asleep. Though Freud never, to my knowledge, says, as Jung does, that we are dreaming all the time, I think Freud uses dreaming as a way of wondering what it might be to be awake. If the dream's function is the preservation of sleep, this makes the dream something that stops us from waking up. If it is a sleeping device we might wonder whether there is a comparable waking device; we know we are asleep if we are dreaming, but what is the complementary sentence? We know we are awake when we are . . . what? Thinking, perceiving, feeling, remembering, daydreaming?

What wakes us up, what causes the dreaming process to break down into nightmare, is, in Freud's view, the failure of the dream-work to make a sufficiently satisfying, a sufficiently settling, dream out of the memory and desire that are its medium. The project is not to be woken up, not to be overly disturbed by memory and desire, and by the memory that, Freud believes, is of desire. But waking up becomes another way, the next way, of not being overwhelmed by these experiences. It is as if the first, preferred container is the dream; the next one, if the dream-work fails, is waking up; and the final one is psychosis. This makes a spectrum or a repertoire out of the series: dreaming, waking, neurosis/psychosis; they all become artefacts for bearing memory and desire. And they could all be described as different forms of sleep, or ways of not being too starkly awakened. And one implication of this might be that the dream is one of the best ways we have of remembering and desiring because in it nothing happens to the dreamer except the experience of the dream. There is no exchange, no one else is present, ideally nothing else happens but the dream. In dreams we desire by ourselves so nothing can happen to us.

'All we know of dreams,' Freud writes in *The Interpretation of Dreams*, 'is derived from consciousness'; so it's not quite true to say that dreams are the royal road to the unconscious, because consciousness is the royal road to the unconscious, even if dreams are particularly good to think with or to speak of in this regard. Dreams thus become emblematic, in the Freudian descriptions, of the fact that all experience is mediated. The unconscious, as far as we can know, is something in this sense derived from consciousness, which could mean, inferred by consciousness, constructed or made by consciousness, of a piece with consciousness. In other words, Freud intimates here (and not only here), we may have thought that there were two discreet, antagonistic realms called the unconscious and consciousness, but one is a derivation of the other. There are continuities, shared projects, even if they are obscure ones; the so-called divided subject might be a convenience for the sake of a certain kind of description. We may be the animals who want to escape from their desire, but this very escape is in the service of preserving the life of this desiring creature. We are divided against ourselves in order to sustain our dividedness. And the dream becomes Freud's best way of talking about this absurd modern predicament; the modern desiring subject desires most successfully when he is immobilized in sleep. His safest satisfactions – and in this sense his most viable satisfactions – are the ones he gives himself when he isn't there.

Dreams, for Freud, are above all functional; they guarantee, when they work, that the individual is not disturbed by his desire. Desiring, he seems to suggest, is something we do best in our sleep. 'When once we have recognized,' he writes in *The Interpretation of Dreams*,

that the content of a dream is the representation of a fulfilled wish and that its obscurity is due to alterations in repressed material made by the censorship, we shall no longer have any difficulty in discovering the function of dreams. It is commonly said that sleep is disturbed by dreams; strangely enough, we are led to the contrary view and must regard dreams as the guardians of sleep.

We must not, Freud implies, be awakened to, be awakened by, our desire; without dreams doing their work we wouldn't be able to sleep. It is, in actuality, a very strange picture. We have a physiological need to sleep, akin to hunger in the sense that without sleep we cannot survive; and yet our desire, our wishes from childhood, are such that without the artistry of dream-work – which is essentially an artistry of disguise and distraction – we would not be able to sleep. Our (childhood) wishes would kill us. Sleep requires its guardians because it is vulnerable to attack, to disturbance. In the dream, to all intents and purposes, we sleep off our desire; we represent it in an acceptable form – that is, in a form acceptable to the censor – and we represent its fulfilment, its satisfaction. A great and essential drama has taken place overnight inside us, but there again nothing has actually happened, nothing has been done in the so-called shared world with anyone else. We have pleased ourselves without including anyone else. We have reversed the dependency of infancy and childhood – gathered it, in psycho-analytic language, within the range of our own omnipotence – and made the fulfilment of wishes a matter of self-contained fantasy.

Now it is self-evident that a meal we dream of eating may be satisfying but it will never be nourishing. We cannot live by dreams alone, even if, as Freud suggests, we want to, and indeed try to each night. At some point, in some way, if we are to survive psychically, desire has to be brought to bear on a real object. At whatever cost, and Freud believes that it is at considerable if not actually unbearable cost, we have to bring our wishes into some kind of exchange with external reality. And a lot of psychoanalytic writing after Freud is precisely about this, about adding to the repertoire of descriptions of what our wishing does to reality and vice versa. But it is clear that for Freud, at least – if not always for his followers and critics – the dream has a special place in his thinking about our relations with reality.

In one version of his account he has what might be called a logical, almost commonsensical, view of the process by which the developing individual gets to reality with its inevitable frustrations, but very real satisfactions. And it is a view that has been taken up, certainly by Winnicott and Bion in the British tradition, and become part of mainstream psychoanalytic thinking. Freud says, in his 'Formulations on the Two Principles of Psychic Functioning' of 1911, that he 'developed' these thoughts in *The Interpretation of Dreams* but is now reiterating them because they are no less than the definitive account of something momentous. 'The state of equilibrium in the psyche,' he writes,

was originally disrupted by the urgent demands of inner needs. At this stage, whatever was thought of (wished for) was simply hallucinated, as still happens every night with our dream thoughts. It was due only to the failure of the anticipated satisfaction, the disillusionment as it were, that this attempt at satisfaction by means of hallucination was abandoned. Instead, the psychic apparatus had to resolve to form an idea of the real circumstances in the outside world and to endeavour actually to change them. With this, a new principle of psychic activity was initiated; now ideas were formed no longer of what was pleasant but of what was real, even if this happened to be unpleasant. This inception of the *reality principle* proved to be a momentous step.

We have an inner need, a desire; we hallucinate, we fantasize its satisfaction; that is, we fast forward the wish to its fulfilment, and this is pleasant for a bit. But then we notice we are still in need, and that the only way we are going to be properly satisfied is by finding what we want in the external world, or by changing the external world so it gives up to us what we want. Reality is our second choice but our best option; we feel it is our worst option because once we move out of self-satisfying states we are prey to a proliferating range of feelings and conflict. We had tried for an efficient narrow-mindedness in relation to our wishing, but we have to open things up; we have to, as we say, get involved with other people; other people who, of course, are engaged in a similar project but from different histories and genetic endowments.

And yet, Freud also says, the dream works because we don't do this; and not only that, but when Freud starts writing exclusively about the dream he begins to wonder what it would be to wake up, and whether in fact it is possible. The story in the 'Formulations on the Two Principles' is really rather reassuring in one, limited sense: it says that there is a reality principle, a reality we can get to; that we can 'abandon' attempts at satisfaction through hallucination; that, in short, it is possible to wake up. That, in Sir Thomas Browne's words, there is a genuine alternative available to us, we don't need to order our affairs by dreams, or 'make the night a rule unto the day'. The dream when we are asleep works because it is the guardian of sleep; the hallucination in waking life doesn't work, indeed must not work if we are to survive. The hallucination in waking life must be abandoned; the dream when we are asleep must not be. But the dream works because we are not in a position to abandon it. There is a difference between containing desire and satisfying it. Freud, we might say, is wondering whether the best container of desire is the one that leads to its real, rather than its fantasized, satisfaction. Freud is considering, through speaking of the dream, whether desire, as it is for modern human animals, isn't often or mostly best satisfied in fantasy, when the individual is effectively immobilized. Hallucination and dream may not ultimately work for hunger – or, indeed, for the need to sleep – but they may work for the desires that are sexual. After all, if unconscious desire is forbidden, is incestuous, where can it better be conducted than in fantasy? Transgression when we are asleep wreaks less havoc than it does when we are awake. Fantasies are, of course, actions, and therefore we can feel guilty about them; but, Freud intimates, the guilt of fantasy may be more bearable than the guilt of action. In dreams responsibilities end.

So, on the one hand, Freud is saying: the safest time and place to desire is at night in your sleep, when you are at your most solitary. And this is not an especially new thought; sex is for daydream, for art, for sublimation; is best done by not doing it. What D. H. Lawrence called disdainfully 'sex in the head' is the best place for it. This acknowledges that for all sorts of reasons sex disturbs us and we will go to great lengths not to engage in it; indeed, one of our best ways of not engaging in it *is* engaging in it, getting rid of sex through sex, as Winnicott called it. But then, on the other hand, there is the more interesting thought that Freud needs dreaming in order to articulate; and this is that it may be impossible for us to wake up to our desire, to fully acknowledge it; that our project is not exactly, as Lacan said, to escape from our desire, but to maintain the guardians of our sleep. It's not that we can't bear reality, it's that we can't bear our desire; and this means, in part, that we can't bear what it leads us into, the labyrinthine entanglements of conflicting feeling. Dreams are simple, intelligible and innocent in their virtuality; reality is complicated, bewildering, and we are never innocent in our dealings with it. No one likes the ways they lose things, so finding is preferred. Dreams are the way we talk about the unintelligibility of reality, and about the ways in which we acknowledge this. Desire, that is to say, makes sense only in dreams. And that is why, Freud seems to suggest, there is no waking up for us.

The Forgetting Museum

. . . moral inertia, the not making of moral decisions,
constitutes a large part of the moral life of humanity.

Lionel Trilling, *The Morality of Inertia*

There is a strange moment, strange at least to the modern
reader, in Rousseau's opening Dedication to his *Discourse on
Inequality* of 1754. He is discussing the Romans, 'that model of
a free people' who were 'in no position to govern themselves
when they first emerged from the oppression of the Tarquins'.
It took the Romans a long time to bear their freedom because
they were 'souls which had been enervated, or rather brutalized, by tyranny'. The traumatic past of the Romans – though
that, of course, would not be Rousseau's word – of brutalizing
and being brutalized, and the difficulties this leaves them
with in relation to their freedom to be self-governing, leads
Rousseau to his strange wish. 'For this reason,' he writes:

I would have sought as my own country a happy and peaceful
commonwealth of which the history was lost, so to speak, in the
darkness of time; one which had endured only such hostile attacks
as might serve to bring forth and fortify the courage and patriotism
of the inhabitants, a commonwealth whose citizens, being long
accustomed to a wise independence, were not only free but fit to
be free.

As ever, Rousseau's contradictions and confusions are as telling as his explicit proposals. Is this wished-for country a happy and peaceful commonwealth because its history is lost? Is it a peaceful and happy commonwealth because it has suffered only the kind of hostility that has brought out the best in it, and if so why would that history need to be lost? With his example of the Romans in mind it is clear that in his view a bad history is bad for a commonwealth, which, of course, has serious implications, as Rousseau and his readers know, because very few, if any, societies have such untrammelled pasts (myths of a Golden Age testify to this fact in their attempt to obscure it). What is strange to the modern reader is Rousseau's stated belief here that a good future, a 'happy and peaceful commonwealth', depends upon a lost past; a past, in other words, that has been forgotten, indeed has to be forgotten because all the evidence for it has been lost.

Today we are more likely to regret, to fear, to avoid and to retrieve our lost pasts. Forgetting, both in personal and political life, is hedged in by a kind of superstitious dread. It is assumed, even by those who no longer believe that we can be saved, that memory can help us, that remembering is our last vestige of the myth of redemption. Attempts to abolish the past, or to dogmatically replace the past with our preferred versions of it, are now viewed by many people with suspicion, even by those who believe that the writing of history can only ever be the rewriting of the past; that all history is revisionist history, the only question being revision to what end, revision with what desires in play? Deniers of the Holocaust are different from those historians who want to work out exactly how many people were killed in the concentration camps, but we still might need to know what exactly it is – wittingly or unwittingly – that they want to persuade us (and themselves) of. What we are urged to remember is bound up with how we are being urged to live. The preferred life has its set of preferred memories. Voluntary or involuntary – that is, encouraged or discouraged – memories always have a future in mind.

So when we are saying that anyone should remember the Holocaust we need to be as clear as we can be about what we are wanting this remembering to do. We know, for example, that to say that those who forget the past are likely to repeat it is not to say that those who remember it will not. In so far as they repeat it at all – and not all traumas are repeated, unless we define trauma as that which repeats itself – they repeat it differently. We tend to think, with this picture in mind, that those who remember the past and repeat it do so as an act of restoration, renewal, celebration, reconsideration, and so on; whereas those who have forgotten the past – or repressed it, as we now say of the traumatized – are likely to do so without knowing that that is what they are doing. We can think of them as helpless, and possessed by something that they are unaware of and driven to re-enact. In this re-demptive myth of memory, remembering the terrible thing – original sin, the cultural or personal trauma – holding it in mind, is presumed to mitigate or even avert its recurrence. To remember the trauma is to re-imagine a life that incorporates it, just as to remember a crime is to remember the law that shouldn't have been broken.

There is a wishful belief underlying the redemptive myth of memory which is that what is to be remembered – if we remember the right things in the right way – is on the side of our well-being, and even of our virtuousness. Remembering done properly will give us the lives that we want. Even that memory can keep us kind. Whereas we know, in another part of our minds as it were, that memory is only ever as virtuous as its users. The Nazis were doing their version of remembering by recycling their myth of Aryan origins; reconstructing, documenting, witnessing, analysing and publicizing atrocities does not seem to diminish their scope or scale. Nazism is now just another iconography and ideology available for use – both for and against – in the cultural field. An obsession with memory blinds us to the abuses of memory and to the uses of forgetting. Of certain things we should be asking – and perhaps the Holocaust is one, if one among many – not how should they be remembered, but how should they be forgotten?

Our (modern) fear is that we won't get our forgetting right, or that forgetting is not possible; it may, of course, be a wish that atrocities cannot be forgotten; that we cannot bear ourselves as creatures who could actually forget such things. We tend to forget experiences that are too much for us, that are, in the reductive language of psychology, either too pleasurable or too painful. We equate the forgettable with the trivial or the unbearable; and in this picture we have a place to put the unbearable; but by the same token we believe that it (the memory, the experience, the desire) is still there, somewhere, and capable of returning. And we have a place for the trivial where it is effectively disposed of ('Remembering everything is a form of madness,' one of the characters in Brian Friel's *Translations* says). There is haunting and there is discarding; and it is not always within our gift to decide which is which. And it is this, perhaps above all, that makes forcing people to remember – rather like forcing them to eat – at once so implausible, and so morally problematic.

In our wanting German people to remember the Holocaust, and to remember it as terrible, we are at best saying to them something like: we are always liable to forget our concern for others, and perhaps it is our concern for others that is the real trauma that we will do anything to forget. You must never forget it again. (No religion has found a way of saying that it is better to be sympathetic than to be right.) At its worst we may, in the nicest possible way, be obeying the law of talion, torturing the torturers, becoming a version of the thing we are horrified by (it is perhaps not incidental that guilt often makes people aggressive, and that therefore making people feel guilty often provokes the very thing it is trying to avert). Making people remember tends to assume that you can calculate their responses to their memories. It tries to engineer solutions when engineered solutions are part of the problem. Forced remembering – the absurd idea that one might learn one's personal history off by heart, and in the correct version – spells a fear of history; a well-founded fear that the past is subject to multiple and shifting interpretations. That what we remember, and where the memory might lead – both what we might do with it and what it might do with us – is unpredictable. So-called liberal democracies cannot escape the fact that some of their members will want to remember the Holocaust for inspiration. Memory, in other words, is not a form of instrumental reason. It is perfectly understandable that when it comes to the Holocaust some people will not want people to have minds of their own; around the Holocaust a consensus is required, anything else breeds terror. So is it possible now for anyone to have what might be called thoughts of their own about the Holocaust? No one, rightly, is militantly encouraging the victims of the Holocaust to recall their unspeakable experiences, and to recall them in a certain way. What then do we want from the perpetrators and their descendants?

One thing we want is a way of remembering that will guarantee the impossibility of a recurrence. But it is possible that this very demand – more akin to exorcism than conversation – is itself at once too intimidating, and too unrealistic. Indeed it may be akin to Rousseau's wish for a lost history. Told what they should remember, and told what they should feel about it, the complexity of each individual German's history and experience is unlikely to be spoken. Where there was conflict – even, or especially, among the millions of so-called bystanders who colluded with the regime by turning a blind eye – there will be compliance. Enforced memory, like all indoctrination, is fear of memory, of what it might come up with, so to speak, when left to itself. All discipline exposes what discipline cannot do for us. To leave memory to itself forgetting is required; the time-lag, the metabolism, the deferrals of forgetting. Forgetting has to be allowed for if memory – non-compliant, unmanufactured memory – is to have a chance. But giving memory a chance may not be the kind of thing we are willing to risk now. After so many memorials it may be worth wondering now what a Museum of Forgetting could be a museum of.

Learning to Live:
Psychoanalysis as Education

I

The only point of writing a note on this simple and not very
good poem is that some reviewer expressed bafflement, and
I want to be consistent in trying to remove all trivial grounds
for bafflement.

William Empson, undated letter to Ian Parsons

'By educating the workers' party,' Lenin wrote in *The State
and Revolution* in 1918, 'Marxism educates the vanguard of the
proletariat which is capable of assuming power and of leading
the whole people to socialism, of directing and organizing the
new order, of being the teacher, the guide, the leader of all
the labouring and exploited people in the task of constructing their social life without the bourgeoisie and against the
bourgeoisie.' This, one could say, is education with a purpose;
Marxism, as an education, has, in Lenin's view, a known, an
inevitable, outcome. It teaches all the labouring and exploited
people how to 'construct their social life without the bourgeoisie and against the bourgeoisie'. Lenin's father was a
teacher; and 'like his father', Beryl Williams writes in *Lenin*,
'he had infinite faith in education. If the working class could
not build socialism, then they had to be taught to do so.' 'The
only socialism we can imagine,' she quotes Lenin as saying,

'is one based on all the lessons learned through large-scale capitalist culture.' For Lenin there are lessons to be learned at each stage of education. Education is the necessary prelude, the precondition for revolution.

Lenin, that is to say, as a man born, like Freud, in the nineteenth century, had an overriding belief in the power of education. Teaching and learning were primary metaphors for progress. When the nineteenth-century word for change was not evolution or revolution or commerce, it was education. Lenin using one of the great nineteenth-century bourgeois capitalist instruments – organized education – to destroy bourgeois capitalism had, what one might call politely, a certain irony. Forms of education designed to consolidate the state could, with the advent of Marxism, be used to dismantle it. Marxism could reveal, as Lenin shows, how the state itself is a precondition for exploitation; how there is a difference – obscured by the bourgeois state – between formal equality and actual equality. There are things people can be shown through education. Through the writing and reading of books.

What Lenin's use of the language of pedagogy exposes is the ambivalence endemic to the nineteenth-century bourgeoisie desire for education. On the one hand, it was clear to liberals and radicals in Europe that one can create democracy or revolution only through the circulation of written texts and spoken sentences. Political ideology, at its starkest, was based on information; people had to learn new ideas. And yet, on the other hand, there was fear of education – called by its critics indoctrination – as the source and stirrer of political unrest. Once there are words flying around in the culture like revolution or exploitation or the rights of man or atheism or trade unionism or, indeed, anarchism, then anything might happen. The desire, say, for freedom may not be containable by the provision of education. People might be prepared to die for their new-found sentences. If cherished traditional ideals are seen to be dispensable – if modern people have appetites for new sentences – then what kind of belief are educated people going to have in beliefs? What education might reveal, as Louis Menand says in a different context in *The Metaphysical Club: A Story of Ideas in America*, is that 'our reason for needing reasons is always changing'. Changing our governments might be like changing our minds. 'In the contemporary condition of society, in which the means for publicizing opinion were ever increasing,' as one early nineteenth-century commentator put it, 'the diffusion may be effected with the instantaneousness of lightning . . . the world has become an immense whispering gallery, and the faintest accent of science is heard throughout every civilized country as soon as uttered' (Philip Connell, *Romanticism, Economics and the Question of Culture*). The proliferating modern print media; the turbulence of political life; the increasing thoughtfulness about and organization of education. All sorts of people and sentences more and more freely associating with each other. This was the world Lenin and Freud – among so many others, and despite the very real difference of their cultural locations – spoke out of. The late nineteenth-century Western European world in which education was both a promise and a threat. What made it seem to be either of these things depended, of course, on how it was assumed education actually worked. On what it was to learn something, and what the consequences of such learning might be. What is called education – like what is called sexuality – are all the sentences that come out of the word; and all the sentences that went into it.

What Lenin proposes, at its most extreme, is a version of education as ideological programming not unlike certain versions of cognitive therapy: informing people in a certain way to make them do things in a certain way. This is a model of education that Lenin would share with his enemies, the reactionary, conservative bourgeoisie who also want education to be a form of indoctrination. If Marxism is taught to the exploited they will no longer be willing to bear their exploitation. Learning about Marxism will be akin to a conversion experience or to receiving orders. It is not assumed, in other words, that Marx's writing might be subject to innumerable competing, and even contradictory, interpretations. On the contrary it is assumed that there is an inevitable and therefore irresistible meaning to these texts that itself leads to equally inevitable and irresistible action; unlike, for example, learning about the facts of life, though possibly more like reading the Gospels. In Lenin's version of education the whole project is extraordinarily calculated; Marx's words are *for* 'the vanguard of the proletariat'; which is itself the only group capable of making the revolution required; and which is itself 'the teacher, the guide, the leader', three titles that become virtually synonymous in Lenin's sentence. Like Freud's sexual instinct, which has a source, an aim and an object, the process Lenin describes has the aura of science about it. It has an impressive inevitability of intention and effect. It privileges clarity of purpose over indeterminacy. It is as though Lenin knows what is to be done and what is going to happen. Even though we are blessed and distracted by hindsight – we can see, in a way Lenin couldn't, the actual consequences of his actions – there is, I want to suggest, a certain Leninism in most models of education. By that I mean that a known object is being pursued. That it is a means to a preferred end. Digression is not privileged; distraction tends to be punished. That, like Lenin, the educator wants something specific to happen to the educated; that there are what we call outcomes in mind. Psychoanalytic training committees do not plan for their students to develop an interest in knitting. The Leninist educator has an aim, which he calls revolution; and a method of education, which is exclusively the means to this end. He takes cause and effect very seriously; and there is, by definition, nothing laissez-faire about him. He is not someone who wants to see what happens; he is someone who wants to make something happen (he would prefer the plans of the day to the dreams of the night). He is a social engineer in so far as he believes in the power of instructing and informing. His wishes have a stark potency; an intractable realism. The problems he foresees – and he is not naive; he knows, perhaps better than anyone, about the nature of resistance – have to be met by force, if not with violence and intimidation. He knows where the recalcitrance is – for Lenin it is called class interest – and he describes it as something that has to be overcome at whatever cost. The Leninist educator has what might be called an immovable object of desire. It might be called, say, mass literacy or eternal life or qualification as a psychoanalyst. The Leninist educator begins, and hopefully ends, knowing what he wants. His omniscience, as omniscience must, extends over time. He may, to some extent, be flexible about his means, but he cannot be flexible about his ends. There are various ways of getting to Jerusalem, but only if that is where you have to go. It is the disarray of life without an aim – or a life in which aims are displaceable – that haunts the politician and the educator. And education, like politics, is unimaginable without ideals and ambitions. For Lenin education is another word for politics; indeed it is education that makes a modern politics possible, even though education means learning Marxism in the appropriate way. And politics means behaving as if, speaking as if, you know what you want. The obscurity of the object of desire has itself been obscured. This is what ideology is for. 'Education,' we are told by Lenin's recent biographer Robert Service, 'was the focal point' for his family of origin; his parents had 'a common passion for education'. They were both trained teachers, and his father was an inspector of schools. It is not surprising that the language of pedagogy came easily to him. For Lenin, Service writes, 'A large part of Marxism's attraction had been its emphasis on scholarship and science. He insisted that Marxists had something to teach the working class and that if revolution was to be successful, there had to be a widespread dissemination of Marxist doctrines.' 'Working-class consciousness,' Lenin writes in *What is to be Done?*, 'cannot be genuine political consciousness unless the workers are trained to respond to all cases of tyranny, oppression, violence and abuse, no matter what class is affected – unless they are trained, moreover, to respond from a social democratic point of view and no other.' And Lenin, of course, is not simply talking about learning from books; actual lived experience has to be described as in itself educative. Like Freud, Lenin is concerned above all with the process of making something conscious; what was soon called consciousness raising. There is something – call it exploitation, call it unconscious desire – that has to be drawn to people's attention. There is something about their lives that they are failing to notice. It is ever present; and it is, apparently unbeknown to them, virtually dictating the lives that they are leading. It is in the language of education that Lenin can describe how people can be shown the nature of their oversight; the blind-spot that hitherto has dominated their consciousness. 'The consciousness of the working masses,' he writes in *What is to be Done?*, cannot be genuine class-consciousness unless the workers learn from concrete and above all from topical political facts and events to observe every other social class in all the manifestations of its intellectual, ethical and political life; unless they learn to apply in practice the materialist analysis and the materialist evaluation of all aspects of the life and activity of all classes, strata and groups of the population.

Lenin, like Freud, is telling us what we should pay attention to if we want to understand and transform what it is we are in actuality suffering from. There is something essential of which we are unaware, and a way has to be found of recognizing it for what it is. And this for Lenin is done by training and learning to improve perception. As this is a scientific materialism the working masses have to be educated in 'observation'. Redirecting people's attention with a view to action. This, not always with Lenin's insistence and certainty, is what is going on in every primary school, in every educational establishment, everywhere. The attempt to transform and/or develop people's preoccupations – to show them what they are ignoring, or have never been exposed to – is the work of every therapist and teacher. Education, like psychoanalysis and politics, is the art of attention seeking (and hiding). And what is at stake in this, to us, most ordinary social practice, is the nature of influence; of how the bodies that are called people work on each other. The entanglements of desire. What people want from each other.

I have dwelled so much on Lenin partly because I think he is of so much interest but also because, as I have said, he represents in particularly vivid, indeed lurid, form one story about education that we have inherited with him, and through him, from the nineteenth century. On the one hand, an incredible confidence in the power of education – in the uses of pedagogy – as a progressive force. That, put crudely, a good education, the right kind of education, makes a good life and a good society. But, on the other hand, and more specifically, underlying this confidence – an assumption that people are extremely malleable, unfixed, suggestible, capable indeed of revolutionary transformations. That what education reveals is the exorbitant effect people can have on each other. That we are more like clouds than stars: that we are fashionable creatures. In Lenin's model of Marxist education, of facilitating the consciousness of the working masses, there is what seems like a relatively straightforward cause and effect at work; a certain kind of education, it is assumed, will inevitably produce a certain kind of consciousness; and a certain kind of consciousness will ineluctably lead to a certain kind of action, and a certain kind of society. We could say that the people who invented communism were the people with the most acute sense of what made communism so difficult (and so necessary). And yet Lenin is committed to a story about education that is akin to something we might call programming; and his critics would call indoctrination. Or, more generously, the learning of a skill. We don't describe heart surgeons or hairdressers or plumbers as being indoctrinated; we think of them as learning what is to be done. They are not being brainwashed, they are being equipped to do something specific. Lenin is teaching the working masses how to do revolution, how to do without the unnecessary oppression of exploitation. But there are grey areas and family resemblances here worth noticing. Being trained in Leninist Marxism, like being trained as a hairdresser, entails either the ends justifying the means (if you want to be a hairdresser this is what you need to know how to do); or at least the end being privileged. It is assumed that it is a revolution that you really want, which is why you are learning this. It is not part of the project that this training is simply a means to an indeterminate end. It assumes, in other words, if not a prior omniscience, then at least a driving preference. Lenin's training is not staged as a setting for too much innovation or improvisation; you can be a maverick hairdresser, you can perhaps have a slightly different interpretation of Marx, but there is still a compass and a map. Revolution is the project. What is not stressed – though it may be partly encouraged – is the eccentricity of individual curiosity and desire or the evolution of wants; what Freud called dream-work (dreaming, that is, as something we are not taught to do). That we can be taught to interpret dreams but not to dream them may be the main point this essay has to make.

So we should take seriously those caricatured reactionaries of the nineteenth century who wanted to censor the distribution of radical political tracts, those contemporary Christians who don't want Darwin taught in their schools. They are at least acknowledging the inflammatory nature of alternative descriptions. But the ambivalence about a too liberal education is often informed by a quasi-religious (but politically motivated) anxiety about conversion. The fundamentalist Christian fears, in a symmetrical way, that the young will be as possessed by Darwinism as they themselves are by the Gospel. The capitalist fears that the worker will become as ruthlessly and extravagantly committed to socialism – to actual as opposed to formal equality – as he, the capitalist, is to profit. If education is not – however subtle and nuanced; however liberal and pluralist – conversion, then what is it? Or, rather, if we understand education in the language of religion (however buried), what kinds of human experience or social practice is education like? I think psychoanalysis is better seen as entering the nineteenth-century debate about education rather than, in one way or another, as a contribution to medicine. Psychoanalysis, whatever else it is, is an enquiry, an opportunity to explore the ways in which people inform each other. And I don't, of course, mean simply transmit information to each other. There is, I want to suggest here, Leninist education in its myriad forms; and there is what Freud would call dream-work and free association and, indeed, psychoanalysis. In the *Standard Edition* translation Freud uses the word 'education' 222 times, and the cognate terms 'educator', 'educative', and so on, another 94 times. The word 'medicine' is used 101 times. There is, let us say, at least a question here. I want to use this essay to see what psychoanalysis looks like when it is described as a form of education, or 'after-education', as Freud himself described it in a rather unusual phrase. And this entails wondering why education has been such a problematic issue in psychoanalysis; both the education of analysts, and psychoanalysis defining itself against education. From the debates between Anna Freud and Melanie Klein to Winnicott's apparently off-hand comment that in doing psychoanalysis he 'interprets', unless he is tired in which case he 'teaches', education is an issue that all too easily becomes *the* issue.

II

Men cannot remain children for ever. They must in the
end go out into 'hostile life'. We may call this 'education
to reality'.

Freud, *Future of an Illusion*

In his late and remarkable essay on and elegy for psychoanalysis of 1937, *Analysis Terminable and Interminable*, an essay so troubled by both the nature and the therapeutic efficacy of psychoanalysis, Freud uses telling children the facts of life as an example for the difficulties of psychoanalytic treatment. It has, of course, always been a wonderful puzzle to psychoanalysis that their interpretations often don't seem to work in quite the way they might have wished. That there is, as it were, a gap between the intentionally given and its reception (it's always easier, of course, to be right rather than to be useful). The so-called patient, just like a so-called person, seems to do his own thing with what is said to him. On the one hand he is keen for orders and instructions, he is a keen student of his own life; but on the other hand he seems to do something the analyst is prone to call resistance, but which is better called idiosyncratic interpretation (refusal is another word for annoying interpretation). The so-called patient, in short, renders himself ineducable; he won't take on, he won't take in, the information. Information, the analyst pleads more or less pleadingly, that is good for him. Freud was himself, in his writing, a good teacher – that is, someone who trades in good examples – and so gives us an intriguing analogy for the obstacles that occur in psychoanalytic treatment. And the example is, one might say, the primal scene of education; if not an archetype, an emblem. An adult telling, the telling that is teaching, the facts of life. Why, Freud wonders, doesn't the child take to this essential, endlessly useful lesson, like a duck to water? Why wouldn't it be, as we say, in the child's best interests to take this in? Why, indeed, should something apparently so natural be so aversive? Children must be quite at odds with what they need to know. 'After such enlightenment,' Freud writes, and it seems, at least in English, the perfect word,

children know something that they did not know before, but they make no use of the new knowledge that has been presented to them. We come to see that they are not even in so great a hurry to sacrifice for this new knowledge the sexual theories which might be described as a natural growth and which they have constructed in harmony with, and dependence on, their imperfect libidinal organization – theories about the part played by the stork, about the nature of sexual intercourse and about the way in which babies are made. For a long time after they have been given sexual enlightenment they behave like primitive races who have had Christianity thrust upon them and who continue to worship their idols in secret.

From a Leninist point of view – not to mention from a psychoanalytic one – this is unpromising. How do you teach someone who doesn't want to be taught is akin to how do you psychoanalyse someone who doesn't want to be cured. Psychoanalysis then becomes an attempt to teach the unteachable. It is as though it begins where the resistance to being taught starts. In the light of this, Freud seems to be saying, how does someone go about influencing someone, persuading someone of something in words, when for good reasons of their own, they would prefer not to be so influenced? Or, to put it another way, what are the children up to; children who, after all, are the main target, so to speak, of our educative efforts? Freud talks of learning the new thing as involving a sacrifice; the children are like so-called primitive races who refuse to be converted, who go on worshipping their idols in secret. So the facts of life are, in Freud's description, something like Christianity, something the child has to convert to. What then is teaching, or indeed psychoanalysis, being experienced as, if it elicits this reaction? And the answer is, it is being experienced as an imposition; what Winnicott calls an impingement, and what could at its most extreme be called a trauma. A trauma is the sacrifice we are compelled to make. It is the sacrifice of our sentience, Freud is saying in his mumbo-jumbo about imperfect libidinal organization, that is against the grain of the child's development. It doesn't suit the child to believe the facts of life at this moment of his life. The child as an intelligent pragmatist knows that the truth is what it is good to believe. It is a tool rather than a necessity; the stork gets him where he wants to be at this moment. The child can be taught only what he wants to know. Of course he can learn to recite the facts of life – he can become a person who 'knows' such things – but it won't much matter to him. He will realize that to be a suitable member of society he has to be a person with the facts of life up his sleeve. There is, Freud intimates, public, official development, and there is secret, informal development. The child goes his own way; and the way to go your own way is to seem to be going someone else's way as well. You can do the real thing as long as you do the right thing. Another word for what Freud calls the child's secret idols are his more private personal fantasies. The medium in which he crystallizes the idiosyncrasies of his desire. Why would anyone ever want to sacrifice these? And the answer, both Lenin and Freud agree, is: you want to give them up only when you suffer too much as a consequence of holding on to them. When the child's story about the stork begins to get him into too much trouble, something has to give. What we call psychoanalysis is an attempt to explain what renders people ineducable – that is, uninfluenceable – and what, if anything, might be done about this. Psychoanalysts have been hampered from seeing this because they have been bewitched by the idea that there is something 'deeper' than education; that in real psychoanalysis they work with the unconscious, where as teaching is, as it were, more cognitive, more like changing or developing something called consciousness.

Teaching, in this story, is about informing people and teaching them methods of psychoanalysis, if not actually trying to persuade them of something; psychoanalysis is assumed to be exempt from persuasion, from suggestion; it facilitates, it enables. People don't come for psychoanalysis to have a lesson on the Oedipus complex; they can, after all, read about that in a book. Psychoanalysis, in other words, is a story about why that doesn't work. Either psychoanalysis is something quite different, or – as I want to suggest – it has found an even better way, an even better form, in which a person can learn how best to live as themselves. Psychoanalysis, that is to say, is also a response to contemporary dilemmas about education; and a critique of what I am calling the more traditional Leninist account of what education is and does. Free association is at once both a new kind of information about the self and a new way of learning about the self; dream-work is the individual's unofficial form of self-education that every educational system always comes up against, the individual's counter-culture where his own pleasures are plotted. The poetry of what he prefers. There is the repeating self that can repeat what he is supposed to know – the facts and fictions that make him a recognizable member of the social group; and there is the dreaming or dreamy self that is making what it wants to out of what it is given. The repeating self adapts – which means seeks requisite legitimation; the dreaming self seeks something else. The dreamer is educable exclusively on his own terms (which is why the pupil always chooses the teacher; and a national curriculum creates delinquency). Freud, I think, could never get over his discovery, his description of the dreamer at work inside the individual. To take this dreamer seriously (not earnestly) involves a radical critique of what we call education; of what it might be to educate someone. Education is our privileged analogy for the ideally beneficial influence one person has over another; parenting is the other. Freud implicitly links them to produce the third term, psychoanalysis; an after-education.

'If at the beginning of any discipline's self-definition,' Marjorie Garber writes in *Academic Instincts*, 'it undertakes to distinguish itself from another "false" version of itself, that difference is always going to come back to haunt it.' Education is the supposedly 'false' discipline that haunts psychoanalysis; and that therefore makes the teaching of psychoanalysis itself such a problematic issue. 'Differentiation,' Garber writes in her book about what she calls 'discipline envy', 'is one strategy that disciplines employ to protect themselves against incursion and self-doubt. But how about the opposite strategy: emulation, imitation, envy?' Or, to put it another way, why are psychoanalysts phobic about 'teaching' their so-called patients? On the one hand there is the analyst's envy of the teacher, his (supposedly repressed) desire to teach. But on the other hand there is the analyst as a new kind of teacher; the psychoanalyst as the one who performs an alternative pedagogy. Freud wanted to show us, in other words, why teaching is impossible (where and how it breaks down); and he invented to deal with this crisis in pedagogy a different kind of teacher: a teacher for whom most of what he teaches he has to learn from the student (that is, the patient). Only the student can teach the teacher how to teach him. A teacher who does something that lets the patient let himself know about himself. Like traditional teaching it was in words and it had a method; unlike traditional teaching there were no texts used in the setting (though texts, of course, informed it). In the interplay between the patient's free association and the analyst's free-floating attention – through the mutual suspension of familiar judgement – something else, something extracurricular, is learned.

'I spent several years,' the critic Harry Berger writes in *Making Trifles of Terrors* about teaching Shakespeare,

entranced by the sound of my moral rhetoric before coming to the realization that what I thought of characters was both less important and less interesting than what they thought of themselves . . . my effort to resist the judgemental impulse [became one] . . . in which one imagines one can 'hear' what speakers hear in their utterances as they listen to themselves and monitor the effect of their speech on others.

The psychoanalyst resists his own judgement to hear what the so-called patient thinks of himself; the analyst teaches not so much a subject, but a form of listening to oneself and others. If there is a subject of psychoanalysis it is whatever obstructs speaking and listening. Freud believes that speaking and listening sometimes require an after-education; which implies that they themselves may have to be learned. Learning to speak and listen – like the experience of dreaming – is quite unlike learning to be a hairdresser or to create a revolution. It has no pre-formed content. It has no predictable outcome. It discovers the object of desire rather than knowingly anticipates it. It experiments with wanting and being wanted, because wanting and being wanted are always an experiment. But unlike scientific experiments they can never be replicated.

Learning the facts of life, like being trained in what Lenin calls 'genuine political consciousness', is apparently the means to a known end. The informer intends to have a specific effect on the informant. Indeed, what is most striking in Freud's example of the unconvertible children – not to mention, of course, Lenin's 'working masses' – is the progressivism of the educative project. To learn such things, to acquire such knowledge and acknowledgements, is the way to a better future. There may not be an afterlife, but there is the potential of the self. The myth of redemption begins to wear a school uniform. Education, the optimistic language of pedagogy, is haunted and taunted by the promise of the future. If only these lessons can be properly learned, these truths accepted, these psychoanalytic interpretations consented to, we shall have a better world, a better future, a better self. And yet, Freud tells us, the bribe for some reason isn't always taken; the lesson of history is that history is not a lesson. Lenin could never predict the consequences of his predictions. Self-improvement doesn't always seem to be the improvement that modern selves are seeking.

Modern Western myths of education, shot through as they are with Christian, Enlightenment and liberal progressivism – with more or less secular and sacred myths of promise and redemption, of the next best thing ahead – keep coming up against what Freud called resistance (and what Lenin and Marx would call the sheer force of bourgeois ideology). Psychoanalysis, in its very belief in therapeutic interventions, acknowledges what so-called education finds itself up against: the idols worshipped in secret have, as it were, the last laugh. Psychoanalysis is literally the impossible profession because it educates us about the impossibility of education. It makes us wonder what it would be to be better. It shows us why getting better isn't always the best thing that we can get; why it is that wherever we go we keep turning round. Don't look back is always a paradoxical injunction.

Why, Freud keeps wondering, doesn't psychoanalysis work better as a treatment? Why is it so difficult for the so-called patient to allow the analysis to have a beneficial effect? Why, in short, isn't a better future what people most want, when it is so obviously on offer in psychoanalysis? And the answer, Freud tells us, is that it isn't always the future that people want; they are often, as it were rather ambivalent about the Promised Land. Indeed, it isn't the future that they most want, it is the past. Psychoanalysis, like education – and as a form of education that turns up when confidence in traditional education begins to falter – is an attempt to lure people into the future, to tempt them to grow up. And yet, Freud tells us – though it is something we have been told in different ways before – the past is an object of desire; suffering is an object of desire; stasis is an object of desire. And, above all, childhood pleasures are the exemplary, the founding (and forbidden) objects of desire. If, as Freud famously wrote, 'The finding of an object is in fact a refinding of it,' then the past must be utterly alluring. It is our virtually irresistible reality. Perhaps after the rigours of a humanistic and religious education we may need psychoanalysis as an after-education in the rather more immediate, sensual pleasures and ordeals of the past.

It is not incidental, I think, that when Freud wants to review towards the end of his life the obstacles facing psychoanalysis in *Analysis Terminable and Interminable* we find the analyst as teacher facing the patient as someone radically ineducable. The analyst, Freud says, is different from a medical doctor. 'As long as he is capable of practising at all,' he writes,

a doctor suffering from disease of the lungs or heart is not handicapped in diagnosing or treating internal complaints; whereas the special conditions of analytic work do actually cause the analyst's own defects to interfere with his making a correct assessment of the state of things in his patient and reacting to them in a useful way. It is therefore reasonable to expect of an analyst, as a part of his qualifications, a considerable degree of mental normality and correctness. In addition, he must possess some kind of superiority, so that in certain analytic situations he can act as a model for his patient and in others as a teacher. And finally we must not forget that the analytic relationship is based on love of truth – that is, on a recognition of reality – and that it precludes any kind of sham or deceit.

It is worth wondering, perhaps, where or indeed how one might 'qualify', get qualifications in, 'mental normality and correctness'. Freud is quite explicit that the analyst, in certain situations, should act as a teacher; and the teacher is implicitly associated with a love of truth; defined as recognition of reality. Teachers possess some kind of superiority. Despite the fact that teachers, presumably, like everyone else have an unconscious, they are exempt from any kind of sham or deceit. They are figures of integrity not victims of self-division. And yet psychoanalytic patients, as Freud keeps insisting, are extremely resistant to the work of these impressive people;

people who themselves have only become analysts, are only qualified, because they have themselves been patients. And the 'bedrock' of this well-nigh universal resistance is what Freud calls 'the repudiation of femininity'. 'At no other point in one's analytic work,' he writes,

does one suffer more from an oppressive feeling that all one's repeated efforts have been in vain, and from a suspicion that one has been 'preaching to the winds', than when one is trying to persuade a woman to abandon her wish for a penis on the grounds of its being unrealizable or when one is seeking to convince a man that a passive attitude to men does not always signify castration and that it is indispensable to many relationships in life.

Women want something they will never have and are unable to relinquish the wish for it. The man, as Freud says, 'refuses to subject himself to a father substitute, or to feel indebted to him for anything, and consequently he refuses to accept his recovery from the doctor'. Men and women, in Freud's view, are allergic to receptiveness. Their potential for passivity – for invention perhaps – horrifies them. They want teachers, but they don't want to be taught. Something in people is unyielding; there are truths to which they will not surrender. But the psychoanalyst is apparently the one who knows why the teaching doesn't work; to learn the lesson too much has to be sacrificed. The analyst, like the teacher, as a teacher, demands a sacrifice. What the analyst and the teacher and the political revolutionary come up against is people's refusal to sacrifice an apparently known pleasure for an apparently unknown one. Better the devil you know, because if you know him he can't be the devil.

'Psychoanalytic treatment,' Freud wrote in 'On Psychotherapy', 'may in general be conceived of as such a re-education in overcoming internal resistances ... for it is education even to induce someone who dislikes getting up early to do so all the same.' It involves, Freud says, 'persuading' someone to accept something they have (because of unpleasure) rejected. It is, though, a paradoxical form of education that is being proposed. It is education to make education possible. Education begins with the word *no*, and begins as the self-education that is called repression; this *no* has to be persuaded to turn into a *yes*, and this requires another person.

The first instance that Freud calls education was the individual's evasion of the pain of his desire. Education was the way he distracted himself from the difficulties of his own nature. Then he suffers from the suffering he couldn't bear. And then he employs a psychoanalyst to re-educate him. Psychoanalysis is an education in the art of unlearning. It teaches you the cost of your education. Because you couldn't bear pain you couldn't bear pleasure. The autodidact, with his repertoire of automatic defences, has to be persuaded otherwise. And Freud is quite clear about the aim of this particular form of education that he has invented to cure the ills of education. The aim is to make the individual a cleverer animal in his pleasure-seeking. The object is to please himself, not to save himself. The enlightenment is in the service of satisfaction, the satisfaction is not in the enlightenment. In this view truth would be worth having only if it gave you pleasure; truth would be recognizable only in its yield of body-pleasure. The extraordinary thing Freud has to tell us is that our pleasure is something that we have to relearn. And that we need someone to teach us. 'Under the doctor's guidance,' he writes in 'Some Character Types Met with in Psychoanalytic Work', the patient 'is asked to make the advance from the pleasure principle to the reality principle by which the mature human being is distinguished from the child.' But, Freud remarks: 'His privation is only to be temporary: he has only to learn to exchange an immediate yield of pleasure for a better assured, even though a postponed one.' It is, he makes it clear, a learning experience, what he calls 'an educative process'.

The analyst plays the part, Freud writes,

of the effective outsider; he makes use of the influence which one human being exercises over another. Or – recalling that it is the habit of psychoanalysis to replace what is derivative and etiolated by what is original and basic – let us say that the doctor, in his educative work, makes use of one of the components of love. In his work of after-education, he is probably doing no more than repeat the process which made education of any kind possible in the first instance. Side by side with the exigencies of life, love is the greatest educator; and it is by the love of those nearest to him that the incomplete human being is induced to respect the decrees of necessity and to spare himself the punishment that follows any infringement of them.

Love and the exigencies of life may be the great educators, but education is the great thing for Freud. Psychoanalysis repeats – or recruits – that education in love, through love, that is parenting. Psychoanalysis is a reminder for the individual of what education used to be like before it was called education. What is original and basic about a person is what the after-education that is psychoanalysis is about. There is, to put it mildly, a scepticism here about sophistication and development. What we want to be is what we are already, Freud suggests; and that is what we need to be re-educated in. Freud is asking us to imagine what happens if we link schooling with love, education with what is basic and original about ourselves. Freud discovered that modern people had to be taught how to re-animate themselves. They were the only animals that had to learn that they were animals. The after-education that was psychoanalysis was an after-education in human creatureliness. An after-education in the question: what is a good life for the animal who is driven by incestuous desire?

If we describe psychoanalysis as a form of education that is, at the same time, a theory about education; and if we take Freud's point that parenting and education and psychoanalysis – his preferred set of terms, with medicine as the ambiguous fourth term – are all versions of a larger question about how people influence and affect each other, how they look after each other, then psychoanalysis as education may seem less of a worry and more of a lead. And what it can lead us to is a recommendation of the aims of education in the light of psychoanalysis, and of psychoanalysis in the light of prior traditions of education. If love and the exigencies of life – and love as one of the exigencies of life – are, as Freud suggests, the great educators, then we have to acknowledge that for Freud, as both the founder of psychoanalysis and as a representative man of the nineteenth century, life (a good life) was conceived as an education. Learning, in other words, was the privileged description of what a life involved. Experience was there to be learned from. Life was a schooling in life.

But Freud doesn't simply describe psychoanalysis as part of some people's continuing education; he describes it as re-education, and it uses, he says, 'one of the components of love'. The psychoanalyst, he says, in 'this work of after-education . . . is probably doing no more than repeat the process which made education of any kind possible in the first instance'. After-education makes people educable. The parents' love opens the child to the world, and the world to the child. It makes exchange possible by fostering an appetite for exchange. And by repeating this, or incorporating it in the treatment, psychoanalysis educates people into becoming educable. What is to be analysed are the obstacles created by the individual to exchange. So in this language trauma is the name we give to the experiences that we find most difficult to learn from; and which hinder learning in the future. What people learn about psychoanalysis is what they have refused to learn about: how and why that education called life keeps breaking down. They learn, in short, their repertoire of ways of sabotaging exchange.

III

We long for a picture of what went wrong in the world.

Susan Neiman, *Evil in Modern Thought*

If psychoanalysis is, as Freud suggests, a form of education called after-education – if its project, broadly speaking, is the undoing of repression, the restoration of vital conflict – it is also unusually mindful of the fact that we have defences for a reason. Psychoanalysis as, in Freud's words, 're-education in overcoming internal resistances' to sexuality, acknowledges the sense in which one's sexuality is constituted, is phrased, by one's resistances to it. Love may be the greatest educator, but Freud forgets to mention here the forbidden love that is incestuous. Forbidden love, he might have said, is also a great educator; though in a rather less pastoral vein. What kind of after-education is possible, or available, after the harsh education of the incest taboo? And the answer would be: education in the various impossibilities of desire, the snags in wanting. To desire now – to desire in the severe wake of the incest taboo – is to learn ruses for the evasion of desire. How we go about so intently not getting what we want, and just what the mortal risks are for us, of getting what we want; this is another kind of after-education.

Psychoanalysis might seem to be, then, an education in forbidden things. Freud makes it quite clear that people don't exactly learn to be incestuously minded; rather, they have to learn not to be. It would be an accurate exaggeration to say that, from a crudely Freudian point of view, education is the attempt to persuade people to lose interest in their parents' bodies; to find fascinations elsewhere, outside the family circle. Education, in other words, wants to teach people to have a future and not merely a past. Psychoanalysis teaches that we must remember our forbidden desires so we can find sufficiently satisfying approximation; so that we can perform that paradoxical form of renunciation called displacement. The lure of the future is that it will be the same as the past, but different. If desire is fundamentally transgressive – and psychoanalysis is an after-education – then psychoanalysis is an after-education in the taking of risks. It would be possible, from a psychoanalytic point of view, to describe the singularity of a person's life in terms of the risks courted and the risks evaded (in this sense, a symptom turns up where an opportunity has been missed, a risk not taken). As Lenin insisted, it is always never the right time for revolution.

There are tremendous satisfactions in learning how, and in learning about. But what we might need an after-education for – the after-education that is psychoanalysis – is to relearn the nature of our satisfactions; the difference, say, between what we want and what we are supposed to want. You can teach people the facts of life, but you can't teach them sex. You can teach people about trauma, but you can't teach them their traumas. You can teach people about dreams, but you can't teach them to dream. You can teach people to listen, but you can't teach them what they will hear. Psychoanalysis turns up when people need to learn things that can't be taught. Or can't be taught by education as traditionally conceived. The unconscious is not a subject. Neither the analyst nor the patient can be supposed to know.

In traditional teaching there is a canon, a syllabus, with ends in mind; and we should ask of any canon, any official reading list, not merely what vested interests is it being used, more or less covertly, to promote, but what have the makers of the canon suffered such that this is their self-cure? It is a more charitable question and it involves us in more complex histories. But there are forms of suffering that the reading list cannot reach. And this is where psychoanalysis comes in; for people to find out about what they cannot learn and why.

When Winnicott dedicated *Playing and Reality* 'to my patients who have paid to teach me' he was acknowledging something very simple: the analyst teaches only through his capacity to learn from people who can't be taught. It is a revolutionary idea that being listened to could be an education.

The Uses of Desire

Religious moderates are, in large part, responsible for the
religious conflicts in our world, because their beliefs provide
the context in which scriptural literalism and religious
violence can never be adequately opposed.

Sam Harris, *The End of Faith*

I

'If we consider just the verbal expression of intention,' Elizabeth Anscombe writes in her book *Intention*,

we arrive only at its being a – queer – species of prediction; and if
we try to look for what it is an expression of, we are likely to find
ourselves in one or other of several dead ends, e.g.: psychological
jargon about 'drives' and 'sets'; reduction of intention to a species
of desire, i.e., a kind of emotion; or irreducible intuition of the
meaning of 'I intend'.

It is, indeed, true that in psychoanalytic writing – which is
more often than not 'psychological jargon about "drives" and
"sets"' – desire often sounds like a strange, rather glamorized
form of intentionality. An intentionality with no identifiable
agent, and with no discernible end. It seems to describe some
kind of emergency about purpose. It seems to be making some

kind of mockery of intention as traditionally conceived and discussed. Or it is another way of talking about something akin to intention that the language of intention can't deal with. In psychoanalytic writing the word is used either as utterly and undistractedly ordinary – as an obvious synonym for strong wanting or biologically based need – or as distractingly privileged. That we desire, that we have desires, is not news; the *OED* has the noun and the verb in Middle English. That there may be something – call it a force or a drift or an energy or a shifty line-up of words – at work inside us or between us despite our best intentions, that has not a mind of its own but ways of its own; that we may be neither masters nor servants in our own houses but something else apparently unheard of; this is, depending on one's inclinations, or perhaps affiliations, either startling or merely mystifying. For some psychoanalysts, using this word keeps them psychoanalytic; and for others, not using it, or using it as though one wasn't particularly using it, has become a statement of intent. And what is at stake here, I think, is something about intelligibility and its uses; and something about that form of intelligibility called prediction. Desire as a keyword – as a term of affiliation, as an attempt to legitimate psychoanalysis as a science of the uncanny – is indeed a queer species of prediction; predicting, as it does at its most glib, unpredictability, and, at its most ironic, predicting hope. In talking about desire, at least from a psychoanalytic point of view, we are talking about the genealogy, the provenance of hope; even when that hope is a hoping for death. We are talking about the unpredictability of aliveness in the human subject; and the forms of death-in-life, the modern forms of death-in-life that psychoanalysis sets itself the task of addressing. Psychoanalysis describes what happens when we live as if our wishes can come true; and what happens when we live as if they can't.

In Laplanche and Pontalis's formative dictionary, *The Language of Psychoanalysis*, there is no entry for 'desire'; but there is an entry which reads: 'Wish (desire)'. A translator's note tells us that 'French psychoanalysis uses *désir* for all these words' – that is, lust, desire, wish – but that desire as an English term is best used to talk about wishing. But then there are two concluding paragraphs of the entry about Lacan's 'attempt to reorientate Freud's doctrine around the notion of desire, and to replace this notion in the forefront of analytic theory' (the translator's 'reorientate' for the 'recentre' of the original slightly lowers the temperature of what is being said and done). In making their brief case for Lacan's *désir* Laplanche and Pontalis are characteristically and pointedly lucid. 'This perspective,' they write,

has led Lacan to distinguish desire from concepts with which it is often confused, such as need and demand. Need is directed towards a specific object and is satisfied by it. Demands are formulated and addressed to others; where they are still aimed at an object, this is not essential to them, since the articulated demand is essentially a demand for love.

Desire appears in the rift which separates need and demand; it cannot be reduced to need since, by definition, it is not a relation to a real object independent of the subject but a relation to fantasy; nor can it be reduced to demand, in that it seeks to impose itself without taking the language or the unconscious of the other into account, and insists upon absolute recognition from him.

What is the problem, then, that Lacan is wanting to solve or to elaborate with the notion of desire? What does he want desire to do for him here? At its most minimal, the problem for Lacan is that there is a misleading straightforwardness, a bewitching empiricism, about need and demand. It is as though both concepts take for granted exactly what psychoanalysis, in Lacan's version, puts into question. Need and demand are such sensible transactions, such pragmatic exchanges, that they are more like contracts, or agreements; more like the kinds of thing people without unconscious desire (or thought) would arrange for themselves. The notions of need and demand are rife with assumptions; the performers of such needs and demands are relatively transparent to themselves and to the people (or objects) they recruit for their quasi-biological rituals. Need has a definite and definitive object, and is satisfiable. Demand – which is essentially and intelligibly a demand for love – is unambiguously formulable – is heard as such by its addressee. The notion of desire is brought in by Lacan to expose, as it were, the unreality of human wanting. The object of desire is a fantasy; wanting goes on in a virtually closed system of wishing; we want something, though we don't know what it is, from someone who doesn't exist. And our needs, as demands, can never be in the form of orders – demanding can never be a straightforward instrumental operation – because language is the language of the unconscious. To speak is to want – and to be heard to be wanting – otherwise than one intends. Indeed, the whole notion of an intention, from this point of view, is a defensive trimming of the way language ranges. With the concept of desire Lacan is showing us the ways in which our wanting cannot be an object of knowledge. He is wanting us to see how psychoanalysis, his version of psychoanalysis, ironizes our favourite idea of knowing what we want. Desire asks us to mind the gap between our wanting and our knowing. When I claim to know what I want – and I would claim this with inflexible rigour in what psychoanalysis would call a perverse state of mind; my so-called perversion is a knowing exactly what I want and need; when I claim to know what I want I have already constituted an 'I' that I recognize by its predictive talents, and by its already familiar and looked-forward-to states of satisfaction; this 'I' has a repertoire of relatively formulable wants, formulable in a medium deemed to be an effective tool for want-gratification. In this picture, whether I am satisfied, whether I get what I want, is to do with my competence, my relative efficiency as a wanter; there is nothing about the nature of wanting itself that is a problem. The machine works if one can find a skilled operator. After all, our survival as one of Darwin's species has meant that something about our wanting has worked, even if Darwin hasn't quite plucked out the heart of the mystery.

Lacan's critique of the 'adaptationism' of American ego-psychology is, therefore, from his own point of view, only a continuation of what Freud started with psychoanalysis: providing certain kinds of description of the unfit between modern people and their internal and external environments. It was only through certain forms of suffering – through the adaptations of suffering – that modern life was bearable. What Lacan's notion of desire adds to our modern picture of our unease is that when we attend to the medium of wanting, language – both our agency and the way our wanting actually works – is put into question. It was clear that Freud knew that language was what psychoanalysis was about; but what he didn't have was the modern science of linguistics. So desire refers, as it were, to the non-instrumental unreason of our wanting. But it also refers to something of Freud's that Lacan took with unusual and insistent seriousness and wit; and this is the incest taboo. The fact that the object of desire is a forbidden object; that what we most passionately want is what we most certainly mustn't have. The medium of desire is enigmatic; and the object of desire is aversive. How we want is baffling, and what we want is impossible. When Lacan says, as a kind of advertising slogan – as an advertisement of the modern – 'man's desire is desire of the Other', he is saying that we desire what others desire (we desire by identification), and that our desire is other to what we think of ourselves as desiring. But this means that our desire is nothing to do with us; that there is desire, but not for us. 'It' comes from a wholly other outside and/or a wholly other inside; the so-called I is a middle man in no man's land. Lacan's psychoanalytic sentences serve to estrange us from what seems most intimate, most immediate about ourselves; it makes our wanting integral by being alien. The concept of desire, one might say, is part of Lacan's estrangement technique; his psychoanalytic attempt to avert the domestication of the drives through ethology and bourgeois morality (and the bourgeois morality that is ethology). Desire, as a concept, keeps something alive in psychoanalysis.

What it keeps alive, I think, is the hope involved in not knowing what we want. Desire, I want to suggest – whether or not Lacan suggests this – refers to the fact that the fantasy of knowing what one wants is a form of despair. And that what the incest taboo compels us to do is to give up both the knowledge of what we want, and to give up on knowing what we want. Because what we know we want is impossible – our psychic life depends upon our not, as it were, getting it – we have to find what it is about our wanting that is possible. We are fully alive only when our wants surprise us. The Oedipus complex says to us: when it comes to wanting you must not be essentialists; you thought hope springs from knowing what you want, but actually it comes from abjuring the magic that

that knowledge is. Desire is the queer form our unpredict-ability takes. Where intentions were, there accidents of plea-sure shall be. Desire, as I am using it, takes our pleasures to be happy accidents, and accidents will happen.

II

I want to suggest that the antonym of desire is what psycho-analysts call perversion, which I would rather call an anxious narrowing of the mind when it comes to pleasure. An intent knowingness – a determined and determining knowing what one wants – characterizes so-called sexual perversions. The person in a perverse state of mind has no conscious doubt about what will excite and satisfy him. He is sceptical, if he is sceptical at all, only about the critics of his object of desire. And he becomes concerned about his unappeasable self-knowledge only when it makes him suffer too much. Scepticism becomes a defeat (for the ego), a fall into too much unhappiness. But, above all, in a perverse state of mind, pleasures can be calculated, satisfactions can be arranged for the self, often by the self. It's a set-up. What psychoanalysts in the past have tended to call perversions – or, rather more circumspectly, perverse states of mind – could also be described as a given individual's self-cure for the problem Lacan articulates in his useful distinction (despite the problems of translation) between need, demand and desire. The individual is deemed to have biological needs, covered by the traditional concept of instinct; but the beginning individual has to make his need known in the form of a demand. And this is where the complications occur; because the infant is not self-satisfying, he recruits, through vocalization, another in order to live. There is, Lacan suggests, a split between need and demand; the finite need to be fed contains within it an infinite demand for love. The mother can satisfy the child's need but she can never fulfil the demand for love. In this meeting of need, and this unmeeting of demand, something insatiable persists; and this Lacan calls desire. In his view there is no such thing as pure need; all hungers are informed by, contaminated by, the pressure of desire. To ask for anything is to ask for everything. Need is the fall guy of desire. 'And just as the symbolic function of the object as a proof of love overshadows its real function,' Dylan Evans writes in *An Introductory Dictionary of Lacanian Psycho-analysis*, 'as that which satisfies a need, so too the symbolic dimension of demand (as a demand for love) eclipses its real function (as an articulation of need).' The question Lacan is asking, is using the concept of desire to ask, is what is the demand for love a demand for? What happens, as in so-called perversions, when the demand for love is pre-empted by or located in an apparently recognizable object? If, say, the demand for love is a demand for hope, what kind of hope is there in a shoe? It's all about keeping ourselves hungry and unharmed.

Lacan is stringent – indeed, at his most starkly insistent – about just how misleading is our desire to recognize the objects of our desire. As though all our talents for representation were to reassure us that representation works. That we can know what we want; and, at least in principle, at least logically, get it. That our terror inspires us to try to reduce all desire to need, and all demand to instrumental reason. That we can know what we want, and because we can know it we could have it. I want to wonder in this essay what the terror is that might make us want to abolish desire in favour of biological need and unambiguous demand. Why, in other words, should we dream of a language that is unbluffing, and of a love that is fathomable?

In Lacan's view, the answer in shorthand is that we are
phobic about lack; that the experience of lack is a kind of
psychic devastation, a destitution that makes us want to believe
that lack is like a question which has an answer. It makes us
simple-minded, literal-minded in our picturing; if something
is empty it can be filled. If something is empty it is empty of
something. We become mathematical and think of pro-
portions and equations; of measuring what's missing; of
making a felt absence intelligible, as in two halves in search of
each other. Or we think in terms of completion or perfection
or closure; whatever it is that would make my life what it
could and should be. Man's project is to escape from his desire,
Lacan famously said, because on the daydream horizon there
is the absence of conflict and the abolition of lack. In Lacan's
– and, indeed, Freud's – anti-utopia there is only the (ironic)
permanence of the wanting Lacan calls desire; the only reliable
object – the only object one can depend upon – is what one is
lacking. And what this lack itself, by definition, lacks is accurate
representation. The perversion version of ourselves seems to
know, seems to register, exactly what turns us on; what
absorbs and possesses us; what makes us dreamy. And yet,
Lacan suggests, this is itself a cover story; this is how we ablate
our terror, this is how we assuage the enigma of our desiring.
Lacan urges us – against the blandishments of American ego-
psychology and British object-relations; against the utilitarian
lures of behaviourism – to face the unknowingness of desiring.
And for Lacan the unknowingness of desiring is not merely or
simply or solely a problem; it is a psychic necessity. All the
so-called pathologies of modern desiring are states of virtual
conviction – conscious conviction – about the object of desire.
Either a person seems to know what they want or, with
equal certainty, not know what they want. The knowing is

apparently intact. For Lacan, at least in his Seminar II, it is precisely such unassailable recognitions that Freud has challenged. 'The domain of the Freudian experience,' he writes,

is established within a very different register of relations. Desire is a relation of being to lack. This lack is the lack of being properly speaking. It isn't the lack of this or that, but lack of being whereby the being exists. This lack is beyond anything which can represent it . . .

We necessarily believe that, at the centre, things are really there, solid, established, waiting to be recognized, and that the conflict is marginal. But what does the Freudian experience teach us? If not that what happens in the domain of so-called consciousness, that is on the level of the recognition of objects, is equally misleading in relation to what the being is looking for? In so far as the libido creates the different stages of the object, the objects are never it . . .

Desire, a function central to all human experience, is the desire for nothing nameable. And at the same time this desire lies at the origin of every variety of animation. If being were only what it is, there wouldn't even be room to talk about it. Being comes into existence as an exact function of this lack, in the experience of desire . . .

The self-conscious being, transparent to itself, which classical theory places at the centre of human experience . . . says – I'm the one who knows that I am. Unfortunately, if it does perhaps know that it is, it knows nothing at all about what it is. That is what is lacking in every being.

The metaphysical incantation of lack and being can be wearying; though the rhythms of Lacan's baroque liturgy seem somehow integral to the void he pursues and is clearly so enchanted by. But I am less interested in the persuasiveness or otherwise of Lacan's quasi-Freudian assertions than I am in whatever it is he is trying to work with; and how he cannot do without the notion of desire. His dual and complementary insistences here – that lack makes being, self-conscious being, possible; and that the object of desire is unnameable, essentially beyond representation – say: if you can name it, it isn't what you want. Desiring is privileged over satisfaction; and desiring depends upon not knowing what one wants. It is perhaps not surprising that for some people this has seemed rather more theological than traditionally psychoanalytic in its affiliations. Once again, one might say, it pits idolatory against true desiring; and even though the desiring being spoken of is irredeemably carnal, it sounds intractably metaphysical. Lacan is ironic but not earthy; he is witty, but like all psychoanalysts he is not bawdy.

Lacan insists that what he calls 'the self-conscious being, transparent to itself' knows nothing at all about what it is. This may overstate the case – and the self-conscious being transparent to itself has surely never quite existed, except as an apt caricature of scientistic, mercantile man – but it may also be a psychoanalytic way of stressing that knowing and wanting go uneasily together. So Lacan is a useful springboard to say something simple that perhaps could not have been said before psychoanalysis, or could not have been said in the same way; that knowing what one wants is a form of terror, and therefore a form of terrorism (of oneself and of others). And so to talk about desire might be to talk about the beneficence of this form of unknowing. We are familiar with what Laplanche in *Life and Death in Psychoanalysis* has called 'the attack of the drives on the ego'; with a human subject constituted by his aversion to his own nature, or thrown by his relation to the forbidden. But there is also a paradoxical kind of freedom in not needing to know what one wants, while knowing that one wants. What Lacan calls desire is the impossibility of such knowing; and yet this is the knowing that we seem to be doing, and wanting to do, much of the time. We have to imagine a wanting not in the form of a knowing.

What psychoanalysts tend to call perversions describe a state of frantic certainty; a knowledge of what is needed for excitement, a fear of its unavailability or of its unavailingness (that is, it's not working); and an often repressed doubt (or question) about its moral worth. Perversion could be construed as the antonym of desire; as the individual's self-cure for desiring. A pre-emptive strike against the differentness of another person – of their unknownness to themselves and to oneself – the perverse act requires accomplices rather than collaborators. As a calculated staging it aims to minimize surprise or shock; as though what is being acknowledged is just how distractable one is when it comes to excitement. It is as though sexuality is only viable, is do-able, so to speak, only when the preconditions for sustaining excitement, for sustaining interest, are known beforehand. A perverse act, one could say, is one in which nothing must be discovered. In this sense perversion might just mean whatever is the enemy of the new, whatever is horrified by the future (the past may be knowable, unlike the future). The hope in a perverse act is that the future will be just like the past. Desire, one can see, has a quite different sense of what hope is: for the desiring subject the future is an object of desire, but the future in all its indescribable promise (the future is not a retirement home for achieved and therefore discarded projects). It would be like hoping for whatever actually happens.

It would be worth wondering, in order to get some sense of what desiring might be, what the preconditions are, from a psychoanalytic point of view, for perversion. What is the terror that informs the need to know what one wants; or that would make a person translate the demand for love into the demand for nameable excitement?

III

In the contemporary non-Lacanian psychoanalytic writing about so-called perversion there is, if not a virtual consensus, at least an overlapping of preoccupations about the provenance of perverse solutions; and, indeed, a shared sense that what are called, diagnostically, perversions are solutions to developmental conflicts. And these perverse solutions are described in terms of revenge, mastery and repair. The emphasis in these accounts is on the mother/infant, mother/child relationship; and they circle around the (relative) helplessness of the child vis-à-vis maternal care, and the hostility mobilized by this helplessness.

'Perversion, the erotic form of hatred,' Robert Stoller writes in *Perversion*,

is a fantasy, usually acted out but occasionally restricted to a day-dream (either self-produced or packaged by others – that is, porn-ography). It is a habitual, preferred aberration necessary for one's full satisfaction, primarily motivated by hostility. By hostility I mean a state in which one wishes to harm an object . . . The hostility in perversion takes form in a fantasy of revenge hidden in the actions that make up the perversion and serves to convert childhood trauma to adult triumph.

'There are those that fuck from desire,' Masud Khan writes more starkly in *Alienation in Perversion*, 'and those that fuck from intent. The latter are the perverts. Because intent, by definition, implies the exercise of will and power to achieve its ends, whereas desire entails mutuality and reciprocity for its gratification.' 'The pervert,' Khan says, 'puts an impersonal object between his desire and his accomplice: this object can be a stereotype fantasy, a gadget or a pornographic image. All three alienate the pervert from himself as, alas, from the object of his desire.' Without intent, without this impersonal object, the person, we must assume, feels radically endangered. For Stoller perversion is sex as hatred; for Khan it is, unlike what he calls desire – it is sex as erotic engineering. In both cases the object wanted is experienced primarily as threat. In other words, the so-called pervert acts as though he knows what to expect; because he knows what other people are like – he knows, that is, what they want to do with him – he has learned how to manage them for his own excitement. It is the immediacy of the other, wanted person that has to be mediated, either by hatred and/or the impersonal object. The satisfactions all seem to be in the direction of distancing and controlling the person who is, apparently, wanted. But it is rather as though the other person is wanted as a kind of excitement experiment; what is being tested is whether one can get excited in the presence of another person and psychically survive. Desire – which in Khan's language involves mutuality and reciprocity – as the alternative to perversion would seem to entail something like wanting the very unknownness of the other person; as though what one desired was their sentient presence. There would, in other words, be two differently desiring subjects in the room; both of whom are unconscious of their desire.

Dehumanization tends to be the term of choice when it comes to perversion, though this, of course, puts the cart before the horse; that is to say, it claims a privileged knowledge of the human in order to do its talking, when it is the human, as Lacan insisted, that is always at stake. But then, by the same token, it is in writing about dehumanization that people can formulate their versions of the human. For Arnold Cooper 'dehumanization is the ultimate strategy' in perversion; and 'the attempt to dehumanize', he writes in an instructive synthesis of Khan and Stoller, 'The Unconscious Core of Perversions', 'is carried out through the use of three specific fantasies':

the perversion is always a result of mixtures of three key unconscious fantasies constructed in the perverse defence against fears of passivity when confronted with maternal malevolence. These fantasies are all efforts to deny the experience of being the helpless, needy baby at the mercy of a frustrating, cruel mother. First fantasy: 'I need not be frightened because my mother is really non-existent; that is, she is dead or mechanical, and I am in complete control.' Second fantasy: 'I need not be frightened because I am beyond being controlled by my malicious mother because I am myself non-human – that is, dead and unable to feel pain – or less than human, a slave who can only be acted upon rather than act.' And third: 'I triumph and am in total control because no matter what cruelty my squashing, castrating, gigantic monster mother creature visits upon me, I can extract pleasure from it, and therefore she (it) is doing my bidding.' . . . these three unconscious fantasies . . . erase passivity by denying human maternal control of oneself as human, by defensively converting active to passive, and by extracting pleasure out of being controlled. These three fantasies deny that the mother has hurt or can hurt the child. In effect the infant says, '(1) She doesn't exist, (2) I don't exist, (3) I force her – now a non-human "it" – to give me pleasure.'

The project in this sexualized process is self-protection and restoration; it is essentially a turning of the tables, a getting even for the victimizations of childhood. And what is most striking in these three descriptions is that the so-called pervert acts as if he knows so much about the person he wants; and so much work, so much psychic work, goes into acting on this supposed knowledge. As if to say: you know the other person, and yourself in relation to the other person, in order to take revenge on them. Knowing oneself and others is in the service of self-protection. Desire, by contrast, could be described as non-vengeful wanting. Its aim is not restoration, but a making new.

The vengeful wanting that is perversion is a return to a scene, to a drama already suffered; the non-vengeful wanting that I want to call desiring has nothing and no one to return to. Vengeful wanting, one could say, is productive of the illusion of invulnerability. Where once I was the object-victim of another's psychic need – another whose need I needed in order to survive – now I can, in Stoller's words, 'convert childhood trauma into adult triumph'. Like someone who cracks codes in order to be able to use them himself, I have become, in a certain sense, knowledgeable about my past. Even if I inflict on others a version of what was inflicted on me, I can now, at least, work the system. Indeed – and this is my greatest triumph perhaps – where once I suffered now I can enjoy. Because I can now, in Cooper's terms, 'extract pleasure' from my mother's domination, it is as though she is 'doing my bidding' (and the pun may be instructive here; a bid is at once an offer, a command and a calling). It is like learning a skill or, perhaps more exactly, it is like acquiring the tricks of a trade. There are, above all, two tricks, two quasi-redemptive magical acts: first, where suffering and confusion were once inflicted and endured, now, by a kind of psychic alchemy, pleasures are made available (now, I am saying, secretly or otherwise, you think you are hurting me, but actually I am gleefully happy, I am delirious with success). And second, where once I was the target, object and instrument of the other person's need, I am now the one in charge; I have made the drama my own; my subjectivity, my sense of myself, is made, is fabricated, out of the materials I have endured. I have, as it were, made it my vocation to convert childhood traumas into adult triumphs; to devise impersonal objects – stereotype fantasies, gadgets, pornographic images, prejudices, hobbies and hobby-horses – to hold myself together as a pleasure-seeker. Of course, excitement itself can become one of these impersonal objects. Above all, in my (excited) dealings with other people I will decide the nature of the exchange that will take place. I will administer the occasion, I will be doing the pleasure deal. And in my dealings, wittingly or unwittingly, I will always have recourse to the past. I will be resorting to the check-points of childhood traumas; I will be driven to go on rescuing myself from situations and exchanges of which I am largely unconscious. My pleasure will be that once again I have survived my history; the confounding rigours of my past, far from undoing me, have glued me together again.

This is why Stoller's term conversion – the converting of childhood trauma into adult triumph – is so apt. Trauma is loss of confidence; the shattering of belief; the traumatized individual (all of us) has to somehow convert himself – usually through converting others – into some kind of triumphalist. What we call perversion is our secular, sexualized, ersatz form of redemption. The so-called pervert – the perverse part of ourselves – lives in an empty afterlife of having survived sexual excitement. Sex is used to get rid of sex, to ditch excitement. Because it was the impinging excitements of childhood – the rages and frustrations and gratifications and confoundments – that couldn't be borne. Those were the experiences of childhood that couldn't be transformed; they could only be stored, like secret weapons, in order eventually to be expelled. Perversion, it would be more exact, and exacting, to say, bears witness to whatever is irredeemable in experience. Revenge is nostalgia.

IV

Perversion, then, is a sacrifice of sorts; it sacrifices surprise, it sacrifices mutuality, it sacrifices the resonance of the other person and oneself. It sacrifices, in other words, the future in the name of the past. By getting even, by attempting to restore an impossible invulnerability, by willing an anti-romance of efficient excitement, perverse acts are characterized, at least in psychoanalytic writing, by their determination, by their ambition. They are like the hauntings that make people mechanical, the pieces of the past that make us feel programmed, or even robotic. It is the redress of the past that makes the past seem ineluctable. It reiterates, through unconscious memory, the trauma it seeks to undo.

I want to suggest – prompted by Lacan, but quite at odds with his account – that desire can be a way of talking about an alternative to what psychoanalysts (and others) have described, albeit unfortunately, as perversion. In my version desire is not so much in opposition to perversion as at odds with it. As a story about un- or non-vengeful wanting it depends upon our being surprised by our pleasures; pleasure ceases to be, as it were, part of our calculations; and is more like luck than justice. In this account we do not suffer from not knowing what we want, because knowing what we want is something we cannot do. Indeed, the phrase 'knowing what we want' is like Anscombe's queer species of prediction. Knowing what one wanted would be like knowing what the future holds; wishing is what we do about the future and this, as Freud went to great lengths to show us, is different from knowing (knowing the future, knowing my future satisfactions, is perverse in the sense that it makes me seem more powerful, more omniscient, than I really am). Desire, in short, is the wanting that comes from the part of ourselves that is without grievance. And if such a part of oneself seems unimaginable it is because perverse wanting is, by definition, such a stark tyranny. When our grudges are suffocating we really know we are omniscient. So my tag would be, not: where id was there ego should be; but: where perversion is, there desire should be. Perversion would be described, would be analysed, as: all the ways I have of keeping myself in the know. Desire would be described as all the ways we can find of replacing knowledge with hope. Falling in love is when what I am calling desire begins (again) to contend with perversion, to stake a claim. Indeed, any experience that would have been described in old-fashioned language as a passion I would describe as a clash and a collaboration between perverse intent and hopeful desiring. For the desiring self it will always be the surprises sprung rather than the programmes entailed that will be the real draw. For the desiring self ideology all too often sounds like more of the same.

By way of conclusion – or perhaps by way of elaboration – I want to suggest that if the term 'desire' should be reserved for the unpreordained, then the two forms of sexuality, the two forms of wanting that I am describing, might be akin to two ways of writing history. Perversion is like a revisionism that keeps failing; it is the 'true' story of a subject people seeking justice and redress. But their zeal is born of terror, so they terrorize. They can't afford their doubts about themselves – about the stories they tell themselves about themselves – because they equate doubt with injustice and intimidation. Perverse history is triumphalist; self-protective and self-justifying. Perverse history is excessively patriotic; it is nationalist propaganda. What other kinds of history could there be, except the history that keeps returning to the scene of the crime, to the trauma that forged the sense of nationality?

Desire, by (my) definition, is unprepared; it has not been equipped or instructed or even inspired by the past. It has nothing substantive to recollect or recycle. It could never be, like perverse history, the history of the future; or a story about how history will reward our intentions. It is not a form of prospecting or divination; nor is it a form of wishing as a conventionally transitive act. You can't exactly wish to be surprised because this would mitigate against the experience of being surprised. The past is carried in our expectations, which make our shocks and surprises possible. But the new is anything that by definition modifies such expectations as we have. And Lacan's notion of lack implies a subject already too knowing – too consciously or unconsciously sensible – of himself as a set; too mindful of himself as a plenitude depleted. From the point of view of desire, in my sense of it, we are not lacking what we find; the notion of lack is our retrospective rationalization, our coherent narrative, about finding as recovering. There can be addition where nothing was previously missing. I would notice, in other words, that what I might call my expectations and assumptions, far from being exclusively baggage from the past, are also forms of omnisci-

ence. The perverse version of the self is replete with expectations.

So the history of my desiring self would also be a history of
pleasurable experiences unwarranted by expectation. It would
not, therefore, be a history of my achieved intentions; nor
could it be a success story in terms of obligations met and
ambitions secured (it would have no truck with the self as
predictor or reader of omens and portents). It would be a story
that would disfigure my wish (or my talent) for coherent
narrative. It would be a story about how my stories were
interrupted or broke down or didn't hang together. It would,
to all intents and purposes, be a history of accidents and
anomalies; all convincingly pleasurable but of uncertain consequence. Not a history of intentions realigned by circumstance,
but a story of lucky coincidences, for which no credit could be
taken by anyone (or anything), and from which no resentment
could ensue.

Need makes perfect biological sense. The demand for love
– however exorbitant, however unconscious its sources, and
however ironic its consequences – is a consoling and exhilarating and sensible intention for people like us who have heard
and overheard so much about love. Need and the demand for
love are indeed the queer species of prediction we are born
into. But desire is wanting as a species of luck.

Nuisance Value

... what they do together is less important than the fact that
they do whatever it is together.

Stanley Cavell, *Pursuits of Happiness*

'Interesting philosophy,' Richard Rorty writes in *Contingency,
Irony and Solidarity*,

is rarely an examination of the pros and cons of a thesis. Usually it is,
implicitly or explicitly, a contest between an entrenched vocabulary
which has become a nuisance and a half-formed new vocabulary
which vaguely promises great things ... it [the half-formed new
vocabulary] says things like, 'try thinking of it this way' – or,
more specifically, 'try to ignore the apparently futile traditional
philosophical questions by substituting the following new and possibly interesting questions'.

For there to be change, whether or not it is considered to be
progress, Rorty suggests, something has had to begin to feel
like a nuisance. But this entrenched vocabulary has to begin
to seem like a nuisance – to seem like an irritant or an obstacle
or a saboteur – for something new to happen. Clearly, at least
in philosophy, people have to be able to have the nuisance
experience. Either this vocabulary becoming a nuisance is itself
an inspiration; or inspiration – or Rorty's version of inspiration,

which he calls redescription – is spurred by the nuisance experience. It is as though one is frustrated into experimentation – 'try thinking of it this way'; or that the old entrenched vocabulary makes some new things sound baffling or implausible. The nuisance effect of the entrenched vocabulary is that it makes one want to ignore it – its apparently futile traditional philosophical questions – and start replacing it with new questions. Certain vocabularies make certain sorts of questions possible. It is not working through that Rorty recommends, it is ignoring and substitution; not mourning but moving off and moving on.

Something about what Rorty calls, in his wonderfully bland and tendentious phrase, 'interesting philosophy' needs a nuisance. So it is worth wondering what it might be about an entrenched or familiar vocabulary that would turn it into a nuisance. You might feel, for example, that there was something that mattered a great deal to you that you couldn't get, or get at, in the vocabulary available; but this old vocabulary would have to exist for you to have this feeling. You would be dependent on the way in which it frustrated you; because this very frustration would be a prompt. The old vocabulary would pester you with what it couldn't do for you, with the roads not taken by that set of words. Indeed, the thing about a nuisance is that, by definition, it won't leave you alone; you can't ignore it until you come up with a way of ignoring that works. If a substitute is a constant reminder of what it is substituting for – if a new lover becomes a compulsory and compulsive allusion to the one you have lost – it is a mixed blessing. When we are talking about something or someone becoming a nuisance we are trying to describe a specific kind of conflict that is called up in us; we are describing being set a task, but a discomfiting one. We don't tend to make claims for our nuisances – people often describe children as nuisances, but ideally no one wants a nuisance, or to be one. What Rorty is drawing our attention to is how the interesting philosopher needs to be able to notice the nuisance value of an entrenched vocabulary. Whether a nuisance is an invitation or an opportunity or more obviously an annoyance, it is always a demand. We may not want to be a nuisance (though why we don't is worth wondering about), but we do, Rorty implies, need to be able to have the nuisance experience. It is a nuisance when we are made to attend to something that we would rather not. Clearly nuisance and the notion of resistance, of preferring not to, go together. But whether the nuisance is, to use an entrenched vocabulary, the cause or the consequence of resistance – whether we resist something because it is a nuisance, or it is a nuisance because we resist it – is never so clear. How we make something or someone a nuisance, and what we use nuisances to do; and what, if anything, this might have to do with what was called, in an older entrenched vocabulary, appreciation of the arts, is the gist of this essay.

Rorty's blithe and impressively light-hearted solution to the nuisance of an entrenched philosophical vocabulary is to regard its traditional questions as apparently futile; ignore them and substitute them with new and possibly more interesting questions. And psychoanalysis is of a piece with this kind of jaunty pragmatism in so far as one of the things Freud showed us was just how inventive we are at ignoring things we don't like, and substituting things we prefer. The only difference is that for Freud this is often the problem rather than any kind of solution; from a psychoanalytic point of view it has always been the best and the worst thing about us that we are able to replace a negative hallucination with a positive hallucination, that we can turn pain into pleasure, at least for the time being. Nuisance, we could say, is the compliment we give to the unacceptable when we want it to be merely annoying; the nuisance never lets go, but it doesn't drive us mad (we don't describe stalkers as a nuisance; we don't say, unless we are characters in an Evelyn Waugh novel, that it is a nuisance to fall in love, or a nuisance when people die). Nuisance, in other words, makes us think of the inconvenient rather than the repressed; and therefore, perhaps, it is not suitable as a term of art. We may at least claim to like art that disturbs us, but we don't tend to describe a poem or a painting or a piece of music as a nuisance, even if their makers often are. We use the word 'nuisance' when there is something that we don't want to be bothered by, but are. The relative blandness of the term is reassuring; it reminds us of our passion for convenience, the narcissism of small conflicts, the wish to be left alone. As a determined pragmatist, Rorty, in passing, also wants us to use nuisance. If something becomes a nuisance you can do something about it. And doing something about it, for Rorty, is doing without it. If a nuisance is something you can't ignore then at its best it will prompt you to find more productive ways of ignoring, better substitutes.

And yet what is odd about the contest Rorty describes between the new more interesting philosophy and the older entrenched vocabulary is that it is a contest in which one party is encouraged to ignore the words of the other. And that, of course, a nuisance is something by definition that you can't ignore; if you could ignore it, it wouldn't become a nuisance. Indeed, that peculiar act of trying to ignore someone or something – the act of seeing and then having to persuade yourself that you haven't really seen, or don't really need to look – is what you start doing with a nuisance. A nuisance is nothing if not good at engaging you and then leaving you with having to deal with all the ways in which one resists being engaged. A nuisance is someone who does and doesn't take no for an answer. But there is, as Rorty intimates, a contest of sorts – an albeit ignoble or mock-heroic one – whenever there is a nuisance around. Though what is striking about nuisance, and so of some interest, is that unlike the art works we would prefer to make and to admire, the nuisance, the nag and the pest don't tend to bring out the best in us, or in themselves. On the whole no one wants to be a nuisance; and yet there are clearly situations and predicaments in which it may be necessary to be able to be one; or, as we say, put up with one.

We don't think of the users or promoters of an entrenched vocabulary as trying or wanting to make a nuisance of themselves; though given how unacceptable it is to be a nuisance perhaps we should begin to notice just how much nuisance artfulness is there to conceal or make more pleasing (the word 'obsession', one could say, pathologizes nuisance just as the word 'preoccupation' aestheticizes it). Every child has to learn to be a nuisance and how not to be; because nuisance is one of the forms demand takes, even if we think of it as a peculiarly unimaginative, monotonous and insistent form. Every child has to make whatever is insistent about them more winning; it is clearly very difficult, for example, to grow up in an environment in which appetite is considered to be a nuisance, an interruption rather than something taken for granted. The child's appetite, one would think, will be a nuisance only if treated as such by the adults upon whom he is dependent; but if it is treated as a nuisance by the adults then the child will have to take on being a nuisance in order to survive. In the face of exasperation and impatience and avoidance he will have to persist; so wherever we make a nuisance of ourselves

– or notice that we are trying not to make a nuisance of ourselves – there is some kind of unmet or unrecognized need (as the psychoanalyst André Green says, in a different context, wherever a grievance is there was a trauma). In this picture, to be unable to complain would be to have abolished one's history. Nuisance and wanting go together even if we prefer them separate. If nuisance is need insufficiently transformed, the bad art of wanting; if nuisance, like many repetitions, is the sign of something thwarted or blocked or stalled, then it would be worth wondering what would have to happen for someone to never need to be a nuisance; or, perhaps more interestingly, for them never to experience someone or something else as a nuisance. Or, to put it the other way round, what are the predicaments in which nuisance is a necessity?

Whenever there is need and a kind of hopeless hope that the need can ever be met – or turned into something else – we will find nuisance abounding. The nuisance, in other words – and the nuisance in oneself – is an interesting figure because of the assumptions he makes. He is living as if he knows exactly what he wants but for all sorts of reasons the other person doesn't want to give it to him. So it is easy for us to think of children, often benignly, as making a nuisance of themselves; and more difficult for us to think, say, of people begging, who, broadly speaking, we experience as a nuisance or try extremely hard to make them and ourselves feel that they are not. If we don't give money to people begging in the street are we withholding something that belongs to them? People divide significantly around their answers to this question; which is also about what it means to find someone else a nuisance, or to manage one's response to them by experiencing them as a nuisance. If someone begging on the street wasn't a nuisance what would they be?

In his chronicle *Down and Out in Paris and London*, published in 1933, George Orwell asks the question 'Why are beggars despised?' He answers:

I believe it is for the simple reason that they fail to earn a decent living. In practice nobody cares whether work is useful or useless, productive or parasitic; the sole thing demanded is that it shall be profitable. In all the modern talk about energy, efficiency, social service and the rest of it, what meaning is there except 'Get money, get it legally, and get a lot of it'? Money has become the grand test of virtue. By this test beggars fail, and for this they are despised . . . A beggar looked at realistically, is simply a businessman, getting his living like other businessmen, in the way that comes to hand.

In Orwell's view we despise beggars because they don't earn through work, and because they are poor. If 'money has become the grand test of virtue' we will be unduly suspicious of those who don't have it. Of course, as Orwell knows, we are duly suspicious also of those who have a lot of it. But the point Orwell is keen to make – which seems slightly odd – is that we despise beggars because what they do is not profitable; because they are not good at what they do. Orwell stresses that there is no 'essential difference between beggars and ordinary working men', it's just that beggars, like children, don't work and don't make money. And this is so despicable that the state makes begging illegal; to get money the beggar has to seem to be actually doing something. 'As the law now stands,' Orwell writes,

if you approach a stranger and ask him for twopence, he can call a policeman and get you seven days for begging. But if you make the air hideous by droning 'Nearer, my God, to Thee', or scrawl some chalk daubs on the pavement, or stand about with a tray of matches – in short, if you make a nuisance of yourself – you are held to be following a legitimate trade and not begging. Match-selling and street-singing are simply legalized crimes.

There are in fact several pages on a street artist in the book in which Orwell is clearly wondering what so-called artists, including himself as a writer, are actually doing now in this pre- and post-war society in which money has become a grand test of virtue, and in which virtue has a quite different kind of purchase on the imagination. But in Orwell's calculated list of match-sellers, street-singers and pavement artists – who are, in his view, on a continuum with all the other businessmen in the culture – it is only by these people making a nuisance of themselves that they can be 'held to be following a legitim-ate trade and not begging'. You have to make a nuisance of yourself to remain within the law; but also, Orwell implies, this is what all businessmen are doing, which is why this has become a test of the legitimacy that is legality. Everyone in this society has to force themselves on other people's attention, and sell them something they don't really want, let alone need. You have to make a nuisance of yourself to get on. Business is like bad art – hideous droning, scrawling daubs on the pavement; someone makes a nuisance of themselves, and gets away with it. The picture Orwell conjures – which, as always with him, is far subtler than he is telling us that it is – is of people paying off these people in order to be able to forget about them. To use Rorty's word, the police can 'ignore' the beggar if he is droning or scrawling or selling matches; and the passers-by give them money so they can pass them by. Beggars make a nuisance of themselves so people will give them money to stop them being a nuisance. Making a nuisance of yourself is an invitation to other people to do something that will stop you being a nuisance. We have to find legitimate ways of begging, of asking for what we need. Orwell is saying that in the society he lives in everyone is a beggar but in order to distract us from this hideous fact we have to be seen to be selling something; and to do that – to, as they say, make money – you have to find a way of making a nuisance of yourself. What the real beggars in the culture make patent is how, in this culture, making a nuisance of yourself has to be redescribed – as being an artist or a businessman or, indeed, a policeman – to make it sufficiently acceptable. The beggar who makes a profitable nuisance of himself is Orwell's representative modern person. In this exchange the beggar gives the nuisance he has made, of himself, for money. It is as though a nuisance is the most minimal thing one can make of oneself. The starkest gift. At the raw end of the spectrum there is being a nuisance; at the cooked end there is being a nuisance without seeming to be one. Criminals, Orwell seems to imply in the book, are the people we punish for being a nuisance; artists are the people we reward for being a nuisance; successful businessmen are criminals disguised as artists.

In *Down and Out in Paris and London* Orwell uses art and artists, including himself, to talk about poverty; both its provenance and its effects. For the people Orwell describes and lived with poverty was not a metaphor, it was not a useful analogy, as it could have been for Orwell himself, who was not without means. It is in a sense the project of the book to stop poverty being used as an analogy; to undo his and our horrified voyeurism of the poor. And the poor, Orwell suggests, are forced to make a nuisance of themselves, and to be seen only as a nuisance. Successful artists and businessmen – Orwell's other two categories that he wants to lump together

– have to make a nuisance of themselves, but in a way that makes them seem to be something other than a nuisance. The artist is the person for whom making a nuisance of himself works. Indeed, works so well that nuisance would be the last word we would use about the work (if not about the artist). So in the context of this essay we might ask: what kind of nuisance is this particular work of art, and why don't we want it to be one? How have we and the artist conspired to stop it being a nuisance so that it could be something else more satisfying? And this would not be to assume that any art work could be reduced to its nuisance value, so much as to draw attention to the nuisance value of the art. Because once we can find the nuisance – like Rorty's interesting new philosopher stuck with the old entrenched vocabulary – we can ourselves begin to get to work. A nuisance, if we can do something with it, gives us something to be going on with.

In a talk given in 1945 called 'Home Again', about children returning home after being evacuated during the war, the psychoanalyst and paediatrician D. W. Winnicott spoke of how these children needed to test the home environment in order to rediscover its reliability. After all, if one has been sent away once one could be sent away again. The child, Winnicott said,

begins to be cheeky, to lose his temper, to waste your food, to try to worry you and to interfere with your other interests. He may very likely try out a little thieving, testing how true it is that you are really his mother, and so in a sense what is yours is his. These can all be signs of a step forward in development – the first stage of a sense of security, although maddening from your point of view. The child has had to be his own strict father and mother while he has been away, and you may be sure that he has had to be over-strict with himself to be on the safe side . . . Now, however, at home with you, he will be able to take holidays from self-control, for the simple reason that he will leave the business of control to you. Some children have been living in artificial and overdone self-control for years, and it can be assumed that when they begin to let mother take over control once more they are going to be a bit of a nuisance from time to time.

Winnicott is describing the developmental necessity of the returning child's freedom to be a nuisance. If the child enacts his personal repertoire of antisocial behaviour and the parents still love him and keep him – if he gives the environment what Winnicott calls 'the full blast of his hatred' and it and he remain in touch and remain intact – then he has discovered a home he can trust in, and entrust himself to. If the parents can't allow the child to be a bit of a nuisance, the child cannot find his way back to the parents. Being a nuisance is the way the child makes a home to return to. But this involves not the parents' so-called unconditional love and acceptance, but the parents being able to experience the child as a nuisance – hate him for it if need be – and giving the child time to become lovable again. In Winnicott's view the object becomes real by being hated; and we can love real people, or discover people to be real, only when they have withstood our hatred. Nuisance is the nice word for the hateful exchange that a relationship can survive; and by surviving can become resilient rather than merely wishful.

What Winnicott calls 'the nuisance value of the symptoms' is always a sign of hope in the child. If the child is prepared to be difficult he is at least hoping that there is a world he can live in as himself, with all his love and hate. 'The nuisance value of the antisocial child,' Winnicott writes, 'is an essential feature, and is also, at its best, a favourable feature indicating again a potentiality for recovery . . .' All the child's so-called antisocial behaviour, one could say – all his stealing, lying, incontinence, and so on – are simply the form his entitlement to have parents takes. The child is living as if, living in hope that, people can recognize, meet and where necessary withstand his need. It is the child who can't be difficult, the child who is too fearful to make a nuisance of himself, that is the child we should be really worried about. The child who is a bit of a nuisance wants more life, wants the better life that can include whatever his development is going to be. The child who is no trouble may have given up hope. For Winnicott the mother's 'willingness to meet the claims arising out of frustration, claims that begin to have a nuisance value' gives the deprived child somewhere to start from again.

But it is clear from this picture that what Winnicott calls the nuisance value of the symptom exists only if the environment both experiences the nuisance and comprehends it as a message, a message about a deprivation. Being a nuisance, in other words, is a precarious process; it demands a great deal of the environment it makes around it. And it is a considerable act of faith. The nuisance value of the symptom resides in the symptom being given value in the way it is responded to. When a nuisance is experienced merely as a nuisance; when a nuisance is taken too literally; when a nuisance goes on being a nuisance, it is a missed opportunity. In an older entrenched language, one might say it takes courage to make a nuisance of oneself. The kind of courage that is involved in being prepared to try to make the kind of world that one can actually live in. For Winnicott, given that deprivation is endemic to human development, the capacity to be a nuisance, and the capacity to bear with a nuisance, are tantamount to the capacity one has to live one's own life. And this involves a willingness to interrupt and be interrupted. So taken is Winnicott by the notion of nuisance that he wants to posit it as a need of what he is keen to call human nature. 'It has often been said,' he writes in a paper entitled 'Integrative and Disruptive Factors in Family Life', 'as a joke and with truth that children are a nuisance; but coming at the right time in a relationship they are the right kind of nuisance. There seems to be something in human nature that expects a nuisance, and it is better that this nuisance should be a child than an illness or an environmental disaster.' Expecting a nuisance of course is different from needing one. It is as if Winnicott is referring to a kind of magic; we expect a nuisance and if we are lucky it will be just that, not a catastrophe. It's a bit like saying we expect to be interrupted, to have our lives disrupted, but preferably by good things. Expecting a nuisance, ideally, is like expecting a child. And expecting nuisance as part of human nature is presumably expecting things not to be as we want them to be; expecting our lives not to be as we expect them to be. For Winnicott nuisance, unlike trauma, is potentially just the right amount of unsettlement.

But to call something or someone a nuisance – and I think Winnicott may be alluding to this – is to be uncertain of its significance. Do we use the word 'nuisance' to reassure ourselves that we have domesticated a trauma, that we have transformed something shocking into something irritating; that nuisances don't link us to our losses and our lapses? Or is a nuisance what we say it is, a low-key disturbance, not a derivative or an echo or a clue to something graver? It is possible that we call something or someone a nuisance precisely when they baffle that distinction, or when they provoke us into ignoring it. A nuisance puts us in this difficult position, the position of wanting something to go away, the position of being forced to take something seriously that one doesn't want to be serious about. When Strachey's Freud in 'The Question of Lay Analysis' refers to 'the fact that neurotics are a nuisance and an embarrassment for all concerned – including the analysts' he is referring to the fact that even psychoanalysts who had found a new way of valuing neurotics didn't necessarily like them. Nuisance may be inspired – by memory, by the meaning that is desire; being able to be a nuisance may be necessary to survival; so-called nuisance value may be another way of describing the individual's stubborn ambivalence about recognition, the baffled nature of his insistent appeal. And yet nuisance, by definition, creates a resistant, if not actually hostile, environment; it invites the avoidance it fears. Perhaps being a nuisance is wanting to start again; or nuisance is the sign of something that wants to get started. After all, an old entrenched vocabulary can be a nuisance, but nuisance always speaks in an entrenched vocabulary.

Waiting for Returns:
Freud's New Love

If the mad Past, on which my foot is based,
Were firm, or might be blotted: but the whole
Of life is mixed: the mocking Past will stay.

George Meredith, *Modern Love*

In the places that I have worked, which have never been universities – child psychiatry departments, child guidance clinics, children's homes, private practice, and so on – I have never heard the word 'modernism' used. And yet, obviously, the psychoanalytic work that I and my colleagues do comes from the work of someone who is considered, by those people who do use the word, to be one of the significant modernist writers. Whatever people think of psychoanalysis, it is relatively uncontroversial to say that Freud worked when and where he did and that his work has been hugely influential. But that there might be connections, say, between Baudelaire and Freud, that there might be books to be written linking Baudelaire, or Conrad, or Gertrude Stein, or Walter Benjamin, and Freud, would until quite recently have been considered irrelevant to anyone doing a psychoanalytical training. For the practising psychoanalyst Freud is not, broadly speaking, an important modernist writer. He is either the source of truths about human nature, which, because they are truths, do not need to be historicized; or he is the source of powerful descriptions of the modern human subject, which must be historicized so as to reassure practising analysts that those descriptions have contemporary relevance. The problem for institutional psychoanalysis – and there is no other kind now – of seeing Freud as a modernist is that he then becomes one among many, a voice, however influential, in a wider cultural conversation. If one permits this – and, of course, by now it has been done many times, but almost entirely within the university – the plot of psychoanalysis, as also the plot of so-called modernism, will thicken and thin in ways not always susceptible to a controlling narrative.

With these preliminary observations held for a while in abeyance, I'd like to consider, from a working position outside the university, what seems to me to be a striking contradiction: namely, that in a period defined by the possibility, indeed by the necessity, of innovation in the arts, Freud was writing about the near impossibility of innovation in the modern individual's erotic life. Where the arts might prosper in their need for the new, the individual was likely to fall sick in his quest for a new erotic object. The modern individual's psychic survival depended, in Freud's view, on finding the new, non-incestuous object of desire; and yet it was the new object, paradoxically, that was the most difficult object to locate. The old object kept returning in the guise of the new; it was precisely in the place of the new that the old parental object kept reappearing. At a time when Gertrude Stein could make a novelty even of repetitiveness, Freud kept seeing the repetition in every apparent novelty. Erotic life seemed to be the realm of cultural activity, so to speak, that was peculiarly resistant, uncannily hostile to the innovative or the improvised. Repetition, Freud kept showing and saying, is always the issue when the modern individual wants to make it new (which in turn might make us wonder both what was new, and what Freud thought could be new, about psychoanalysis. Its novelty might be that it exposed the modern resistance to novelty.).

Moreover, the repetition that is mimesis, which was anathema to so many of the modernists, Freud began to describe as the modern individual's only hope. The new object of desire could only be an object of desire at all if it was, in some sense, a copy of the original, incestuous object. Indeed, for Freud, the copy functions as the necessary cover story for the new; in erotic life the new is possible only by way of the copy. Freud promotes, as we shall see, the necessity of mimesis in the construction of the new; and insists on the new as the stomping ground for the repetitions of the past. We are likely to be at our most repetitious, Freud proposes, when we think we are at our most innovative.

Many of the tags and captions and clichés of modernism that are most often repeated are about repetition, from Marx's infamous opening to 'The Eighteenth Brumaire of Louis Bonaparte' – 'Hegel remarks somewhere that the great events and characters of world history occur, so to speak, twice. He forgot to add: the first time as tragedy, the second as farce' – to Freud's 'The finding of an object is in fact a refinding of it' in his *Three Essays on the Theory of Sexuality*. From Benjamin's talismanic title 'The Work of Art in the Age of Mechanical Reproduction' to Eliot's notorious quip in his essay on Massinger, 'immature poets imitate; mature poets steal', new questions are being asked about reproduction. In the period supposedly covered by the term, the significance of the new technologies of reproduction – the photograph, the cinema, the print and

mass-production generally – was that news stayed news. Progress in the sciences was founded on, was defined by, the repeat-
ability of experiments; there were only proofs, results and
refutations in science because experimental conditions could be
reproduced. In the so-called arts there was, on the one hand, an
acute sense of the stultifying repetition of the past – of tradition
as foreclosure – and so, on the other hand, an impetus, in
Pound's words, to make it new. 'The world' between the wars,
Wyndham Lewis wrote in *Blasting and Bombardiering* in 1937,

was getting, frankly, extremely silly. It will always be silly. But it
was getting into a really suffocating jam – no movement in any
direction. A masquerade, a marking time. Nothing real anywhere.
It went on imitating itself with an almost religious absence of
originality; and some of us foresaw an explosion.

The craving for the new was not, of course, itself new; nor
the sense that an absence of originality was a religious absence.
What was gaining momentum was the sense that imitation
was a form of servility rather than civility. Lewis, as one of
David Trotter's so-called paranoid modernists (see 'Paranoid
Moderns', pp. 263–76), was, he writes, involved in 'an all-out
assault on social [and aesthetic] mimesis'. In Lewis's view, as
Trotter makes clear,

Capitalism has to make people the same person so that they will
consume the same things, which can therefore be produced en
masse; and it has to overhaul this person periodically so that he or
she will consume even more of the same things, or the same things
done up in a different fashion. The revolutionary impulse does
capitalism's work for it, because it encourages people to overhaul
themselves periodically.

The same things, and the same things done up in a different fashion, become at once the modernist problem and the modernist solution. Freud, as we shall see, was wondering what the difference was, and if it was a difference that made a difference. In erotic life it was peculiarly difficult to make people consume the same things; under the cover of consensual objects of desire there were always the more troubling idiosyncrasies of personal history. Those modernists tyrannized by mechanical reproduction had to, as it were, invent their own repetitions or be oppressed by another man's. When T. E. Hulme, for example, was sponsoring the new avant-garde work of Epstein and Bromberg as a revival of Byzantine art; or Eliot was rediscovering the metaphysical poets; or Yeats was idealizing the quattrocento, they were all trying to repeat through re-creation, to recycle a preferred past. These are calculated and calculating repetitions to offset, to revise the more stifling – the more automatic – repetitions of contemporary life. There are – though these are not quite the right words – the imposed repetitions, and the apparently chosen, or preferred, repetitions. There are the coerced identifications, and the inspiring identifications. The question is not only who owns the means of reproduction, but what are the means of reproduction? There is a preferred past, a past as an object of desire, a past that for various reasons – conscious and unconscious – one wants to repeat, to revive; and a past that repeats itself anyway, and as persecution. Does the modern individual have anything akin to a choice about whether he repeats himself, and about what he repeats; repetition being, by definition, of the past? It is only, of course, because there are repetitions that there is something we want to call choice.

*

The image of the ivory tower, so prevalent in the period of modernism, memorably expresses, as Peter Nicholls writes in *Modernisms*,

the desire to evade the pressure in a modern democratic society to conform and identify with others. Writers and artists at this time were increasingly aware of a mimetic principle at work in bourgeois modernity, in its fondness for representational art, in its parasitic dependence on 'tradition', and in the psychology of emulation underpinning a culture in which moral continuity was insured by institutionalized habits of imitation. Bourgeois culture thus seemed to ground itself in the awkward paradox that we become truly ourselves only by copying others . . . our words, our actions, our most intimate desires always seem to bear the trace of an other who was first on the scene and whom we unwittingly copy.

The paradox that Nicholls refers to – 'that we become truly ourselves only by copying others' – puts into question the singularity, let alone the originality, of the modern individual. Indeed, one might think that the idea of individuality only ever emerges at the point at which it begins to occur to people that there may be no such thing. For Freud – and not only Freud, of course – this is what modern people are talking about when they talk about love. In fact, talking about love is the modern individual's way of talking about such things as repetition, imitation and identification. There were the virtually automatic forms of repetition – akin to hypnosis – that made possible mass-production and consumption, the mass market of commodities and ideologies; and the technology required to produce and sustain them. All of this belongs with what Nicholls calls 'a mimetic principle at work in bourgeois modernity'. There were also those apparently automatic forms of repetition called symptoms, which were only called symptoms – diagnosis in such terms was only possible – because these discernible, describable kinds of behaviour that modern people suffered from (and with) were reproduced with minor variations in many people's lives. Illnesses and their complementary treatments caught on like fashions (you could discover a new species of bird, but it was contentious as to whether you could discover a new species of so-called psychological illness). The same things, or the same things done up in a different fashion, were precisely what Freud seemed to be observing in his clinical practice: hysteria, obsessional neurosis, paranoia, and so on, were usable diagnostic categories and yet they were also, in Freud's view, ways of reproducing the past. The idiosyncrasies of individual histories repeated themselves in similar forms, as though symptoms were forms of unconscious cultural consensus about how history had to be told. Just as there were techniques of mechanical reproduction there seemed to be unconscious techniques of historical reproduction. A hysterical conversion symptom, for example, reiterated in disguise, in compromised form, a desire *from* the past, which was also an (albeit conflicted) desire *for* the past.

But why, given the suffering entailed, would the individual want to repeat the past in this way, at once obscuring that it is the past that is being repeated, and not wanting to know that this is the case? The symptom is the research project of the unwilling modern historian. The symptomatic modern and modernist individual wants to make it old. Or, in striving to make it new, none the less keeps making it old.

Freud asks two fundamental questions about modern European men and women. First, what are their conscious and unconscious repetitions of the past in the service of; why, in other words, is the past something – an object of obscured desire – that they want to repeat, even or especially at its most painful? Second, what is the desire to imitate, to identify, a desire for? And the answer, in brief – and we will come back to this – is that the modern individual copies to avert – and/ or to master, to rework – a catastrophe from the past he is unconscious of. He copies in order to be able to desire. Identification frees him to desire by rescuing him from the full terrors of incestuous desire. This, at least, was one of Freud's answers to the modern individual's profound ambivalence about making it new. Psychoanalysis might be a technique for dispelling – or understanding through redescribing – the modern individual's techniques for reproducing, for repeating the past. For Freud's modern individuals were living, unconsciously, as if the future was not an object of desire; or as if the future was an object of desire only in so far as it was an opportunity to go on repeating something of the past. If the new is traditionally the discovery of a new object of desire, and that discovery is itself discovered to be a recovery of a past object; if a new love is a remake of an old love – even if the new is a wished-for recycling, as it was for so many modernists – how is the new to be newly conceived? In Pound's injunction 'make it new', what is the *it*? Freud's version of modernism, if there could be such a thing, was more about the modern individual's repertoire of resistances to the new. If desire, as Freud was describing in his myth of origins, was incestuous – if desire was, by definition, desire for a forbidden object – 'make it new' becomes a super-ego demand, at once a necessity for psychic survival and a defeat. Freud's so-called mechanisms of defence are techniques for a compromise between the old and the new.

In his book on *Early Modernism*, Christopher Butler cites as the 'common feature in all the [canonical] works' their 'emphasis on individual style' and their 'experimentalism of technique'. Psychoanalysis, one could say, was itself an experimental technique – and an experiment in the idea of technique – designed to investigate the contemporary constraints on individual styles of loving. It was, after all, in love that the individual's singularity was at stake. An object of desire must have something special about it, otherwise it is nothing special. An object of desire in an age of mechanical reproduction can be mass-produced; there are consensual objects of desire. And yet love singles people out; the modern people Freud treats are nowhere more picky than in their erotic lives. What Freud calls their 'preconditions for loving' are peculiarly exacting; there is an unofficial but no less scrupulous rigour about object-choice. What, Freud seems to be asking himself, are the modern individual's criteria of the new? Domesticating the drama of modernism – making it, as it were, a family matter – Freud is wondering how the modern individual gets from desire for the parents to desire for the unfamiliar. When modern people fall in love, what's new? When it came to love, in what sense could modern people make it new; what, if any, experimental techniques did they have, other than symptoms, to find an individual style of loving? Might not an individual style of loving simply mean: one that was sufficiently satisfying?

Freud found himself treating people so to speak, for incestuous desire, for trauma, and above all for the – in his view universal – trauma of incestuous desire. For love as the shock of the old. Whether or not the replacement of an old, original, prohibited object of desire with a new, less forbidden one was akin to the modernist project of innovation and experimentalism, Freud was above all mindful of the modern individual's resistance to the old and past as incestuous, and her resistance to the new as insufficiently incestuous. In his view the modern person's struggle for the new was tantamount to a struggle for survival; and yet nothing seemed more difficult, nothing seemed more painful, nothing seemed more impossible than desiring, let alone finding the new. It was as though it was hubris, in modern form, to desire anyone other than the parents; and since the parents were forbidden objects it was hubris to desire at all. Symptoms seemed to be the modern individual's techniques – experimental or otherwise – for the always compromised and compromising work of desire.

II

It would be a sad day indeed when there should be something new to say.

Henry James, 'Venice' (*Century Magazine*, 1882)

The word 'new' is used in Strachey's Standard Edition translation of Freud's work 1,422 times. (The word 'pleasure', for example, by way of comparison, is used 1,088 times.) And it is in love – in his patient's erotic relations – that the enigma of the new turns up. The Oedipus complex, of course, Freud's central myth, is a story about the difficulty of finding new objects, and the difficulty of finding that new objects are in fact old objects. The further you get into the future the more embroiled you are in the past; the more radically you seek the new, the more the old – the past – comes to meet you. The neurotic, for Freud, is the person who keeps arriving at the place he is trying to get away from. The psychic need for the new – the sense in which the modern individual's psychic survival as a developing and reproducing organism depends upon finding sufficiently new objects; and the apparently equal if not more powerful need to resist, to attack, to abolish the new – was the defining tension, the constitutive split in Freud's modern subject. Indeed, how the modern individual goes about destroying the new – and often in the very ways in which he tried to make it new – became Freud's abiding preoccupation. The past, he sometimes seems to be saying, is what we use now to destroy the future; indeed, that is what the past has become for the moderns: whether it is the mythic past of the fascist ideologue or the incestuous screen-memoried past of the contemporary neurotic, a regressive, embittered nostalgia is masquerading as a promising future.

Typically in Freud the object of study is the developing individual and the difference in development consequent upon the difference between the sexes. 'In the case of the male,' he writes in 'Female Sexuality',

his mother becomes his first love-object as a result of her feeding him and looking after him, and she remains so until she is replaced by someone who resembles her or is derived from her. A female's first object, too, must be her mother: the primary conditions for a choice of object are, of course, the same for all children. But at the end of her development, her father – a man – should have become her new love-object ... The new problems that now require investigating are in what ways this change takes place, how radically or how incompletely it is carried out, and what the different possibilities are which present themselves in the course of this development.

The mother, Freud writes, remains the boy's first love-object 'until she is replaced by someone who resembles her, or is derived from her'. The new object, in other words, is a kind of copy; her newness resides presumably in the fact that she is not in actuality the mother but that, unlike the mother, she resembles the mother. The advantage of the new object is that it can be like an object that is in actuality absent. The problem with an original is that it can never be a copy. Newness is being *like* by not actually *being* something or someone else. The new that makes the kind of desire possible that will facilitate the individual male's development is in the disparity that makes the resemblance possible. Because the new woman is not the mother she is free to be like her. Desire for the copy, for the resemblant, is the only viable kind of desire – the only desire with a future – for the modern male. Desire for the original, or original desire, is deemed to be catastrophic; and catastrophic means annulling the future. At the level of the individual one could describe this as disillusionment with the original; the sense that the original desire, or the original object of desire, is degenerative. The new becomes a replacement, something or someone that resembles or derives from an endangering original; to sustain desire, the copy, the new woman, must not be rendered identical to the original woman, the mother. The question becomes, how to maintain a resemblance; if the new woman becomes too like the mother she will become undesirable. She may have to be news that stays news, but she also has to be a copy that stays a copy. When it comes to modern newness, you have to have just the right amount. It is not a problem, for the modern man, that the only women he can desire are, from his point of view, imitations of his mother – similar things done up in a different fashion: it is the solution. Imitation is the name of the game. But from the desiring male subject's point of view, the copy has to be just right; and copying itself has to be a peculiarly recondite art.

But the girl's development, in Freud's view, is more complicated. First, it is implicit in his description of male development that in order for a girl to become a woman who is desirable to a man she has to become someone who resembles a man's mother. But second, as a desiring subject – or rather, as Freud's normative version of a desiring heterosexual woman – she has to change her love-object. She has to experience, as it were, two degrees of newness; the first new object is the father, who, we assume (or presume), doesn't have to resemble the mother in order to be desirable, who is apparently, by definition, not a copy of the mother; and then presumably she has to replace the father with a man who resembles or derives from him. Either a woman has to desire a copy of a copy; or, for the developing girl, there is an excess of newness, two objects having to be replaced, two lots of newness, which means two lots of sufficient resemblance to be dealt with. Normal Freudian man goes from mother to similar new woman; normal Freudian woman goes from mother to father to new man. If at the end of her development, as Freud puts it, her father should have become her new love-object, how, one wonders, will she have the strength – the emotional and imaginative resilience – to get to another new love-object?

'The new problems that now require investigating,' Freud writes, 'are in what way this change takes place, how radically or how incompletely it is carried out, and what the different possibilities are which present themselves in the course of this development.' The modern individual, clearly, must find a way to get to the new love-object on which his or her development depends. The modern individual has to be a copy in order to be desirable; in the man's case, he must remind the woman sufficiently of her father and behind him of her mother, and in the woman's case she must remind the man of his mother. He or she will be able to desire only if a copy becomes available. The original, in this description, has the status of the forbidden, of the prohibited, of an object that it is impossible to desire and impossible not to desire. The modern individual is on a quest for resemblances that work, that sustain desire. But this quest for resemblances and derivations is shadowed, in Freud's view, by a hatred, by a resentment of the new *because* it is the new and *not* the impossible original. The new is that about which one bears a grudge, or that which evokes a nostalgia, or that which one seeks to convert back to the lost original. For some modern people, those Freud calls neurotics, making it new, when it works, means making it old. The patient in psychoanalysis attempts a virtually mechanical reproduction of past loves, a work of art that Freud calls transference, because it involves transferring something of the past into the future. In other words, the medium of the so-called cure of psychoanalysis is the patient's capacity for repetition. The obstacle to development – to involvement with and recognition of sufficiently new objects – becomes the instrument. Psychoanalysis is an experimental therapeutic technique for the transforming of repetitions, a technique itself, of course, being something that can, by definition, be repeated.

What Freud was discovering from his patients was that there was nothing more regressive than the wish to make it new; nothing more mimetic – at the level of identification, at the level of the reproduction of images, of styles of loving from the past – than desire. Modern love, in Freud's account, takes people back rather than taking them forward. Indeed, it is only the apparently new that discloses the past, that makes it available. But it is not merely that the new in all its shocking immediacy has to be resisted; it is that the new can't be found. The new is everywhere – call it, say, the city, where, in Baudelaire's words, 'modernity consists in the transitory, the fugitive, the contingent'; but for Freud's patients, in their erotic lives, it is the newness itself of their objects that is transitory and fugitive. The experience of Freud's patients trying to love outside the family circle seemed to restore and reinforce earlier patterns of familiar desire. If anything, the past is consolidated, is constituted by the quest for the new. There was nothing like a new object of desire for reviving an old object; as though the new object was there, was desired, merely as an opportunity to restore the past. This resolved itself, for Freud, into a clinical question that became a question about psychoanalytic technique: are there two kinds of love, old love and new love, or only one kind? And if there are two kinds, is there a technique that can release the patient from the grip, from the repetition, of the old forms of loving? Can the modern individual find new love, and what would be new about it? This seemed imperative to Freud because what his patients seemed to be suffering from, what they albeit ambivalently demanded to be cured of, was repeating the past. What free association as a method revealed – and free association as an injunction to speak in a certain way was itself anti-realist, anti-mimetic, undoing the traditional conventions of narrative – was the insistence of the forbidden desires of and for the past.

The patient, Freud writes in an appropriately entitled paper, 'Remembering, Repeating and Working Through', 'does not remember anything of what he has forgotten and repressed, but acts it out. He reproduces it not as a memory but as an action; he repeats it, without, of course, knowing that he repeats it.' What free association revealed, for Freud, was the unwitting repetition. But the implication is that remembering is at least potentially the cure for repeated actions. That compulsion is the site of a forgetting. The patient is living in the past, can't get to the new experience, because he has repressed something, or that something he has repressed keeps returning. All he knows is that he keeps doing the same thing, and he doesn't know what it is. At a manifest level it may be that he keeps falling for the same kind of woman, that he keeps buying books, that he steals, and so on; but the repressed has been displaced on to these actions and repeated. Memory, Freud wants us to believe – the right kind of remembering – makes the new available; or makes it, the desire for the past, new. Remembering the past stops you living in the past. The wrong kind of remembering, of course, is a way of living in the past. The possibility of new love depends upon a certain kind of remembering; and upon a certain kind of interpreting of, of conversation about, memories. A new love, even if it had to resemble or be derived from the original love of the mother, would have something unique about it that would, of necessity, call up an original style of loving. The new, if one could find it, would be that for which one was (relatively) unprepared.

'The sense of and pleasure in nuance (which is real modernity),' Nietzsche wrote in his 1886/7 notebook, 'in what is not general, runs counter to the drive that takes its pleasure and force in grasping the typical.' The patient in psychoanalysis, Freud tells us in his paper 'Observations on Love in Transference' – one of the papers on technique – will begin to treat the doctor as typical of his previous love-objects. The pleasure and force of the patient's transference will be in grasping the analyst as someone representative of a past love. The sense of and pleasure in the nuance of the new object that is the doctor will be ablated. The patient's drive is not to see the doctor as unprecedented; it will be the nuances, the subtle differences that will elude him. The passion for nuance – Nietzsche sees it as definitive of real modernity – is what the treatment ideally must disclose. Psychoanalysis becomes the therapy for making people modern, or for finding out how modern they can bear to be. That is, how singular they can bear to be.

The English translations of the title of Freud's paper dramatize the issue. Strachey entitles his Standard Edition translation of the paper 'Observations on Transference Love', as though there was a kind of love that can be distinguished from other kinds of love. Alan Bance in the recent Penguin translation entitles the paper 'Observations on Love in Transference', which suggests that there is something called love that is also at work in transference. The question Freud is working on in this revealingly confounded and confounding paper is whether it is possible for modern people to distinguish two kinds of love: on the one hand, a form of loving from and for the past that recurs in psychoanalytic treatment and that is given a technical name, transference love, because it itself recurs in psychoanalytic treatments – indeed, psychoanalysis is defined by its use of the repetition that is the transference; on the other hand, a form of loving that derives from the past but is not foreclosed by it, that is new. Call it, after Nietzsche, the love of nuance. Freud is unsure whether all love is what he calls transference love – 'reissuing old components and repeating infantile reactions', he writes, 'that is always the essence of falling in love. Everybody repeats childhood patterns.' Or perhaps transference love is what the individual suffers from, and that he needs to be released from by analysis. The drawback of what Freud calls transference love – and it is a misgiving that is radically under-emphasized in the paper – is that transference love is counter-developmental. Development seems to depend upon the finding of new love-objects; and yet transference love, which may be the only kind of love modern individuals are capable of, makes this impossible. What they call love is the inability to leave home. If there is another kind of love, a new love that people are capable of, it would be – and this is where Freud's utopianism begins to show through – a form of love that would be a medium for growth. If there is one thing that the modern individuals that Freud saw in his consulting room couldn't bear, it was their own development. The new as the sign of growth, or at least change – in the contemporary sciences of developmental biology as much as in the arts – had become a phobic object. If the only love modern humans were capable of was averse to the new – to the non-parental – then there was a profound self-destructiveness, a pervasive unconscious despair in the culture. God may have been dead, at least for some, but the parents – as incestuous objects, as protective objects – were very much alive. When it came to erotic life, to development, what Christopher Butler called 'experimentalism of technique' was to be avoided at all costs.

For Freud, in this crucial paper, the heroines or the anti-heroines of this main drama are the people he calls 'women of elemental passion'. These are the rather more difficult patients who don't accept the doctor's distinction – upon which his work as a psychoanalyst is based – between transference love and the other love. These women believe, as it were, that love is love; for this 'type of woman', Freud writes forlornly, 'the attempt to preserve the love-transference for us in the analytic task, but without satisfying it, is doomed to failure'. These are the patients who won't play the psychoanalytic game. They, in other words, are the saboteurs of their own development; unless, as Freud also considers, they are right. 'With this type,' Freud writes – needing to see them as a type, not nuanced – 'you [the analyst] have a choice to make: either return her love or suffer the full hostility of a woman scorned. Neither case furthers the cause of the therapy.' The love that makes psychoanalytical therapy possible has already, in effect, accepted the distinction that is in question. Psychoanalysis, Freud says, works as long as the patient and the analyst accept that there is such a thing as transference love, and that it is to be worked with, to be analysed, for there to be any kind of cure. The patient, in other words, has to accept the very thing she cannot bear, the idea of a new love.

Is this 'implacable love', as Freud calls it, of these women of elemental passion what love is really like? Freud thinks not, and for two reasons. First, this love is 'unmistakably', in Freud's view, a form of resistance; it is being used by the patient to resist cure, to sustain the suffering of her symptoms. It renders the doctor ineffectual and the patient impervious. What Freud calls the patient's 'supposed infatuation' is an unconscious ploy to prevent her recovery. But it is the second reason Freud cites that is more pertinent:

The second argument against the authenticity of this love is the assertion that it bears not a single new trait arising out of the present situation, but is composed entirely of repetitions and pale imitations of earlier reactions, including infantile ones. [The analyst must] undertake to demonstrate this to the patient through a detailed analysis of her stance in love.

The analyst, Freud continues, works towards 'exposing the infantile choice of love-objects and the fantasy that was woven around it'. The choice is inauthentic in the sense that it is regressive, 'it bears not a single new trait arising out of the present situation'; and the present situation, as are also the psychoanalyst and the treatment, is itself new. The infantile choice ablates the new in the service of repeating the old – 'it is composed entirely of repetitions and pale imitations of earlier reactions' – while being unaware that it is doing so. Just as in the dream, where the dreamer used details of the new day – what Freud calls 'the dream day' – to call up, to evoke the desires of the past; so the patient in psychoanalysis uses the doctor to reconstitute her past desires. Modern people fall in love, Freud is saying, as a way of resisting the new; that may be what falling in love is for the modern individual, a staving off of contemporary reality, a fear of the future. Falling in love is the defence that psychoanalysis is organized to cure. Is there, Freud wonders, a kind of love, a kind of falling in love *now*, that is a desire for the new? Freud's critique of transference love, in other words – and his fear of its triumph, of the analyst being seduced by it – is that it creates a world in which there is no such thing as the new. Psychoanalysis, Freud intimates, is a treatment to cure people of their hatred of the new; to initiate them into the real modernity of nuance by showing them their resistances to it.

But towards the end of his paper Freud, oddly, reneges on his crucial distinction, siding with the women of elemental passion. 'That is always the essence of falling in love,' he writes:

Everybody repeats childhood patterns. It is precisely what stems from its conditioning in childhood that lends infatuation its compulsive character, with its overtones of the pathological. Perhaps love in transference has slightly less freedom than the love that occurs ordinarily in life and is called normal; it shows more clearly its dependence on its infantile predecessor, and it proves to be less adaptable and flexible, but that is all – the differences are not essential.

Transference love, Freud suggests, is marginally less responsive, 'less adaptable and less flexible', than ordinary love; but the differences are not essential. Modern love – or rather the love talked of and reproduced by his patients in psychoanalysis – is a resistance. This is what modern people do when confronted with the new, they fall in love; falling in love is a self-cure for living a contemporary life, for facing and making the future. Love is the enemy of change, growth, development, progress; of any of the available teleologies. 'Sexual love,' Freud writes, 'undoubtedly has a prime place among life's experiences . . . everybody knows this apart from a few weird fanatics, and arranges his life accordingly; only in scientific circles does anyone make a fuss about admitting it.' And yet this love, Freud asserts, also betrays the modern person's hatred of the future.

And if we ask what, if anything, do shifts in aesthetic practice have to do with changes in erotic relations, we find illuminating parallels at least. But what differentiates Freud's work from the work of other writers is that he seems to be giving an account not only of *why* the new may be impossible, at once sought after and risky; but also of why the new may be unbearable to the modern individual. By virtue of being new, the new object may be insufficiently desirable; without its echo of the past it is invisible; if it is too new it is out of the visual field. And it may involve too much loss, too much renunciation of the libidinal ties of and to the past. The new at its best is an opportunity to viably desire a version of the old; the new at its worst is the defeat of original hope. Because you can't have the old object you must have a new one; but because you must have a new one you must give something up that was once everything. Freud's patients were people who, one way or another, couldn't bear the losses entailed in making it new, while modernist artists were at least committed to experimental techniques that allowed them the sensation of newness without having to confront at every turn the losses entailed in the procedure. In Freud's view, in Freud's language, being unable to desire the new made modern people sick; but desiring the new revealed and revived, like nothing else, the desire for the past. In a very long book called *Psychoanalysis*, on the resolution of the Oedipus complex, Freud adds to the injunction 'make it new' the question: what would it be about the new that might make it bearable, given that it was necessary for psychic survival? 'Make it new' was too blithe a demand for Freud's patients. But in attending to the casualties of that particular modernist demand Freud invented psycho-analysis. It was, and clearly still is, a traumatic demand. It is not obvious now what it would be to recover from it.

Two Lectures on Expectations

I Great Expectations and First Impressions

All this, I saw in the first glance after I crossed the threshold
– child-like, according to my theory . . .

Charles Dickens, *David Copperfield*

Writing enthusiastically to John Forster in September 1860 Dickens mentions that 'a very fine, new, and grotesque idea has opened upon [him]' such that he wonders whether 'he had not better cancel' the short piece he is supposed to be writing for the *Uncommercial Traveller*. By October he is writing to Forster to tell him that he has planned the new book, and has 'made the opening, I hope, in its general effect exceedingly droll. I have put a child and a good-natured foolish man, in relations that seem to me to be very funny.' The book, which will be *Great Expectations*, begins well, in the author's view, but he has one reservation: 'to be quite sure I had fallen into no unconscious repetitions, I read David Copperfield again the other day, and was affected by it to a degree you would hardly believe'. Dickens's initial impression of his new work – and, he hopes, the reader's – is good; but that very first impression makes him fear a fall. His very first impressions of this 'very fine, new, and grotesque idea' remind him that they may not be first impressions at all; the book may not be a new idea at all, it may be an unconscious repetition. And this haunting suspicion leads Dickens back into rereading *David Copperfield* and being profoundly affected by it.

Great Expectations, as it turns out, is a book that is to a remarkable degree about first impressions. Just as Dickens believes that the book works because of the reader's first impressions of it – 'Pray read Great Expectations,' he writes to Mary Boyle in December 1860, 'it is a very great success and seems universally liked – I suppose because it opens funnily and with an interest too' – so, in the same force-field of preoccupations, Dickens seems fascinated in the book by how first impressions work; by what first sight portends for the future and can do to the past; by what it is about a first moment that makes us think of it as the first moment. 'All this I saw in a moment,' Pip says coming upon Magwitch for the second time, 'for I had only a moment to see it in,' as though there could have been something else he could have seen it in. Having described his first impression of Miss Havisham Pip remarks, 'It was not in the first moments that I saw all these things, though I saw more of them in the first moments than might be supposed.' The first moment is shocking because it betrays an uncanny competence; a taking in all of something when there is seemingly no time to take anything in. When Pip says 'I saw more of them in the first moments' he intimates in the ambiguity of the phrase that, at least for some things, the first moment is the best moment, even though you may not know it at the time. Being caught off guard is an opening: powers of memory and perception and anticipation are summoned in a death-defying second. Repetition, the self-cure for the trauma of first moments, is a great deadener. You lose sight of what you saw, because repetition is the consumer of shock. Asked by Jaggers, two thirds of the way through the book, 'What do you suppose you are living at the rate of?' the now jaded Pip is flawed. 'I had looked into my affairs so often, that I had thoroughly destroyed any slight notion I might ever have had of their bearings. Reluctantly I confessed myself quite unable to answer the question.' Dickens feared at the outset of *Great Expectations* that he might be looking into his affairs again, and so too often; that he might be unconsciously repeating *David Copperfield* in repeating the story of a boy growing up. There is a way of looking too often – call it habit, call it a mechanism of defence, call it a repetition compulsion – that can destroy even the slightest notion one has ever had of the bearings of one's affairs. Bearings meaning both what one has borne and had to bear; and also in the sense of losing one's bearings, of losing ballast and direction; the necessary tropisms of desire and assurance. The fall into unconscious repetition can be a fall from, a fall away from, the plenitude of first impressions, that first moment in which we see more of things than might be supposed. Even if what we see we see in fear. It is because an appetite of sorts has been stirred in that moment that we call it a first moment; even if what it is an appetite for is, of necessity, obscure.

I want to note that a novel Dickens called *Great Expectations* is full of first impressions; is indeed packed with firstnesses of all kinds, and so much occupied and preoccupied by what repetition is for, or does to what we are tempted to describe as firstness ('Joe felt, as I did, that he had made a point there, and he pulled hard at his pipe to keep himself from weakening it by repetition'). How is it – and what is it – that repetition weakens? Or, to put it in Pip's terms: if Joe's point would be weakened by repetition, what would serve to strengthen it? Pip and the author of the novel are continually exercised by what, if anything, has to be done with first experiences, and what it is to repeat something. For something to be repeated there has to be some acknowledgement of its first having happened. Indeed, it may be a sense of repetition that alerts us to something having originally happened. And for something to be repeated there must, we assume, be a reason.

What are repeated on the first page of *Great Expectations* are three of Pip's first impressions; and each of these first impressions is enigmatic. His name, his parents and the place he grew up in are all, he tells us, in different ways, made up by him out of the difficulty of his initial and initiating experiences. His 'infant tongue', he tells us in the opening paragraph, could not pronounce his father's family name, Pirrip, nor his own first name, Philip, so, as he puts it, 'I called myself Pip, and came to be called Pip.' His sense of who his parents were he got from their graves. 'As I never saw my father or my mother, and never saw any likeness of either of them (for their days were long before the days of photographs), my first fancies regarding what they were like, were unreasonably derived from their tombstones.' Pip effectively invents himself through these acts of transformation; it is what he makes of what he is given – and how unreasonable these necessary, founding acts of transformation are – that Dickens impresses upon our attention. First impressions are material to work on. Unlike the first impressions we get of a character in a nineteenth-century melodrama – theatricals that particularly appealed to Dickens – the first impression we get of Pip is of someone bemused by his own first impressions. Pip is someone we are introduced to as a person preoccupied by what he calls his first fancies. He names himself, and construes his parents from singularly unpromising beginnings. We are introduced to Pip at the outset making himself up out of these first impressions in order to become recognizable to himself. If those popular theatrical melodramas that were so important for Dickens's art of characterization worked by reassuring their audiences that their very first impressions of the characters were accurate, in *Great Expectations* Dickens immediately calls these assumptions into question. Our first impression of Pip is of someone who needs to tell us about his first impressions, and how these are integral to his sense of himself. Dickens, in short, is telling us at the beginning of *Great Expectations* about the creation of character.

The first thing that Pip wants to tell us about the place he grew up in is what he calls his 'first most vivid and broad impression of the identity of things', with the inevitable implication that there will be further impressions, but that the identity of things has something to do with the 'first most vivid and broad impression' (Dickens's phrasing here is characteristically subtle; it is not clear whether it is the first and *also* the most vivid and broad impression, or whether it is most vivid and broad *because* it is the first). Not merely reflecting on his impressions but reflecting on his *first* impressions is Pip's singular concern. What we have come to call the inwardness, the inner complexity and idiosyncrasy of character, Dickens describes as this imaginative work done by Pip on his first fancies; his inventive reaction to an inheritance. The only thing that is transparent about (modern) character, Dickens seems to be saying, is the sheer scale of self-invention. Orphans are people who have lived before the invention of photography. They are people without pictures of their past provided by other people. Their first impressions are, so to speak, first hand.

There are of course here, as we shall see, suggestive links with Freud's work. In *Great Expectations*, we might say, Dickens is psychologically minded; he is telling us stories about what could be going on inside people. But he has to make this compatible with the kind of caricature with which he made his name. So it is not strictly speaking true to say that Dickens's exploitation of contemporary theatrical melodrama in his creation of character is straightforwardly a critique, a suspicion, about the inwardness of character as elitist and socially divisive. In melodrama, Juliet John writes in her instructive book *Dickens's Villains*,

Character . . . is normally transparent. The audience cannot fail to understand immediately . . . a character's destined role in the play and his or her ethical substance . . . This objectification of emotion is in keeping with melodrama's communal, anti-individualistic agenda. Emotions are robbed of the unique status often accorded to them in post-Freudian culture; they do not 'belong' to the individual experiencing them but to common experience.

This is useful but it is fairer to say, I think, that as a genre – and this is what Dickens picks up on in his fiction, and particularly in *Great Expectations* – melodrama works with and on our wonderings about transparency, immediacy and first impressions; and especially our first impressions of other people. The drama of character, the suspense of character, is about what drama does to our expectations about character. Melodrama, as described here, says your expectations about this character are well founded; indeed, your first impressions and your expectations are at one with each other. Here you can relax because the expectations that inform your initial impression are confirming rather than disfiguring or distorting. The audience's first impression of a character in a melodrama is a true but diminished thing because it cannot develop; impression conforms to expectation and vice versa. For Pip in *Great Expectations* Dickens wants to show us that his first impressions are true (and sometimes false) in ways in which he would never have expected. He is always seeing more than he realizes, and never quite sees what he does realize. So it is also instructive to see John as wanting, by way of explication, to set Dickens against Freud, and to stage this as a drama, if not a virtual allegory, of the communal in its war with an exclusive elite, the outward bound versus the inward. 'Pip's deviant characteristics,' she writes,

can be read as directly linked to secrecy and self-obsession; his apparent growth to 'maturity', therefore, for the most part involves an attempt to escape from or even forget the self, rather than the kind of inwardly focused self-analysis so valued in our own therapy culture. Events or actions, rather than Hamlet-like introspection, are always the starting-point for self-knowledge in *Great Expectations* . . . The introspective individual prominent in high romanticism was to Dickens constitutive of, and constituted by, a culture of exclusivity.

Hamlet's introspection was not, of course, unrelated to certain events and actions. If as John concedes self-knowledge is an issue in *Great Expectations* – though not of the 'Hamlet-like introspection' kind, or the 'inwardly focused self-analysis so valued in our own therapy culture' kind – then this self-knowledge devolves into knowing what any particular self has in common with all the other selves in the culture. And at its most caricatural these selves would be like the characters in nineteenth-century theatrical melodramas that Dickens so much enjoyed: transparent, immediately recognizable, unintrospective. Not the kind of people who make special claims on behalf of their inner complexity; not the kind of people who mystify themselves and others by believing in their own obscurity to themselves. Not the kind of people, in other words, who need to explain themselves.

And yet the one thing that does make Pip at all Hamlet-like, the one thing that does make Pip puzzling to himself – and not only to himself, of course – is the first time he does something, the first time something happens to him (so-called growing up is, after all, one first time after another). 'I never have been so surprised in my life,' Pip relates of his fight with 'the pale young gentleman' in Miss Havisham's garden, 'as I was when I let out the first blow, and saw him lying on his back, looking at me with a bloody nose and his face exceedingly foreshortened.' With this first punch Pip's perspective changes; the consequences of Pip's action are looking at him. With *Great Expectations* the antinomy of Dickens and Freud proposed by John more exactly suggests the link. For both these writers of the nineteenth century we are at our most self-revealing – our most self-surprising and surprised – in our first impressions, and in what we do with them. And what is revealed is precisely our expectations, great and otherwise. For Freud, as we shall see – and in this he is clearly what Juliet John refers to as a high romantic – psychoanalysis is about the fate of early impressions; about the ways in which those early impressions are informed by those expectations called appetites, and the ways in which they are themselves transformed into expec-tations, great and otherwise. A trauma, we need to remember, is a species of first impression. And the great expectation that is desire is, in Freud's view, a type of trauma.

*

If, in melodrama, our first impressions are sufficient – 'the audience cannot fail to understand immediately . . . a charac- ter's destined role in the play and his or her ethical substance' – then anyone, or indeed any genre, not satisfied by first impressions, or not interested in the relationship between first impressions and consequent impressions, is going to be wondering where to start; or where the story starts from. In melodrama the audience can take something for granted – 'character is transparent' – and they can take it from there. They don't have to suffer the so-called inwardness born of scepticism. There are foundations – being able to recognize people accurately – from which the drama can proceed. They are free from the obligation of a certain kind of suspicion. They can relax into the entertainment. It is this that Dickens is looking into through the growing child Pip, whose life, like all children's lives, is riddled with first impressions; and in *Great Expectations* the word 'first' is used with inordinate frequency, as a troubling reminder. 'When she first came to me,' Miss Havisham says to Pip about Estella, 'I meant to save her from misery like my own. At first I meant no more.' 'Well, well!' Pip replies 'I hope so.' To put it as blandly as possible: first impressions, rather like first intentions, Dickens intimates in this novel, are informed by great expectations. What hap- pens at first turns out not to be the first thing that had happened.

Perhaps there is a book to be written about first impressions in the nineteenth century, about the fate of first looking into, of first seeing and hearing and touching and smelling. In an age of such technological innovation there were clearly many opportunities – as in the well-documented accounts of people first seeing or travelling on the railways – for unprecedented experiences. Of course, people had always travelled, but they had never travelled in this way; just as they had always fought in wars and communicated with each other over great distances, but were now struck by the shock of the new methods of warfare and long-distance communication. My guess is – and this is only an impression; I am thinking here of, say, Ruskin's teachings on seeing and drawing, or Baudelaire's dandies – that in the nineteenth century at least some people were peculiarly exercised by the enigma of first impressions. And I want to suggest in this essay that Freud's work of psychoanalysis, whatever else it is, is an enquiry into the nature and status of the first impression; that not only is Freud very interested in firstness – the word 'first' is used in Strachey's Standard Edition translation 3,766 times ('pleasure', by way of comparison, is used 1,088 times) – but that also, for Freud, first impressions have to be redescribed as great expectations. For Freud, nothing is more revealing of our ambition and our history than what we think of as our first impressions. The notion of transference is Freud's tribute to a paradox that is at the heart of psychoanalysis; that one's first impressions are a (disguised) disclosure of one's personal history. There is nothing more anachronistic than a first impression. From a psychoanalytic point of view there is often nothing *less* first than a first impression; indeed, the word 'first' in this context is a misnomer, a disavowal of the past.

In simple language one could say: we call them first impressions because they are not. Or, we want them to be first impressions because the phrase conjures us into starting afresh, persuades us of novelty to muffle the echoes. What Freud is saying is that we have what we refer to as first impressions only because there are antecedents to this firstness; not causes, exactly, but preconditions. It is as if, unbeknown to ourselves – that is, often quite unpredictably – our individual histories predispose us to respond in specific ways to specific signs. Just as the dream-work works the dream day in ways that can never occur to us (there is nothing we can do to work out what, if anything, from today will turn up, in whatever form, in our dreams); and we can be sexually aroused without knowing the provenance of our excitement; and amused, as Freud says, without really quite knowing what it is that has got to us; so our desire, and what it might latch on to, is an unknown quantity. From a psychoanalytic point of view we can never get the measure of ourselves because we can never quite know beforehand what we will be drawn into. When it comes to what Freud calls deferred action we can never be ahead of the game. Any scene, any apparently new experience – and especially, perhaps, anything we need to go back to as a first impression – may remind us of a trauma that until that moment, until that so-called first impression has called it up, was, to all intents and purposes, no trauma at all.

'Only the occurrence of the second scene,' as Laplanche and Pontalis put it in *The Language of Psychoanalysis*, 'can endow the first one with pathogenic force.' As Freud suggests in the case of Emma in the 'Project for a Scientific Psychology', what makes something so strikingly a first impression – in a sense, what constitutes something as a first impression – is that it is at once the belated revision of a trauma that through revision constitutes the prior experience as an experience. 'A memory is repressed,' Freud writes, 'which has become a trauma only by deferred action.' These first impressions impress one because they make the past present in refigured form; these first impressions are history in the making. Indeed, to have a certain kind of so-called first impression is the only way through to the constructing of personal history. In Freud's language these shocking or troubling apparently new experiences are secular epiphanies: revelations not of God's grace but of the history of our desire. They link us to our losses. The shock of the new is how uncannily old it is, how secretly reminiscent of what we preferred to forget.

Emma, Freud writes,

is subject at the present time to a compulsion of not being able to go into shops alone. As a reason for this she produced a memory from the time when she was twelve years old (shortly after puberty). She went into a shop to buy something, saw the two shop assistants (one of whom she can remember) laughing together, and ran away in some kind of affect of fright. In connection with this, she was led to recall that the two of them were laughing at her clothes and that one of them had pleased her sexually.

All Emma experiences on first entering the shop is an utterly unintelligible fear; something has struck her, something has occurred to her that she must resist, and she is now unable to go into any shop unaccompanied. In other words, she would have had no first impression worth noting – nothing she would bother to call a first impression – if she had not been in some way unconsciously stirred by the scene in front of her. In a less dramatic way we might take this scene as emblematic, and wonder what makes anything or anyone strike us at all (we might, for example, ask of any writer, what it is about the language that strikes her). We might wonder what, unwittingly, we are bringing to the scene – two shop assistants laughing together – that makes it into a scene at all.

This makes such a strong, such an unavoidable, impression on Emma, Freud writes, because, without her realizing it at the time,

On two occasions when she was a child of eight she had gone into a small shop to buy some sweets, and the shopkeeper had grabbed at her genitals through her clothes. In spite of the first experience she had gone there a second time; after the second time she stayed away. She now reproached herself for having gone there a second time, as though she had wanted in that way to provoke the assault. In fact a state of 'oppressive bad conscience' is to be traced back to this experience.

Like the young Pip, the young Emma in Freud's account is surprised at first by the shopkeeper's desire, and then by her own desire revealed by her returning to the shop. Years later she is shocked on first entering another shop; and the link, Freud proposes, of which she is unconscious, is that the laughter of the shop assistants reminds her of the grin on the original shopkeeper's face when he sexually assaulted her. The 'new' impression she is left with conceals a memory. You know something as a first impression, Freud intimates, because it isn't the first impression, it is a reworked memory, and the memory is of forbidden desire. Emma is, in the words of the song, the first to find out and the last to know. Calling it a first impression would be to obscure it; would, in fact, be integral to the defence. The first is not so long as we can say it is the first. So long as Emma can think of her initial experience in the shop as a first she can hold her history at bay.

As anyone knows who has read this significant, indeed formative, vignette in the 'Project', Freud has more complex things to say about how this second scene makes up, and makes up for, the first traumatic scene. For the purposes of this essay there are two things to be said about deferred action; one trivial, the other not. The trivial one is that they are rightly called first impressions in so far as what they lead to, under psychoanalysis, are the truer first impressions of desire and its prohibition. What we call first impressions are stand-ins or cover scenes for earlier, more traumatic experiences. From a psychoanalytic point of view first impressions are the equivalent in the present of screen memories (perception is constructed and selected according to the disguised memory of desire; what we see is what we want and mustn't have). The non-trivial is Freud's implication that in order to have a past we have to have new experiences. New experiences and first impressions are above all reminders; moments when our always traumatic personal history becomes real, but only through its return. Our first impressions, in other words, are always intimations of repetition. The first impression is always at least a second impression – scene one, in Freud's language, can return only through scene two – and that is why we call it a first impression. What is deferred in deferred action is the import of what has been recognized but not seen.

It may be worth distinguishing between genuine first impressions and the other kind, the déjà-vu, as it were, of genuine first impressions. As Dickens is clearly so struck by in *Great Expectations*, a child growing up has a series of genuine first impressions of himself and the world, and also becomes capable over time of reflecting on the whole notion of first impressions. Indeed, given how many first impressions there are for the child, the ones that get dwelled upon, the ones that seem worthy of comment, the ones plucked out for reflection, assume an inevitable significance. In his moments of self-reflection on these experiences – of meeting Magwitch, of meeting Miss Havisham, of punching the pale young gentleman – Pip ceases to be a 'transparent character' out of a nineteenth-century melodrama, and becomes a person who can't help but surprise himself, who can, as we say, reflect upon himself. One can surprise oneself only if one has been living (unconsciously) by a false description of oneself. The self that can surprise itself is subject to revision. Genuine first impressions, and so-called first impressions, are always, whatever else they are, opportunities for self-revision. Given half a chance they are invitations to a redescription of ourselves. Omniscience, one could say, is the conviction that there is no such thing as a first impression.

For Freud, and for Dickens in *Great Expectations*, the first impressions that matter are the ones that for some reason make us work; like the dreams that stay with us when we wake, some of our first impressions preoccupy us, make us think, trouble us. We may tell other people; we may even write them down or, indeed, write about people having these particular impressions. Whatever we do, we have to do something with them; we can't let them go. And by the strange law of repetition we are prone to think that whatever haunts us, whatever stays with us, whatever keeps repeating itself, must matter. The first impression that goes on impressing us must, we feel, be significant even if, or especially if, its significance is obscure. We may even think that the enigma of our individuality, the idiosyncrasy of our histories, resides in these specific hauntings; that who we are is what we are struck by. And Freud confirms this by showing us that we can unravel our histories by analysing these uncanny, traumatic and seemingly first encounters.

But there is one genuine first impression, Freud believes, which we all share; one first impression in which we pool our differences; one first impression, he believes, we can't help but have even if each of us makes something quite different of it. Like Henry James's definition of the real, that which it is impossible not to know, castration and the fact of there being two sexes is the Freudian child's paradigmatic first impression; every child's formative trauma. The Freudian child's great expectation is that everyone has a penis, and that it is impossible to lose one. Freud, in other words – and he may be unique in this – offers us a kind of primal scene of the first impression; or even, perhaps, a supreme fiction about the nature and significance of modern first impressions, which he calls castration. Indeed, I want to suggest, for the purposes of this essay, that what Freud calls the castration complex is as much a theory, a way of describing first impressions, as it is a theory about the provenance of psychic life. What is a first impression like? Freud asks. It is like noticing that there are two sexes. A first impression is the difference between two kinds of genitalia.

In his paper 'The Infantile Genital Organization', Freud returns to the ongoing issue of the sexual researches of childhood. Nearly twenty years after writing the *Three Essays on the Theory of Sexuality*, Freud is emphatic that there is one experience, one observation, above all that informs the child's curiosity and organizes his subsequent development. 'In the course of these researches,' he writes,

the child arrives at the discovery that the penis is not a possession which is common to all creatures that are like himself. An accidental sight of the genitals of a little sister or playmate provides the occasion for this discovery. In unusually intelligent children, the observation of girls urinating will even earlier have aroused a suspicion that there is something different here. For they will have seen a different posture and heard a different sound, and will have made attempts to repeat their observations so as to obtain enlightenment. We know how children react to their first impressions of the absence of a penis. They disavow the fact and believe that they *do* see a penis, all the same. They gloss over the contradiction between observation and preconception by telling themselves that the penis is still small and will grow bigger presently; and they then slowly come to the emotionally significant conclusion that after all the penis had at least been there before and taken away afterwards. The lack of a penis is regarded as a result of castration, and so now the child is faced with the task of coming to terms with castration in relation to himself.

When it comes to the difference between the sexes the child's reaction to his first impression – that is, seeing the absence of a penis – is to see his expectation instead; in Freud's words the child 'glosses over the contradiction between observation and preconception'. The child's expectations are there, effectively, to stop him having to take in his first impression. Great expectations protect the child from his first impressions. Pre-conceptions are the self-cure for (painful) observations. How do you know when a first impression is traumatic? Freud asks. You know it is traumatic because you immediately disavow it, you replace a fact with a wish; you know it is traumatic because you have to do something with it, you have to transform it into something else; though not merely into *something* else, but into something it isn't. Traumatic first impressions are the ones that have to be turned back into expectations; where the child had a first impression he has to persuade himself that there was no first impression; that there was nothing there that could impress him, nothing unexpected, nothing out of the ordinary. Where there seemed, at first, to be no penis there was, or had been, one. A traumatic first impression is the one that the child is unable to sustain as a first impression. When it comes to trauma it appears to be the case that there are no first impressions. The traumatic first impression is precisely what the psychic work is there to abolish. The story of castration is the elaboration, the continuation, of the psychic work that has to be done to the formative first impression.

Faced with this genuine, and genuinely traumatic, first impression, Freud proposes a three-stage movement. There is the first impression, the absent penis; the disavowal of this accurate impression; and finally a story – the story of castration – that explains and justifies the disavowal: everyone has a penis, but some people have had them cut off. (It is interesting, by the way, to wonder why Freud doesn't offer, as one of the child's options, the story that no one has ever had a penis, but that some people have had them attached.) At its most minimal, we could say story-telling is integral to the work we do on traumatic first impressions. Without a good story, disavowal would be impossible; it wouldn't be sufficiently persuasive, adequately reassuring. Theories (or stories) about first impressions – those first impressions that stay with us because they are redolent of trauma – are stories about story-making. A good story, Freud suggests here, is reactive to an unbearable first impression. What, we might ask, is the unbearable first impression that any given story is the attempted cure for? For Freud, first impressions, disavowal and the making of fictions are inextricable. We have great expectations – what Freud calls preconceptions – to make some of our first impressions bearable. The child's discovery of the difference between the sexes and his reaction to it are Freud's picture for the modern enigma of the first impression, the first impression that never lets go.

On completing *David Copperfield* in October 1850 Dickens wrote a Preface to the book in which he reflected on his first impressions of having finished it. 'I do not find it easy to get sufficiently far away from this book, in the first sensations of having finished it,' he writes in the first sentence, 'to refer to it with the composure which this formal heading would seem to require.' Attentive as ever to first sensations, first fancies, first impressions, Dickens links here – as Freud does, but with a different vocabulary – composure with first experiences. This, one could say, is one of the defining features of a first impression: that one's composure is somehow called into question. What might make a first impression seem like a first impression is that one is unprepared for it. Indeed, the question, what would it be to prepare for a first impression, in its virtual nonsensicalness, focuses the point. Dickens has been working away at *David Copperfield* for well over a year – in fact, as one of his editors surmises, 'the genesis of the novel may well go back to June 1845' – knowing that in all likelihood it will one day be finished. And yet he is quite unprepared for his first sensations of having completed it. And, of course, he has finished books before, but not this one. What is at stake is a loss of composure. And loss of composure is as good a definition as any of a symptom; at least from a psychoanalytic point of view. What the ego composes the unconscious disposes. Or, rather more accurately, one might say, symptoms stem the tide, are a kind of damage limitation, in the face of such losses of composure. Composure, albeit against the odds, is the project of the ego. First impressions – because they are first impressions, or because they lead back to the original traumatic first impressions – are a threat to our composure. Unless, that is, we can incorporate them into what we have composed. Psychoanalysis shows us, if we needed showing, just how precarious the artefact of (modern) character is.

If you want to see the fragility of the ego, Freud says, look at the way the child deals with his first impression of the difference between the sexes. If you want to see just how much of an artefact character or identity is, Dickens says, look at what Pip does with his first impressions of his own name. Faced with these first impressions the child replaces reality with his own invention. In both cases the first impression is a misnomer in so far as the first impression – the names Pirrip and Philip; the absence of the penis – is that which is concealed by what is recorded or represented as such. These disturbing, difficult-to-take-in first impressions make liars of us all; we disfigure the truth to sustain our composure. You know you are having a first impression when you are using all your imaginative resources to persuade yourself and others either that you are not having a first impression or that the first impression is merely novel but untroubling. When Pip names himself Pip, when the Freudian child believes penises are the order of the day, reassurance is at hand. What, we may wonder as we consider this issue of first impressions, do we need so much imaginative reassurance about? What are these first impressions felt to be if they demand so much of us? One answer is that they expose and, by the same token, threaten to destroy our great expectations. Our hopes for ourselves. Our desire, one might say, putting it melodramatically, is at the mercy of our first impressions. By calling himself Pip, Pip can go on being the seed of himself.

How do you make a (psychically) sustainable future out of the series of first impressions that are one's childhood? How does one transform the traumatic first impression into something, in William James's words, to go on from? Because the problem of the shocking first impression, as Freud describes it, is that it is something one keeps going back to. 'Instead of looking back, therefore, I will look forward,' Dickens concludes his Preface to *David Copperfield*, in the full knowledge that certain first impressions are a perpetual temptation; we want to look forward from them, but we keep looking back at them. And yet, Dickens goes on to suggest, his first sensations on finishing *David Copperfield* may be a clue to the future. 'I cannot close this volume more agreeably to myself,' he writes, 'than with a hopeful glance towards the time when I shall again put forth my two green leaves once a month, and with a faithful remembrance of the genial sun and showers that have fallen on these leaves of David Copperfield, and made me happy.' 'Faithful remembrance' is a useful redescription of our strange loyalty to certain of our first impressions; it suggests that we should abide by these particular impressions – or that they are themselves abiding – because they are the seeds of the future. They haunt us because we are haunted by the potential futures they portend. No one could ever recover from the difference between the sexes any more than they could stop themselves going back to it. Dickens goes back to *David Copperfield* when he starts writing *Great Expectations* because his first impression of the beginning of the book is that it may be a repeat, and in going back to it he was 'affected by it to a degree you would hardly believe'. The problem, in other words, is not repetition in and of itself; it is how to make repetition work for us, as a pragmatist might say; how to make repetition sufficiently generative ground for innovation and improvisation. Whether we can, as it were, keep going back to the difference between the sexes for inspiration and appetite; whether we can keep what we think of as our first impressions fresh and pregnant with meaning. Clearly the idea of screen memories, the idea of deferred action, the idea of transference itself, each of these makes us return to our so-called first impressions with other thoughts in mind. If psychoanalysis has done anything it has given us a way of redescribing first impressions as unerringly resonant historical moments. If one of the aims of psychoanalysis is not merely to abolish repetition but to keep it productive, then this is done by showing us the sheer scale and scope of appetite and personal history disclosed and concealed in what we refer to as our first impressions.

What may be worth considering, by way of conclusion, is that when it comes to impressions we talk of our first impressions, and sometimes of our second impressions, but never of our eighth or our forty-fifth. Whether or not I have kept my first impression of the difference between the sexes, however disguised, I certainly don't have my sixteenth. Beyond a certain point, after a certain amount of experience, what we call our impressions cease to be distinct: we stop counting. Pip eventually called himself Pip and by so doing he, in a sense, settled the issue of his name; just as we are eager to settle the differences between the sexes, usually through essentialist formulations, however provisional or ironized (women are passive, men are active, and so on). In other words, the thing we are inclined to do with first impressions is to settle them as an issue; to come to conclusions about them; to defend ourselves against them. Psychoanalysis should perhaps be the art of unsettling our first impressions, and unsettling what we make of them.

II *First Impressions and Second Thoughts*

I am loath to display a litter of variants, and hold up a still
target for the critic who knows that most second thoughts,
when visible, are worse thoughts.

Robert Lowell, Note to the New Edition of *Notebook*

First Impressions, a novel that on second thoughts was called
Pride and Prejudice, is about, among many other things, how
pride and prejudice is a better way of describing first impressions. Because the so-called first impressions that Elizabeth
and Darcy most prominently have of each other are not merely
skewed or distorted by their personal pride and their prejudices
but constituted by them, it is as if Jane Austen is saying: if you
want to find out about your pride and your prejudices –
if you want to reveal your most cherished preconceptions
about yourself – then it is your first impressions you should
attend to. And not, of course, any old first impressions, but one's
first impressions of an object of desire. Where there is desire,
where there is unusually intense interest – of a positive or negative kind – there are no innocent eyes. The innocent eye may
see nothing, but the desiring eye sees too much. It sees too much
of itself, too much of its past – for which the words 'pride' and
'prejudice' are as good words as any – and it is seen by itself, if it
is lucky enough to be the desiring eye of a fictional character in
a progress narrative, to have been self-preoccupied. To desire
someone else is to fall back in love with oneself. It is to ignore
the other person – to misread them, as we say – in the interests
of self-preservation.

In *Pride and Prejudice* Austen explores what the preconditions might be, what might serve as both an opportunity and a temptation, to revise a first impression; and how, if at all, modern people are led to change their minds, given their minds have already been changed into the settlement we call their character, which Jane Austen, with no obvious religious intent, wants us to think of as prone to getting fixed into pride and prejudice, self-idolization and dogmatic, principled exclusions. Our first impressions disclose our histories, our characters – our preferences and aversions – but at the cost of the object or person we are apparently impressed by. At its most extreme a bizarre picture of social life is conjured by Austen in this novel; of characters radically unaffected by each other. They may flirt and elope like Lydia; they may parent like the Bennets; they may fall in love like Bingley and Jane, and so on; but they remain intractably themselves. Indeed, they are not interested in themselves as, do not desire themselves to be, people seeking what we might call inner change; they may want to marry, but they do not want to be transformed. To be interested in first impressions, I want to suggest – to begin to wonder why they are so designated and what they might portend – is to be interested in a secular version of what were once called conversion experiences. Elizabeth and Darcy, unlike Mr and Mrs Collins, and indeed Jane and Bingley as far as we know, are not seeking through their union merely to consolidate who they have always been and want to continue being. They seem to have a different version of what Austen calls in a letter 'self-consequence'.

Elizabeth Bennet, Tony Tanner writes in his book on Austen,

identifies her sensory perceptions as judgements, or treats impressions as insights. In her violent condemnation of Darcy and the

instant credence she gives to Wickham, no matter how understandable the former, and excusable the latter, Elizabeth is guilty of
'Wrong Assent or Error', as Locke entitled one of his chapters
[of his *Essay Concerning Human Understanding*]. In it he gives some
of the causes of man's falling into error, and they include 'Received
hypotheses', 'Predominant passions or inclinations' and 'Authority'.
These are forces and influences with which every individual consciousness has to contend if it is to make the lonely struggle towards
true vision, as Elizabeth's consciousness does; and the fact that
whole groups and societies can live in the grip of 'Wrong Assent or
Error', often with intolerably unjust and cruel results, only helps to
ensure the continuing relevance of this happy tale of a girl who
learned to change her mind.

The use of Locke and the allusion to Blake in the phrase 'true
vision' is at least suggestive of the complicated knot of cultural
preoccupations that Austen's apparent comedy of manners is
engaged by (and with). Both Blake and Locke, Blake's supposed
antagonist, are joined in their belief that it is possible to see
things more or less clearly, even if they disagree both about
the nature of seeing and about what there is to see. In order
to love, in order to be in some sense with the person you most
want, Austen intimates in *Pride and Prejudice* – but only if you
are a certain kind of person, a person like Darcy or Elizabeth
Bennet – you need what Tanner refers to as 'true vision'. You
have to see people as they are; and this means as not suiting,
as not fitting in with, one's pride and prejudices. For these
people, the people we truly desire, are, by definition, at odds
with our first impression of them. Indeed, the drama of this
kind of love depends upon the protagonists being able to,
which entails wanting to, transform their initial impressions
of each other. A certain amount of inconveniencing has to go

on; people have to begin to think of themselves as self-deceivers, as people whose vision requires revision. Not settling for first impressions is the mark of a certain kind of character; one who, for example, believes that whatever a first impression may be, it uses the past to shield out the present; and by doing this – by seeing the past in the present; what Locke calls 'received hypotheses', 'predominant passions or inclinations' and 'authority' – precludes desire for the new; indeed precludes the idea that desire might be desire for the new.

One can be converted only to something that already exists. In those new secular conversion experiences called falling in love (or desire) – which requires, as we shall see, a first impression followed by a second thought, or an illusion followed by a disillusionment – the object of desire is a new object. Elizabeth and Darcy have never met each other before. They have, we know from the novel, loved other people – Elizabeth we are told on several occasions has an affinity with her father – and we assume that they have fantasized about the people they might want. All the couples in *Pride and Prejudice*, and there are surprisingly many, at some point met each other for the first time; and 'first', not incidentally, is a word used many times in the novel, as though something about the order of events is being drawn to our attention. And yet with Elizabeth and Darcy, something more romantic seems to be happening. It is as if they have to understand something, to learn something about their first impressions of each other in order to get on. The reflected-upon first impression; the first impression held on to and then modified by experience – that is, conversation with other people – these are what Freud was to call the preconditions for loving. Or at least loving in this more romantic way. Your first impression has to be wrong;

and you have to have the appetite and the luck to discover its wrongness. This love, in short, begins with a formative misrecognition that is transformed into an accurate recognition; and in this progress myth – this myth in which one's perception and capacity for love are reunited and redeemed – it is an accurate, realistic sense of oneself and the other person that is supposedly acquired. Love requires self-revision.

In *Pride and Prejudice*, a novel about first impressions, the phrase 'first impressions' is never in fact used (for Austen you often get the impression that the explicit is the taboo). The other phrase in this essay title, 'second thoughts' – being what we should have about our first impressions to stop them sticking, to stop them repeating themselves – is used, but only once. Elizabeth's uncle, Mr Gardiner, and her father have gone to London to find the eloped Lydia and Wickham, and are finding it difficult to track the illicit couple down. If you want to find someone you have to first find someone who knows them. After all, when people conceal themselves what is one to do? 'I have written to Colonel Forster,' Mr Gardiner writes to the Bennets,

to desire him to find out, if possible, from some of the young man's intimates in the regiment, whether Wickham has any relations or connections, who would be likely to know in what part of town he has now concealed himself. If there were anyone that one could apply to, with a probability of gaining such a clue as that, it might be of essential consequence. At present we have nothing to guide us. Colonel Forster will, I dare say, do everything in his power to satisfy us on this head. But, on second thoughts, perhaps Lizzy could tell us what relations he has now living, better than any other person.

The reader knows that Wickham has concealed himself not only in a part of town but also in a part of himself that lies about who he is. The reason that Mr Gardiner on second thoughts thinks Lizzy might know better than anyone else is because she has spoken so highly of Wickham in the past. His first thought was that a fellow soldier would know; his second thought is that a woman who likes and values Wickham is likely to know better. Elizabeth, we are told, 'was at no loss to understand from whence this deference for her authority proceeded', but she has no information. Here, we might say, is the one place in the novel in which a perfectly intelligible and quite explicit second thought turns out to be wrong; at its most abstract Mr Gardiner assumes that a fond woman will know something about a man that other men will not know. In a novel implicitly committed to second thoughts, to the revision of initial judgements, the only explicit second thought in the novel is a misrecognition.

In a novel in which second things are always better than first things – 'Georgiana had the highest opinion in the world of Elizabeth; though at first she often listened with an astonish-ment bordering on alarm at her lively, sportive manner of talking to her brother'; in a novel in which it is as though the characters have to get through their first impressions to come to their best senses – 'after the first exclamation of surprise and horror Mr Gardiner readily promised every assistance in his power'; in a novel in which first things are continually being drawn to our attention in order to be superseded by preferred second things, we are warned peripherally at this moment to wonder about the second thought and why we are inclined to value it. As usual in this novel an important clue comes in a letter. Austen is suggesting through Mr Gardiner that we may need to revise our (and her) beliefs about revision.

The cherished second thought, which apparently makes a more sophisticated story out of a too immediate first impression, can be as misleading as the first conclusion jumped to.

It is important for certain characters in Austen's novel to believe they can revise themselves, but it is also possible, Austen intimates through Mr Gardiner's letter, that this may be merely a deferral of the problem. That when it comes to first impressions and second thoughts – which is, of course, the ordinary language version of what philosophers call the mind–body problem – there may be no progress myth available, no settling of preferences. After all, what is it about the second thought that leads us to value it over and above the first impression? It could be the rhetorical force of the word 'thought' over the word 'impression'; coming second, second-hand objects and information, the second hand are not our automatic choices. Or, to put it a little more formally, what are our criteria for belief or assent or agreement such that the second thought satisfies us more than the initial impression? If we set aside for a moment the absurdity, the impossibility, of counting our thoughts at all; and at the same time forget the fact that we don't talk of fifth thoughts, or indeed eighth impressions, it is worth considering what it might be that makes us so keen on these particular phrasings of our experience; why first impressions become enigmatic and in need of interpretation, and what, if anything, is resolved by a second thought.

When Elizabeth eventually realizes the scale of her misrecognition of Darcy she has a vocabulary immediately available to her to explain what has happened:

'How despicably have I acted!' she cried – 'I, who have prided myself on my discernment! – I who have valued myself on my abilities! Who have often disdained the generous candour of my sister, and gratified my vanity, in useless or blameable distrust – How humiliating is this discovery! – Yet, how just a humiliation! – Had I been in love, I could not have been more wretchedly blind. But vanity not love has been my folly . . . Till this moment I never knew myself.'

It is perhaps remarkable, or just worth remarking on, how quickly, given the opportunity, Elizabeth understands herself; the inner critic is immediately at hand, with its fluent moral certainties. James Wood has commented in his essay on Austen, 'Jane Austen's Heroic Consciousness', that her 'heroines are the only characters whose inner thought is represented. And this speaking to oneself is often a secret conversation, which Austen almost invented a new technique, a precursor of modernist stream-of-consciousness, to represent.' What is perhaps worth adding, at least in Elizabeth's case, is that this inner conversation is rather more of a monologue than Wood suggests. Elizabeth is so of a piece, so identified with her inner critic (or moral censor) that it sounds like stream of consciousness, or stream of criticism, in this sense is more accurate a description than conversation. Her second thoughts about Darcy, when they come, are utterly clarifying; and she never goes back on them. Knowing yourself, she realizes in this moment of revelatory solitary thought, is knowing how your vanity distorts your judgement, your discernment. And, to add insult to injury, the very thing you most value about yourself – 'I, who have prided myself on my discernment!' – is the thing that undoes you. But, as often happens in Austen's writing, there is a strange and disturbing candour in the incisive clarity of mind she values. 'Had I been in love,' Elizabeth says to herself, 'I could not have been more

wretchedly blind. But vanity not love has been my folly.'
Vanity is not offered up here as the saboteur of love, which
one might expect; rather, Elizabeth tells us, both love and
vanity make us blind. So love and vanity, at least in this sense,
are similar; but the question raised is what kind of relationship
with oneself or others does not make one blind? Through
what way of feeling for oneself or others can one achieve what
Tanner called 'true vision'? There is a choice of follies, vanity
or love; and there is discernment, which is proof against
neither of them. We can't help but wonder – despite, or
perhaps because of, the power of the revelation and the happy
resolutions of the plot – what Elizabeth is going to rely
on now. Rather like Mr Gardiner's second thought about
Elizabeth, Elizabeth's second thought about herself may not
be quite as reassuring as it seems. 'Till this moment I never
knew myself,' she concludes; but does she know anything
grander than that she made, initially, a mistake about Darcy's
character and so about herself, no more and no less? And, after
all, her first impressions of Darcy as arrogant and difficult were
not, as he himself acknowledges, completely wrong; nor was
her first impression of his aunt, his portrait or his family house,
Pemberley. The self-knowledge so keenly proclaimed by Elizabeth may be rather desultory; sometimes one's first impressions are right, sometimes they are wrong. Or perhaps, as
modern self-knowledge goes, this is rather profound. It is a
rivetingly low-key conclusion; and something as important as
a marriage depends upon it. Austen, I suspect, didn't end up
calling her novel *First Impressions* because it would have given
the game away; and then she could give the game away a bit
more through Mr Gardiner's and Elizabeth's second thoughts.
Sometimes our first impressions are the whole story, sometimes they are not; but it is the whole story that we seem to

want. The way Austen concludes, ties up, *Pride and Prejudice* creates the illusion that, to all intents and purposes, the whole story has been told. We may be charmed but we are not fooled.

It would be as absurd to say that there were no first impressions until the nineteenth century wrote about them as it was when Wilde said that there were no fogs in London until Dickens wrote about them. But it is my impression, given the sheer scale and momentum of newness in the nineteenth century, that there was the beginning of a new-found curiosity about the nature of first impressions; and a concern about their consequences: about where they might lead and about what, if anything, we might do with or about them. There were, to put it as crudely as possible, more new things and people around for more people than ever before; but there was, as it were, a complementary doubt about whether new experience was possible; about the adaptability, the improvisational skills of the modern individual. And with the privileging of first impressions came the questions: what do these new experiences, these first impressions, call up, evoke in these modern people – involuntarily, as it were? What are they turned into? And what resources might these people discover; what choices might they make to deal with this torrential novelty?

There is no first impression, one might say, without a second thought (or, in the case of a trauma, without at least initially the impossibility of a second thought); without imaginative work being done. Indeed, sometimes – and this is where Freud's psychoanalysis might come in – you may have to reconstruct the so-called first impression from the second thought, in the way that the desire has to be derived from the defences against it. Second thoughts, as I said, are what we should have about our first impressions to stop them sticking, to stop them merely repeating themselves, to stop us being overwhelmed by them. But informing this fascination with first impressions is a scepticism about second thoughts, about what we have to set against the first impression which seemed, to more and more people, to have a life of its own. Indeed, a life, in so far as it could be narrated, was the tracking or the reconstructing of the fate of certain first impressions.

Elizabeth and Darcy in *Pride and Prejudice*, Pip in *Great Expectations* and the people in Freud's case histories are all in a long line of fictional and non-fictional characters who are going to have to change if they are to secure the pleasures they desire. And change is contingent upon what they make of certain key first impressions. There is no pleasure without self-revision; the life of at least one version of modern desire entails a transforming of the desires of and from and for the past. Desire in this sense involves a change of character, and a change of character involves a retrospective reconsideration of who one takes oneself to be. First impressions, particularly of an object of desire – which can be a person, a book, an ideology, an idea, etc. – unearth, expose, undermine, waylay, redirect character; ourselves as we know and wish ourselves to be, which Freud called the ego (and Lacan referred to as our constitutive misrecognition of ourselves). You know when modern people like Elizabeth Bennet sense real pleasure in the offing, feel real desire for someone, because their first reaction is to recoil from it, to repudiate it, to deny it. As Freudians we might say her first impression of Darcy was of desire for him, which, because it was problematic, was turned into aversion; so her first conscious impression of Darcy – her intense though flirtatious dislike of him – had to be transformed. So if we are these Freudians we would, by inferring unconscious desire on Elizabeth's part, say that she did not in fact change. Her second thought was simply her recovery, her working through to her first impression, which was her desire for Darcy. On this reading second thoughts are in the service of first impressions; first impressions are of desire, and first impressions are the resilient ones. To recover from the first impression of desire, it is the desire that has to be recovered. From a Freudian point of view, what Elizabeth didn't do was radically change; she simply, over time and through experience, rearranged herself around her desire, a desire that was intrinsically troubling to her but upon which a good life for herself depended. Second thoughts become the realization of first impressions. We are fighting a losing battle with our desire and we call it thoughtfulness or self-reflection. This, at least, would be the crude Freudian view. The question is: if second thoughts seem truer, more valuable, less impulsive, what is it that they are truer to?

'In every man,' Ford Madox Ford writes in *Parade's End*, his novel about the Great War,

there are two minds that work side by side, the one checking the other; thus emotion stands against reason, intellect corrects passion and first impressions act a little, but very little, before quick reflection. Yet first impressions have always a bias in their favour, and even quiet reflection has often a job to efface them.

It is the persistence of first impressions, and there being something about 'reflection' that wants to efface them, that strikes Ford. In his carefully staged sentence with its series of equivalences mapped on to each other, first impressions are of a piece with passion and emotion and at odds with, corrected by, intellect, reason and reflection. First impressions perturb and disturb and need to be worked on, if not actually got rid of. And then there is the strange phrase 'Yet first impressions always have a bias in their favour'; there is something about first impressions, by virtue of their being first – and the Great War, the First World War, was, of course, full of first impressions – that tips things in their favour. A 'bias', it should be noted, is a swerve away, the *OED* having also 'predilection; prejudice'. The intimation is that first impressions pull you away from something, and their influence, their effect, can be ineluctable. What, it has to be asked, does a first impression prejudice you in the direction of? And what can second thoughts – those new-found resolutions born of reflection – do in the face of such force? What they can't do, Ford makes clear, is restore the status quo. There is no going back to before the first impression. One has been branded or wounded or marked by something; one is being pulled away but it is in a direction without a determinate end. This was what the Great War did. The first impression of the war, the first impression that the war was for every participant, both military and civilian, could never be effaced.

As shorthand one could say: first impressions are radical; second thoughts are conservative. The new is registered and resisted; but the resistance is itself the sign of registration. Contemporary ethologists have a good picture or emblem of this in the concept of habitat-tracking. When the habitat of a species is destroyed the individuals of the species do not simply adapt to the new environment or become extinct; in the words of Niles Elderidge in *Why We Do It*, they

simply track habitats that provide a close enough fit to their already in place economic adaptations, their fundamental needs for making a living, whatever they were . . . The key to surviving episodes of climate change even as monumental as the Pleistocene glacial advances is to find a place where existing adaptations (familiar prey for a bobcat, suitable soil chemistry for a fern species) can be put into use.

New adaptation, in the first instance, is resisted; the desire is not to change. You know things have changed, are changing, when people are trying to keep things as they are. The fate of the first impression, the shock of the new and its repercussions, is the new story. We don't talk of first thoughts and second impressions.

Faced with episodes of climate change – that is to say, with significant changes of environment – the animals go in search of an environment in which their previous adaptations still work. They have registered this great change, from our point of view, through their very quest to restore the status quo. If, for the sake of analogy, we anthropomorphize them, we can say: their first impression was an accurate one, something essential has changed. If they are lucky enough to find an environment that works for them – that is, if they don't need to change – they might in time forget what I am calling their first impression, accurate though it was. But if they can't find a suitable environment then their second thought would be an intensification, a realization, of that first impression: things have really, unavoidably changed, and they are going to have to change to deal with the change. This second thought is a facing up to something real.

In Ford's description we may remember quick reflection is there to deal with, to stand against, to correct and even to try to efface the first impression; but it is the first impression that, in one form or another, abides: 'first impressions have always a bias in their favour'. But there is something about them that we resist. They are a paradoxical version of Henry James's description of the real; they are both that which it is impossible not to know, and that which it is impossible to know. First impressions, we are encouraged to believe from a variety of modern sources, are indelible; they may be transformed, they may be denied and refused, but they persist. Second thoughts, we might say, at their best give first impressions a chance; at their worst they are wrong or misleading, or simply misfire when they betray first impressions or fail, in some difficult to define way, to keep faith with them. We may want to think of love at first sight as the real thing; but we should remember that there has always been a first sighting.

And yet putting it like this, taking the argument in this direction, reveals, I think, how confused we are by these issues. One version of common sense tells us that first impressions, virtually by definition, are unreliable and need reflecting on; the body (the senses) without the so-called mind brought to bear on it is known to be unreliable. First impressions, even when they turn out to be accurate, need second thoughts to tell us this; first impressions are inchoate, unformed, patchy, in short they are impressions; second thoughts are coherent, articulate, narratable, in short they make sense. So how can first impressions have a bias in their favour, be somehow more revealing, more immediately illuminating, even essentially more accurate, more truthful than our more thought-out or worked-through reactions to them? And why should it be that what we call second thoughts can be both preferred, encouraged and trusted – and by definition plausible – and at the same time be objects of such suspicion? We don't know which to believe in; or perhaps it would be more accurate to say that we don't know how to believe them, how to believe them in different ways. Our faith in first impressions is never the same as our faith in second thoughts. If we put our money on our first impressions we are left wondering what to make of an incoherent thing; first impressions, after all, come in bits and pieces, they are unformed into intelligible objects. If we put our money on second thoughts we are left wondering – though perhaps not as often as we should – what to make of a prepared thing. One way of putting this is to say it is the difference between the unrehearsed and the rehearsed. When it comes to certain kinds of experience we don't like to think of ourselves as forever in rehearsal, as unprepared.

Our first impression, whatever else it is, refers to the moment when we haven't worked something out. In what we call our second thoughts we have at least begun to. In our first impressions our desire, our project – what, if anything, there is to be worked out – is unclear; a second thought tends to be a project formed (when we are advised to sleep on something, or to not act impulsively, we are led to believe that the project has formed too quickly for our own good). In our first impressions we are at a loss; our second thoughts are more decisive, more intent (so-called theory could never be a first impression of anything). When a first impression is fluently articulated we assume that it has been rehearsed, that it is being treated as something more recognizable than it could ever be; if a second thought is not articulated fluently enough we assume that the first impression has not been sufficiently recovered from. Second thoughts take time; they are like a convalescence. First impressions also take time, but it is unacknowledgeable; you can never tell when your first impression has finished or is complete except, perhaps, by saying something like 'but on second thoughts . . .' Second thoughts, in other words, have a certain finish that first impressions can never have. Not that this, in and of itself, makes them either more truthful or more useful; it just makes them more conventionally persuasive. Incoherence, obscure or non-existent narrative, vague bulletins, phrasings that lack confidence, contradictions that lack explanation and fleeting states of conviction do not make a good argument or a convincing news item. It is a question of what kinds of speech act work for us; the tentative and unformed or the thoughtful and considered. A rule of thumb might be: a first impression doesn't make a good story; the better the story the less of a first impression it is, the more it has been worked up. We assume, in other words, that this process, this picture that we envisage of first impressions becoming second thoughts, is an elaboration, even if the labour in this elaboration is obscure.

The picture is something like this: something novel strikes us, we have an experience that, like many of our experiences, particularly when we are children, is unprecedented. This is a shock to the senses, a stirrer of latent desires, a disturber of our familiar equilibrium. It is envisaged that some kind of work is then done on the feelings called up; acts of transformation, however unconscious, are performed, and these veer between exclusion and inclusion, between incorporating the new and expelling it (the *it* being a foreign body). The phrase 'first impressions' refers to the inauguration, the initiating, of this process (if that is what it is); 'second thoughts' refers to something later, to some work done. This process – and even to call it that is to ascribe a teleology, if not a progress – satisfies our desire for origins but not, it should be noted, for endings; there may merely be accretion, accumulation rather than clarification or refinement.

The psychoanalyst W. R. Bion in a book called *Second*

Thoughts – in which thoughts are much considered but second thoughts never mentioned – uses the example of writing notes after a psychoanalytic session with a patient. 'It is usual to think,' he writes,

that a report written within an hour or so of the events has a special 'built-in' validity and superiority over the account written many months or even years later. I shall suppose simply that they are two different accounts of the same event without any implication that one is superior to the other. A technique is needed which will reveal the nature of the contrasting stories and of the contrasting elements in them. Historians are familiar with the uses of contemporary history and history written sufficiently long after the event for 'passions to have cooled' and perspectives to have matured. A psychoanalyst will require some more precise definition of the realities behind these distinguishing formulations.

Bion alerts us with subdued irony to the problems in play. Whether or not Bion really believes that there could be a technique to distinguish how our stories, our accounts of events, change over time, the familiar idea of passions cooling and perspectives maturing seems to beg all the questions. What he calls the 'usual' view speaks up for the validity, the accuracy of the earlier impression, its supposed 'superiority' to the later more considered view that I am calling, as shorthand, second thoughts. Bion's supposition is that they are merely two different accounts, and that we don't yet have a way of evaluating which is more useful for what. Perhaps we should be asking not which is more accurate, which is more truthful, the first impression or the second thought; but, rather, for what purposes, in which situations, should we prefer the first impression to the second thought, or vice versa? We should be asking not which is superior, but which is superior for what? We should, in short, be asking a pragmatic question. A scholar looking at early drafts of a poem clearly has a different project than the reader of the completed poem in the book. Contemporary history – the contemporary history, say, that is journalism – is a different genre from history written sufficiently long after the event. Acting on a first impression – treating it as instructive – gets us somewhere different than our acting on a second thought. It is a question, in any given situation, of what we would prefer to be led by.

If for Freud a first impression – at least one that is noticeably striking – is never only or merely a first impression but a gathering of one's history in a moment when passions have not cooled but perspectives have been prepared, then what I am calling second thoughts are more akin to what Bion calls 'history written sufficiently long after the event'. It is inevitably a revisionary history because something – what I am calling a first impression – has been revised. Bion's suggestion that a 'psychoanalyst will require some more precise definition of the realities behind these distinguishing formulations' reflects just how integral these issues are to the work of psychoanalysis. At the end of my last essay I suggested that 'Psychoanalysis should perhaps be the art of unsettling our first impressions, and unsettling what we make of them.' It would have been more accurate to say, I think now, that psychoanalysis is the art of redescribing what we think of as our first impressions, and unsettling what we make of our redescriptions. If unconscious work has always been done to make a first impression possible it presumably continues – even if it is unconscious work of a different kind – in those reconsiderings we call second thoughts. It is, of course, very often the case that for a second thought to occur, or when a second thought does occur, passions have cooled, we are calmer. Calmness, like passion, is better for some things than for others. The preconditions for a second thought are the lessening, the regulation, of excitement. The assumption here, broadly speaking, is that being aroused is potentially misleading. What is so misleading about desire is that we want to be misled by it. Or at least as Freud among others will suggest, there is a part of ourselves that wants to be misled. Second thoughts we might think of as a form of damage limitation. If our first impressions – from a Freudian point of view – present us with an albeit disguised awakening of our unconscious desire, second thoughts are ways, are formulations that make this desire sufficiently bearable. 'It must give pleasure,' Wallace Stevens said of the supreme fiction. It is also what Freud says of our desire: 'it must give pleasure'. It is the aim of our so-called second thoughts to redescribe our desire as sufficiently pleasurable. And we need to do this because our desire is by nature so utterly disruptive. It is easy to feel that sexual desire, whatever else it is, must be a desire for suffering. This is what Freud is hearing from his modern patients; that where there should be pleasure in their lives there is too often suffering. If the first impression is a kind of trauma, the second thought is a kind of self-cure. Some self-cures, of course, are so radical that it seems as though there was no initiating trauma; some second thoughts are a burial ground for the first impressions that prompted them. Freud's emblem for this is the dream.

When Darcy and Elizabeth meet, so shocking is the desire in the encounter that a mutual antipathy ensues. They antagonize each other, we would say, so as not to yield to each other or yield to their desire for each other. What they don't notice, in the first instance, is their wanting each other, even though 'It is a truth universally acknowledged, that a single man in possession of a good fortune, must be in want of a wife'; what is not universally acknowledged is just how difficult it is for some people – some modern people, like Darcy and Elizabeth – to acknowledge their wanting when it occurs. Wanting a husband or a wife, Austen intimates, is not always as easy as it looks; especially if you want something more than most of the other couples in the novel seem to want. What Freud formulates, through his description of the dream-work, is that for desire to be experienced it must not be noticed; or it must not be noticed as desire. Some modern people can desire only by not knowing that that is what they are doing. Their first impression is recoil; everything depends on the fate of the second thought. The dream is a version of a second thought. The first impressions that inform it, that quicken it – what Freud refers to as 'the day residues' – are very often unknown. There are first impressions we are unaware of having and of having had.

In what Freud calls 'the dream day', the day before the night of the dream, unbeknown to our conscious selves the dreamer inside us is finding things that are recruited because they both stir and formulate unconscious desire; things heard, things seen – but rarely the things in the day that our conscious selves have been struck by – are collected to be worked up into the dream. The dream will use them to make that bizarre, because censored, visual presentation of our least acceptable desires; and if the dream works we will not be disturbed – that is, woken up – by these desires; we will, as it were, sleep through them. In the day, but unbeknown to our (conscious) selves, our more unconscious desires are being stirred; and in the second thought that is the dream they are formulated in a way that we will be unable to comprehend and that will not, ideally, be too disturbing; and that will fade on waking. Unless, of course, you take your dream to a psychoanalyst; with whom, if it all goes according to plan, you will – through free associating to the elements of the dream – reconstruct the undeclared first impressions and work out what the second thoughts that are the dream have done with them. What Freud adds to the picture is that it is our so-called second thoughts that need interpreting. We need to interpret our own interpretations of our desire because we are the animals that hide from themselves, that conceal from themselves what it is they want; that have to work to make what they want bearable to themselves. For Freudian people second thoughts are never going to be enough; and second thoughts will be the ones that count, the only ones we count up to.

In his recent book *Blink: The Power of Thinking without Thinking*, the science writer Malcolm Gladwell, perhaps unsurprisingly comes up with the conclusion that our first impression can be both astonishingly accurate and perceptive, and profoundly misleading and prejudiced. We have to learn, he suggests, to use our best version of our capacity for first impressions. 'Our unconscious reactions,' he writes,

come out of a locked room, and we can't look inside that room. But with experience we become expert at using our behaviour and our training to interpret – and decode – what lies behind our snap judgements and first impressions. It's a lot like people do when they are in psychoanalysis: they spend years analysing their unconscious with the help of a trained therapist until they begin to get a sense of how their mind works.

At our best, well trained, we don't need what we call second thoughts, our first impressions tell us everything we want; at our worst our second thoughts, our misread first impressions, baffle our access to this unique survival skill. Unburdened by Freud's picture of us as divided against ourselves, not on the side of our own desire, Gladwell is upbeat about our first impressions (he refers to a therapist who within seconds of either meeting a couple or watching them on videotape can predict with a high degree of accuracy whether their relationship is going to work). The question is – if we are counting, and we are not – how many thoughts do we need to have about ourselves? What, if anything, do what we call our first impressions require of us? What Austen and Dickens and Freud – and Gladwell in his enthusiastic way – show us is just how much depends on how we develop our first impressions, how much goes into forming them and how much can come out of them. Our first impressions, they tell us, are what we make out of them.

Paranoid Moderns

But what tyranny is so hideous as that of an automatically
ideal humanity?

D. H. Lawrence, *Psychoanalysis and the Unconscious*

What is now called trauma theory informs contemporary
biography as much as it does the academic art of literary history.
Belief in trauma as a kind of agency, as a cultural force – belief
in events as the real heroes and heroines in life stories – turns up
historically when people were beginning to lose faith in God
and character and cause and effect. Despite the fact that the
relationship between being shocked and being changed is indeterminate – many shocking things make little real difference,
and the unnoticed and the unnoticeable can have astonishing
repercussions – the idea of trauma reassures us that we can find
a beginning, and that there is a beginning worth finding; that
some causes, as it were, are worth taking seriously. All the new
thinking, like all the old thinking, is about wanting to understand change; and about wanting change to be a drama. Trauma
theories, at their crudest, tend to recycle old ideas (just as
trauma itself is usually described now as a form of recycling; it is
trauma that makes us so repetitive). Trauma has become *the*
great change that makes change impossible. It is the change that
stops us changing. This is clearly an attractive story for people
who are beginning to feel that there is too much change.

*

T. E. Hulme believed that something terrible had happened in the West called romanticism, and that we needed to recover from it. In his view we needed to get back to a time before human nature was deemed capable of radical change, before the idea of progress distorted our reality sense. He loathed anything without the ballast of original sin in it, and was one of the first people to defend the modernism of the abstract art of Bomberg, Epstein and Gaudier-Brzeska against the apparent progressivism of Roger Fry and Bloomsbury. He had found his preferred version of human nature in Byzantine art, and its recovery in these abstract modernists. One of the many things that is so interesting about Hulme, and which Robert Ferguson is illuminating about in his thorough biography of him, *The Short Sharp Life of T. E. Hulme*, is his redescription of original sin as the best way of talking about ineluctable human limitations. Hulme in his own combative unacademic way was trying to work out why original sin, even in its secular versions, was an idea we shouldn't be trying to do without. And clearly no modern writing has yet been able to do without a version of this original trauma, either as something to be properly acknowledged, or as something to be properly defied. The problem of original sin, secularized as the problem of innate unsociability, has been remarkably resilient.

David Trotter believes that what we have learned to call modernism is more akin to a cumulative trauma, the trauma of secularization (the loss of a plot, a fear of a life without magic, the profitable displacing the meaningful). If we can't get a wholly convincing sense of the beginnings of modernism, Trotter says in his *Paranoid Moderns*, we can get the next best thing: a sense of what the modernist generation thought they had lost (life as a coming to terms with loss is integral to the trauma/original sin approach). What the modernist artists felt they had lost, among other things, was the assured place of the artist, his or her necessary significance within the culture. The writers who concern Trotter – Godwin, Wilkie Collins, Conrad, Lawrence and Ford Madox Ford –

wrote about professional identities under extreme pressure. They were themselves, as professional writers confronted by a rapidly developing literary market-place, under extreme pressure. So they wrote about madness, and they went a little mad themselves . . . the literary experimentation by means of which they hoped to achieve a degree of magical power can be understood as a psycho-pathy of expertise.

Paranoia is the self-cure for insignificance. Trotter's paranoid modernists are marked, above all, by a sense of what is unbearable about modern life. Although these writers were not exactly trauma theorists themselves, much of the writing of the period has a manifesto-like quality, and the manifesto is the paranoid genre par excellence. Naming the madness of modern life, as Trotter shows in fascinating detail, was sup-posed to be part of the professional expertise of psychiatry. And psychiatry was a profession in a way that novel writing was not. But its claim to expertise lay only in its (linguistic) descriptions of the relationship between heredity and trauma, and heredity as trauma. 'Trauma' enters the language as a magic word, a technical term invested, so to speak, with the psychopathy of expertise, at around the turn of the nineteenth century. Two world wars and the new-found prevalence of sexuality as trauma consolidated its rhetorical power. Trauma made both accident and intention newly meaningful.

Trauma has become one of the last essences that even the most radical anti-essentialists won't do away with because not believing in trauma can sound very like not believing that people suffer. The notion of trauma helps us to go on believing that lives turn on significant events, and that we need to be able to recognize them as such. We have to be able to do the trick of turning good and bad luck into meaning and substance, cause and effect, beginnings, middles and ends. As David Trotter's remarkable book makes remarkably clear, luck and chance have never been quite good enough for us. Trauma theory puts a plot, if not a plan, back into modern lives. No longer believing in providence all too easily begins to seem like a huge piece of bad luck.

And yet even the most committed modern trauma theorists must be wary of the ways in which such theories smuggle the sacred back in in the guise of the secular. The idea of something beyond our control intervening in our lives in a way that ineluctably changes them (for better or for worse) is not exactly news: nor is the sense that radical unpredictable change confounds us, and usually makes us ask what we have come to think of as deep questions about life. Trauma theory becomes properly secular only when it stops needing to be morally reassuring; when it stops having to put a plot back in. When we were being told that the world will never be the same after September 11, that we will never forget that day, we were once again being reassured – that is, coerced into believing – that we can still recognize a meaningful event when we see one, and that our capacity for prophecy is undimmed. It is a difficult fact of life that we can be horrified by things that we do not find meaningful, that don't matter to us despite our wish for them to matter (and with so much horror around, not caring becomes a kind of forbidden pleasure). We may have finally begun to notice that the only thing we can predict politically is the unpredictability of events; but our relish for a sense of inevitability – for things having to happen in a certain way known to someone – is hard to give up. It is always too soon, and always just the right time, to tell whether the French Revolution has worked. There is something we should now call paranoid modernism, Trotter suggests – and Hulme is an exemplary instance of this – because many of the most important modernist writers were writing out of the fear that they must make their own systems or be trapped in a world without system. 'The beginning of paranoia,' Trotter remarks in one of many arresting formulations, 'is the deep sense that it all hangs together'; 'paranoiacs . . . find themselves by eliminating muddle'. To become modern, to sustain a belief in cause and effect and plotted orders of meaning, was to become paranoid. Outside the paranoid map there was the mess of contingency, and the contingency of mess. Off the (paranoid) map there was the real, unintelligible world of chance events. Paranoia, in other words, was the modern, the modernist, word for sanity. It was sane to believe that life made sense, and that the sense it made could keep us going.

Trotter has a complicated story to tell, but he tells it with admirable lucidity. And it is part of the artfulness of his book, to state and understate what it might mean to tell a story about paranoia that all hangs together. His scrupulous and always generous acknowledgement of debts and sources and references – the scholarly apparatus of telling us where things come from, and where they can be followed up – can't help but make us wonder in this context whether gratitude and an accurate sense of indebtedness are not themselves ironically of a piece with the paranoid strategies of modernism that Trotter unmuddles for us. It is one of the many boons of this erudite and exhilarating book that Trotter makes a case for paranoia that is never merely the case against it. If anything,

Paranoid Modernism shows us that paranoia as a solution is a remarkably imaginative recognition of the problem. The paranoiac is the person who has really noticed what a mess we are in and knows that the only sense he is going to get is the sense that he can make. 'Nothing is bad in itself except disorder,' Hulme remarked. As one of Trotter's paranoid modernists, Hulme would have no truck with the idea that what might be bad in itself was the inability to bear disorder; or that being unable to bear disorder was being unable to bear what life was really like. The modern paranoiac has realized that since God is dead someone has got to be god. Someone has to know what is going on, and there has to be a something that is going on.

Most of the (academic) stories about so-called modernism are trauma theories; theories about what certain writers couldn't bear in the early decades of the twentieth century, and the ways they found of bearing it. Trotter's story began with a series of fascinating sketches – of Turner, Melville, Dickens and Degas, among others – in *Cooking with Mud: The Idea of Mess in Nineteenth-Century Art and Fiction*, which is an elaborate prelude to his more focused but no less eloquent *Paranoid Modernism*. It was in the 1860s that mess became a preoccupation in art. The litter in Turner's landscapes, the spitting that goes on in *Moby-Dick*, the chance occurrences in Flaubert's *Sentimental Education*, are all evidence for Trotter of various chaoses being kept at bay. And determinism, what Trotter refers to as 'the method in paranoia's madness', becomes a grand consolation, as well as a grand narrative, in a world in which people seem to be doing nothing more coherent or impressive than taking their chances. The great nineteenth-century determinisms – the economic, the evolutionary, the psychoanalytic – were the secular plots that

replaced providentialism. There was, in the nineteenth century, Trotter writes in *Cooking with Mud*,

a determinism hell-bent on the excavation of cause from effect.
Determinism, while it may demand a prodigious expenditure of
energy and intelligence (indeed, precisely because it demands all
that), is the easy option: the choice we make without knowing we
have made it . . . Determinism is never not productive, and we
should be thankful for the bounty it brings. But the hardest thing of
all to think about is chance, which denies the very form and purpose
of thought itself. Mess makes this possible.

What the determinisms have going for them, despite their
apparent rupturing of the sacred order, is their continuity with
it; they satisfy our desire for inevitability, and, as Trotter says,
they are a comforting form of bad faith (if we can't help it, we
can't help it). In *Modern Art and Its Philosophy*, of 1914, Hulme
wrote that in the modern revolution of 'sensibility', 'there
seems to be a desire for austerity and bareness, a striving
towards structure and away from the messiness and confusion
of nature and natural things'. Paranoia is a solvent for messiness and confusion; ripe with certainty, it is a hotbed of
convictions (once God is dead plausibility replaces revelation).
To value clarity and coherence, or meaning and purpose, was
to be on the side of the paranoiacs. The question was, and still
is, faced with the messiness and confusion and pointlessness
of nature, is there a viable alternative to paranoia for us as a
way of life? The composure of abstraction – towards structure
and away from messiness – is an unpromising cure for contingency, for the no-sense we are faced with. It is to the 'representational strategies' of the great literary modernists, Lawrence,
Conrad, Ford and Wyndham Lewis, that Trotter looks for the

working out and the working through of these new dilemmas. 'The writers and painters of the period acknowledged,' he writes, 'by the interest they took in mess that a realism that did not want to know about the operations of chance would be no realism at all.' Once you get interested in chance, your sense of human agency – your sense of what the idea of human agency was invented for – begins to change. If chance is the medium that agency operates in, agency is a diminished thing, merely reactive. People have to find ways of describing the (new) fact that, like everything else in nature, they are nothing special. And even the people who are deemed to be especially good at this, the writers and painters, are nothing special either.

The paranoiac is at the centre of a world that has no centre. The history that Trotter tells suggests not merely that the so-called 'crisis of modernity' was a legitimation crisis, with writers as simply the most articulate complainers about the fact that people, and not merely writers, are now utterly marginal because (secular) nature is all margin and no text; but also that the sense of hierarchy within the human world was increasingly constituted by a new kind of magic. The divine magic of the divinely ordained ancien régime had to be replaced by that contradiction in terms, secular magic. With the gradual redistribution of wealth went the redistribution of magic (it's clearly possible to be enchanted by the disenchant-ment of the modern world). 'During the nineteenth century,' Trotter continues,

the status the upwardly mobile professional classes sought for their expertise was the status of a magical power: a status previously or otherwise afforded to qualities such as wealth or warlike valour. They did not always find it. Sometimes, when they did not find it, they made it up. Paranoia is a delusion of magical power . . . Paranoia, the psychiatrists maintained, was the professional person's madness of choice.

Paranoia, one might say, is the ambition to go on believing in ambition. And the ambitions of the modernist novelists are exemplary, for Trotter; these novelists, and the heroes of their novels, are insistently preoccupied by the nature, if any, of their expertise, by the ironies of their ambitions. What, these writers wonder, is the ambition to be a novelist an ambition to be? What kind of symbolic capital do writers have that bankers or lawyers or psychiatrists don't? In what sense is writing a profession? Birkin, Lord Jim, Lewis's Tarr, all are men of uncertain worldly status (a character asks of Tarr in the novel, 'What sort of prizes could he expect to win by his professional talents? Would this notable arriviste be satisfied?'). They are the kind of people, one might say, who aren't properly qualified. The other characters in their novels can't ever be quite sure of their trustworthiness, of whether they are sound or fraudulent. And you often get the sense in these novels that the novelist isn't quite sure either. Hulme, one of the most strident unofficial theorists of modernism – who, as Robert Ferguson shows in telling detail, was unable to get or stay qualified or licensed in anything that mattered to him, such as philosophy or marriage – is an example of the self-assertion required by the modern man without (officially legitimated) qualities. Indeed, Hulme emerges in Ferguson's shrewd biography as uncannily like the intense, vagrant heroes of Conrad, Lawrence and Lewis. He was, Lewis wrote in *Blasting and Bombardiering*, 'a very rude and truculent man. He needed to be.' He always carried a knuckleduster, Ferguson tells us. And he was determinedly explicit about what he couldn't bear ('I believe in original sin . . . I can't stand romanticism . . . and I am a certain kind of Tory'). It was the progressivism, the perfectibility-of-man stuff, that Hulme couldn't take. Belief in original sin has always sanctioned bad behaviour, and Hulme's life sometimes seems like a series of sexual and intellectual scrapes; as though he didn't want to be better than he felt himself to be, but was quite happy to be a bit worse.

One of the most striking things about the great British and American modernist writers, other than Joyce, is the scale of their contempt. Like people in shock, there was a great deal that they found unbearable. Their scorn for the masses or democracy or women or Jews or Bloomsbury or romanticism is, at least in retrospect, staggering. Not since the Augustan satirists have fear and loathing so defined a literary moment. Suspiciousness of motives, a kind of sceptical hauteur, is everywhere in the writers Trotter deals with. 'All arguments on reasons given,' Hulme wrote, 'is absolute waste of time, for the real reason is something not given.' Just to know this, of course, singles you out, keeps you ahead of the game; but only a belief that there is such a thing as the real reason makes such insights possible. It is the paranoiac's primary project, as Trotter shows in such interesting detail, to single himself out; never to be, at least in his own eyes, merely one among many. So hatred and the provocation of hatred, which always go together, are integral to the structure of paranoid modernism. 'Paranoid symmetry,' Trotter writes, 'adjusts the degree of fantasized grandeur to the degree of fantasized persecution . . . They hate me because I am special; I am special because they hate me . . . the degree of persecution becomes the only appropriate measure of the degree of achievement.' If paranoia is the assertion, the quest for recognition of one's significant status, one will be reassured only by the most urgent forms of attention. The (modern) paranoiac invites persecution out of a fear of invisibility. To be hated makes him feel real; he has made his presence felt. To be unforgiveable is to be unforgettable. As an object of hatred one is exceptionally vivid to other people. Being memorable to others is a reminder that one exists.

There is a by now familiar before-and-after story here, a historical trauma theory. There was a time when people had a place and knew their place; and then there was a time, which we are still living in, when for various reasons they didn't. In this story, once status is no longer safely embedded in social structure – once there has been the reformation, the rise of capitalism, the French Revolution, and so on – recognition becomes the name of the game in a quite different way. More and more people have to find a place in the world instead of simply inheriting one. Prestige is up for grabs. The project of the modern, unmoored, displaced individual is to find his value in the eyes of other people, and to resent this. It is a predicament that breeds new forms of megalomania and new forms of servility. The whole notion of ambition, of what people might want for themselves, is transformed. In Trotter's view, using Bourdieu's notion of symbolic capital, and Harold Perkin's story about the 'rise of professional society', there is, in certain writers of the nineteenth and early twentieth century,

attention to the very specific problem of identity which afflicts those whose capital is symbolic through and through: those who have only their own integrity and an esoteric knowledge guaranteed by certificate to sell, rather than muscle, or the possession of land, or existing wealth.

It is Trotter's contention that the writers he discusses were acutely aware of all this because, as writers, they had a profession that wasn't one. Their capital was symbolic, but there was no available certification (Hulme, Ferguson writes, 're-mained an untrained thinker'; you could train, then, to be a thinker, but not to be a writer). There was no institution available – other than the market, which is a kind of counter-institution – to tell writers that they were the real thing. And this, of course, exposes the secular magic of being guaranteed by certificate. Once qualifications beg the question; once the value of recognition becomes the issue rather than whose recognition it is that one seeks, it is the lightness of being that has to be borne. Paranoia was the self-cure for those who couldn't bear it, for all those modern and modernist writers with substance anxiety. One is in a paranoid state of mind when one's insignificance is unthinkable.

The aesthetic consequences of this are an aversion to mimesis, and a sense of the unavailingness of institutions. 'The paranoiac wishes above all,' Trotter writes, 'and at almost any cost to be recognized for what he uniquely is, and the loss of identity which mimicry always entails is fatal to his project.' In novels such as Godwin's *Caleb Williams*, Collins's *The Woman in White* and Conrad's *Lord Jim*, Trotter shows how the protagonists and antagonists 'share the conviction that private judgement is superior to the judgements delivered by individual law'. This idealizing of private judgement, of inner superiority, was hardly conducive to a politics of consensus. What Trotter calls the 'charismatic professionalism' of the modernist writers he discusses – charisma being a magical (modern) form of self-legitimation; qualification without examination – tended towards a paranoid politics, which he wants to call, perhaps hedging his bets a little, post-liberalism.

Post-liberalism becomes a kind of preoccupation with the violence that seems to make democracy impossible. 'We still want to know,' Trotter writes, 'why radical literary experiment proved conducive to flirtations with fascism.' Part of the allure of fascism is that it satisfies contradictory impulses; it is perhaps not surprising that for writers like Lawrence and Lewis the utter anonymity of the masses and the unprecedented singularity of the leader seemed like having it both ways, having the best of all possible worlds.

In the legitimation crisis that is paranoid modernism the self exists only in its assertions of itself (performative utterance is the emblematic speech act of the unlegitimated). The paranoiac is the person who has realized that he is no different from anyone else. So his singularity – and the importance of singularity – becomes his hobby-horse (the contemporary preoccupation with finding one's voice is clearly a derivative of this). The idea of individuality may emerge at the point at which it begins to occur to people that there may be no such thing. People may be unique, but their uniqueness may be insignificant. Finding the right tone to write of, or to write off, the utter inconsequence of modern human life became the modernist project. Post-liberalism, Trotter implies, is a sense of the irrelevance of politics, of the political as an exhausted project; a doubt about the value of values. Fascism as despair about politics. Lewis and Lawrence are the heroes of Trotter's book because they were able, at least occasionally, in his view to 'own up' to their paranoia. As though they were able to see their paranoia as an option rather than a truth. And yet the paranoiac is always, by definition, the one who knows the truth. Owning up to paranoia might be like owning up to just how right one really is. Or boasting about one's vulnerability.

'Paranoid modernism,' Trotter writes, 'was markedly –

though by no means without exception – English, male and novelistic.' This could lead one to believe, and Trotter intimates as much, that the story he wants to tell about the 'crisis' of modernism was, whatever else it was, a crisis of masculinity; that it was the utter inconsequence of the inherited forms of masculinity that was preoccupying these particular writers; and not, of course, only them. Paranoia wasn't so much the modern word for sanity, it was the modern word for masculinity. *Paranoid Modernism*, as Trotter acknowledges, is a book about male writers; male writers for whom mess, disorder, luck (good and bad), accident, contingency and waste were all words descriptive of femininity. Male paranoia demands female abjection. The man who is happily nothing special – the man who feels himself to be no one in particular but is still able to desire and be desired – is the secret sharer of Trotter's paranoid modernists. Not the man without qualities, whose very qualitylessness makes him unique, but a man for whom uniqueness is no longer the point. With the invention of singularity comes the desire for anonymity. Ferguson tells us that Hulme's 'favourite injunction' to a woman was 'forget you're a personality' (the man, as usual, addressing to the woman what he can't bear to address to himself). There was more to paranoid modernism than this. But 'forget you're a personality', in its various versions, was the modernist motto. Personality has proven rather difficult to forget. Paranoiacs keep reminding us what a desperate business it is.

The Analyst and the Bribe

'What has he done, if no one can name it?'
'He has done everything.'
'Oh – everything! Everything's nothing.'

Henry James, *The Wings of the Dove*, Book Second

In her book *Lacanian Psychotherapy with Children* Catherine Mathelin describes a child analyst who had been

seen in consultation by a father who said to her, while taking out his chequebook with an expansive gesture, 'Ask any price you want. My son doesn't talk. So do whatever you want as long as you make him talk, and then let's not talk about it any more.'

This apparently absurd vignette is used by Mathelin to illustrate the way in which contemporary analysts can 'find parents handing over to them responsibility for their children's upbringing'. 'In former times,' she writes ruefully, 'patients were caught off guard at the first meeting with an analyst. Today they think they know what they are getting into.' Money, I want to suggest, is, from a psychoanalytic point of view, a way of thinking that we know what we are getting into. And, of course, a way of knowing what we are getting. We know what money is by what we think we know it can do for us.

So what, then, is absurd about the man with the cheque-book? What is so ridiculous, so patently misguided, about his flaunted chequebook? If we are amused, Freud would say, we are also somewhere troubled. There is what he calls 'the laughter of unease' – if not also 'the narcissism of minor differences' – in our reaction to the spectacle this man makes, not only of himself but also of the analyst. After all, what is it that the analyst is being supposed to know about children that can be bought? And what must this knowledge, this skill, be like if the more you pay the more you get? The man seems to have made a category mistake – treating psychoanalysis as though it were a service in which, if the analyst gets the amount of money she wants, the client/father will get more of what he wants: his son talking, and no more talking about the problem. His money will instrumentalize his wish.

It is sensible to assume that if you pay for psychoanalysis it must be like other things you pay for; and unlike things you don't pay for. The more you pay a prostitute, a car dealer, a hotel, the more you get; you don't, in the ordinary way of things, pay your friends money to get more friendship from them. What might amuse and disturb us about this man with his chequebook is that he assumes his money – 'Ask any price you want' – permits him to disregard the wishes of the analyst and, indeed, of his son. Money, he assumes, can make his wishes the wishes of everyone involved. His money is a solvent of difference: it makes whatever is taboo apparently accessible. This father at least behaves as if he knows exactly what he is getting into. And he is being staged, if not actually set up, as an example, by the analyst, to reveal something about the nature of psychoanalysis, of just what it involves. If the man with the chequebook has got it wrong, what would it be to get it right? The father said to the analyst, 'Ask any price you want. My son doesn't talk. So do whatever you want as long as you make him talk, and then let's not talk about it any more.' It is implied he should have said something like, 'I can pay your fee. My son doesn't talk. I want you to use the skills you have (by virtue of your qualification) to enable him, if possible to talk; so that we can understand our part in his symptom.' We are being told, in other words, that psychoanalysis is different from – has even, perhaps, been able to exempt itself from – most other services in the culture. And the difference, at least in this example, resides in our attitudes to and assumptions about the relationship between psychoanalysis and money.

I imagine the analyst balked at three of this father's assumptions: first that the analyst wanted as much money as possible from the father; second, that the more money she got the more successful she would be, in the father's terms; and third, that the amount of money asked for would permit her to, as the father said, 'do whatever you want as long as you make him talk'. That, in short, it was above all the father's money that the analyst wanted (that is, the father already knew, without asking, what the analyst wanted); that the amount of money invested would dictate the success of the venture (which the father also already knew: success would be the son talking, and no more talking about the son not having talked); and that it would be money alone that would free the analyst to do what she wanted (which was, in fact, to do what the father wanted). The analyst, in reporting this incident, seems to be saying: there are some things money can't buy; there are some things money can't do. These, one might say, are at once both banal and novel suggestions; as though psychoanalysis knows something (perhaps new) about money that can show us where money doesn't work. You can, to put it crudely, buy a psychoanalysis, but you cannot, in the same sense, buy something that the analyst or the patient considers to be a successful psychoanalytic treatment. You can't bribe someone to have a dream or to be cured.

If money, in this culture, seems to guarantee our expectations (if I pay this much for a car it entitles me to expect, to look forward to, certain things); that is to say, it can seem to turn us into knowing predictors of at least bits of our future. Therefore, when we pay money for something, we are making a (secular) prophecy. If the analyst is the one who is supposed to know, so too is the consumer. He may not know exactly what he's getting for his money, but he has some idea. The person who goes to see an analyst goes to get something for their suffering. And they too, from their past and from their culture, have ideas about what transforms suffering. They have what Peter Reder and Glenda Fredman call a (long) relationship to help. And they didn't, of course, begin as children by paying for what they needed. They might find themselves, as adults, paying for something akin to this earlier concern and interest. When Freud said – and we will come back to this – that the reason no adult is really satisfied by money is because money is not something that satisfies young children, is not something that children want, he was alerting us to the idea of money as a substitute-satisfaction; money as a derivative as opposed to an original (or orginary) satisfaction (as, say, being stroked, fed, caressed and cuddled are). But he was also making us wonder, from a psychoanalytic point of view, just what it might be that is added to the nature (and experience) of exchange by money.

There is the obvious question: in what sense are the original pleasures of childhood better (and in what sense are there original pleasures)? But if we don't pay our parents for their love – even though we may find ourselves paying them back for their love – what do we then make of the things we do have to actually pay for with money? In so-called growing up there is the elaboration, the sophistication, of forms of exchange; food, excrement, smiles, sounds, caresses, words and, eventually, money. The currencies multiply – both the objects exchanged and the ways of exchanging them – and then, we might feel, they narrow. When the father with the magic chequebook and the dumb son meet the psychoanalyst, at least two languages collide. For the father, money, as the measure of all things, makes all things possible. For the analyst, in this allegory, how money is assumed by this man to work is taken to be a misleading description of things, and may, indeed, be symptomatic; the father believes that it is money that talks – and that talking money is the best way of talking about talking; and his son doesn't speak. And in the example as given it is as though we are waiting to hear what the analyst might say, might reply, to all this omnipotent magical money-talk. What the father seems to want, above all, is that his money will work. It is as though he knows what he wants – that is, he has no wants of which he is unconscious in relation to his son and the analyst – and that money makes such wanting efficient. After all, if money can't, literally as it were, get his son to speak, what can?

What makes this scenario so resonant, what gives such a new twist to old clichés – every man has his price, money can't buy you love, and so on – is that it is a psychoanalyst who is being addressed and a child who is being bargained over. A son who can't or won't speak to his father. Isn't everyone struck dumb now by belief in money? Or, to put it another way: can anyone think of anything else to talk about? Are there now any alternatives, is there anything more persuasive, than the money-cult? The way in which this father uses his chequebook, like a fetishistic object, makes it very difficult for everyone, including him, to work out just what it is we are valuing when we value money. (If money talks, persuades, moves, in the way his father seems to believe, then what, the son might wonder, is the relationship between money and words, between money and desire?) The father's very insistence on money as the key to, as the prime mover in, his son's treatment both conceals his doubts about money and narrows the repertoire of what else could be of use or significance.

If money won't work, this frantic representative man seems to be saying, what will? (The father says to the son: my money will make you talk; but what if it doesn't?) What the analyst's presence in this drama of exchange and its refusal makes us wonder is whether we can recognize any more the areas of our lives in which money won't do the trick; in which the belief that money is the answer is a misrecognition of the question. The psychoanalyst is being offered up here as someone who speaks a rather different language regarding money, or another language within the current language. After all, the psychoanalyst must be in an extraordinary, extraterritorial, if not culturally privileged, position if she has something that a chequebook can't reach. It would be to misunderstand the nature of psychoanalysis to believe that if you paid your analyst more than his fee you would get a better session. And to understand why that should be so would be to say something about the nature of analysis, and of the significance of money. What the analyst has to offer is paid for; but more money doesn't buy you more of it. More money can buy you more of the analyst's time, but not more of this other thing that is being sold. The analyst, in other words, is selling something only some of which can be bought. Perhaps one of the reasons

– one of the poorer reasons – that psychoanalysis is under attack is that it is a service, a commodity, that exposes, or puts into question, our fantasies about monetary value.

The analyst is a charlatan because he can't tell you what it would be to get your money's-worth from an analysis. And that is because the phrase 'getting your money's-worth' implies an omniscience that can be part of the problem; it is a misplaced knowingness. To have got one's money's-worth can be to betray an uncertainty about how to value one's experience (what something is worth to me may be incommensurate with what it cost me in money). The father will get his money's-worth if the son speaks; but it wouldn't make sense to ask what it would be for the boy, or indeed the analyst, to get their money's-worth in this situation. The analyst, it is assumed, makes a minimal, market-based self-evaluation and establishes, with some flexibility – a minimum and a maximum charge – her fee. If the patient negotiates with the analyst about the fee, it is not assumed that the quality of the treatment is being negotiated. If the analyst works in good faith the quality of her attention and intervention will not vary according to fee (when so-called better analysts – those who are apparently more senior, more experienced, more talented, more famous – charge more money than the rest they compromise this principle). That is to say, the way psychoanalysis is managed – both arranged and practised – sets it against, or at odds with, the father waving his chequebook.

If the analyst, here, can't be bribed – not because she is so morally scrupulous but simply because more money is in some way irrelevant to the enterprise; is actually a misunderstanding of what goes on in psychoanalysis – what then is money, from a psychoanalytic point of view, such that it can be not so much resisted as rendered impotent? When it comes to psychoanalysis, the wish to pay more (or less) for what you are getting would itself be psychoanalysed; would be deemed to be symptomatic of something or other. Money is a different currency within the context, within the setting, of a psychoanalytic treatment. A psychoanalyst is someone you pay to not tell you what you will get. Not because she *won't* tell you, but because she *can't* tell you. She does not know quite what will happen when she and the so-called patient start talking and listening to each other. The patient is paying for something, but he can never know what the product will be. He pays for a means but not for an end. The analyst will reliably provide him with time, space, attention and her skill; but the net result is not definable beforehand, and may never be.

'In former times,' Mathelin wrote, 'patients were caught off guard at the first meeting with an analyst. Today they think they know what they are getting into.' They think they know what they are getting into, in her view, because there is so much psychobabble – so much spurious psychological knowingness – circulating in the culture. But also because psychoanalysis has entered, or begun to acknowledge that it is competing in, a market-place of therapies, in which people are wanting, in the homogenizing language of that market-place, to get their money's-worth. And when the analyst is asked the standard question – what will my money be buying me? – he cannot, by the lights of his own profession, answer this question simply or easily, if at all. Indeed, the psychoanalyst is one of the few people left in the culture who might interpret rather than straightforwardly answer that question. And once this traditional question is not straightforwardly answered, the patient cannot know – or cannot know very much about – what he is getting into. The use value of an analysis is indeterminate, and bears a peculiarly mystifying relationship to its exchange value.

It is not, I want to make it clear, that psychoanalysts, by virtue of their profession, are somehow more morally upright, so to speak, than any other professionals. It is just that it is at least possible to bribe, say, a judge or policeman or a politician with money; money over and above what they would ordinarily be paid. If you bribe a policeman he may be able to do something for you, to arrange something you want. But what can you bribe a psychoanalyst to do? What would more money be being exchanged for? And, obversely, if a patient (or a patient's relative, as in this case) were to attempt to bribe or just to offer more money to the analyst, the analyst would not treat it, in the ordinary way, as a bribe. She would respond quite differently than the judge or the policeman or the politician. The offer of money would be treated neither positively, that is, accepted as a bribe, or negatively, as a breach of decorum or an affront to civilization as we know it. In exchange for the offer of more money, the patient would be given an interpretation, which would also be a refusal of the money itself. The patient would find his money, and his words about his money, taken in an unexpected direction. He thought he would be able to buy more of something (other than the analyst's time, that is) or a better version of something, and what he has been given back has cost him the original price. When it comes to the ordinary bribery of everyday life, the patient will be caught off his guard; he will be getting into something that his offer of money probably hasn't prepared him for. He will find himself paying money in order, among other things, to have the meaning of his money shown to him (cash for questions). This is not usually what his money does for him; this is not how it is supposed to work.

It is, of course, hardly news that when you go to a psychoanalyst your words will not be treated at so-called face value. This is what psychoanalysts do, they interpret. And yet there is something peculiarly paradoxical both about paying for the meaning of paying for things; and about a professional practice that puts into question what, from one's own point of view, one's money entitles one to.

Perhaps it should be stated baldly, as we imagine the analyst and the son (as nominated patient) listening to the father's words – 'Ask any price you want. My son doesn't talk. So do whatever you want as long as you make him talk, and then let's not talk about it any more' – can the unconscious be bribed with money? Or, to put the question at a different angle, what are we wanting when we want money? And that means not only, of course, when we want more money, but also when we want less. Is there a part of ourselves for which money is not, indeed never can be, the currency? And is this part of ourselves, however described, progressively silenced in a culture that speaks in money, and is therefore progressively driven to distraction?

In Rome, in 1869, the young Henry James wrote to his friend Grace Norton, 'I *have* seen today one really great picture – one of those works which draw heavily on your respect, & make you feel the richer for the loss: the portrait of Innocent X by Velasquez at the Doria Palace.' James has been describing the wealth of the Vatican – 'To the Vatican I have paid of course many visits . . . Its richness & interest are even greater than I supposed' – and Rome, or rather the wealth, in both senses, of its art and its visible, suggested histories, has made him money-minded. It is as though writing in Rome, about Rome, has invested his sentences with what Melville calls, in 'Bartleby', a 'paramount consideration'. It makes James write in the language of profit and loss. 'It is,' as he says in the letter, 'poor work writing from Rome.'

It is not strange that writing about money would be, for James, a way of writing about aesthetic experience. There is what he describes as an exchange going on between himself and the sights the city has to offer. And he can't help but wonder as a young American in Europe just what is to be gained from all this accumulating history, all the artistic riches that are everywhere to be found. 'It doesn't do to stand too much alone,' he writes to Grace Norton, 'among all these swarming ghosts of the past & there can be no better antidote to their funereal contagion than a charming modern living feminine letter.' The past is also like an illness – even a plague perhaps is suggested by the 'swarming ghosts' and 'their funereal contagion' – though quite what James is fearful of catching, apart from his death, is not clear; but it is something that a 'charming modern living feminine letter' is an 'antidote to'. Not a charming modern living woman, it should be noted, but her letter, her writing. The feminine letter, he jokes, will protect him from something fatal; he feels, however whimsically, endangered in Rome; at some kind of loss. But then there is, among so many riches, the one really great picture, the Velasquez Pope. With this painting, paradoxically, James's loss of something is his gain. His lessness in front of this painting does not diminish him, but the way he puts the experience is characteristically contrived. There is, as it were, a sting (and a surprise) in the tail. It is, he writes, 'one of those works which draw heavily on your respect, & make you feel the richer for the loss'.

On the one hand, James is simply saying: this painting makes you respect it a great deal. But, on the other hand, he is also saying: this painting draws so much respect out of you – like money out of a bank account – that you have very little left (for anything else). It actually depletes you of the thing you want to give it, *and* you feel all the richer. James is saying here that he is, in a certain sense, all the richer for having spent so much respect on this painting. How, we may reasonably wonder, does this work? Perhaps respect gets in the way of the exchange, of the appreciation, of these works of art; so by drawing heavily on James's respect – like drawing out a sting – James is freer to do something else with the Velasquez, something that makes him feel richer. It might be reminiscent, for example, of what Freud writes about in 'On the Universal Tendency to Debasement in the Sphere of Love'; the way in which, for some men, having a high regard, too much respect, for a woman is counter-erotic; indeed, renders them impotent. 'As soon as the condition of debasement is fulfilled,' Freud writes, 'sensuality can be freely expressed, and important sexual capacities and a high degree of pleasure can develop.' There is no plausible evidence that this is what James is somehow describing – and a lot of inferential evidence that he would have found such a parallel unlikely – but James is saying that he is all the richer when his funds of respect are so drawn on (and therefore depleted). He spends a lot of respect on the Velasquez, and gets a greater sense of its greatness. Fore-shadowing Frost's remark that 'strongly given is kept', the more respect James is able to give, the more appreciation he gets back. He feels the richer for the loss, as he says, because he is losing something in order to gain something else. The noble word for such a transaction is sacrifice; the other word for it is a bribe. You give up something, you hand over something you value, for a greater good. It is what we have come to think of as the obvious good deal. And it is part of the deal, as it were, that it reveals to us what it is, supposedly, that we most want. If we can bear to have less of one thing, we might have more of something else. So investment is a wonderful notion because, if you are lucky and shrewd, you can have more of the thing you have less of by making the investment. James, of course, doesn't say anything as vulgar as that he has invested or even spent his respect on the painting; he just says he has drawn heavily on his respect. Where the funds come from, and what they are now doing, is omitted from the description.

I have taken this detour via James in Italy in 1869 just to point out something rather obvious; which is that money enters the verbal equation, enters the exchange – as analogy in James, or starkly in the patient's father's attempt to bribe the analyst – as a way of describing a wish to get more, licitly or illicitly. Like Viagra, money is the means to what is deemed to be the pleasure we seek (clearly in our culture more life is associated with more money). But it is of necessity – or in so far as it is a means and not an end – what Freud calls a fore-pleasure. The pleasure that is the route to the object of desire. 'You cannot give money,' John Forrester writes in *Truth Games*, 'in the gratuitous sense of giving, because money is pure exchange.' Even if you hoard it, even if it is never used, in fantasy it is buying you a future good. Money, that is to say, is something we can't help but do something with. It is the material of (and for) our most compulsive dream-work. It is our ultimate, inert transformational object: it can make us feel better. Money has become one of the best ways of describing the more that we apparently want and the lack we most apparently feel. It is instrumental in the acquiring of objects.

James gets more aesthetic pleasure by drawing on his funds of respect; as though respect like money can be successfully invested. But he will also, paradoxically, be richer for the loss of respect entailed. The analogy, James's figure of speech, is characteristically resonant; it makes one wonder about the ways in which he is wondering what is going on when he looks at this painting. He is finding ways of describing a peculiar kind of exchange that has happened to him. And he is describing not so much an intention as what feels like an effect. If anything it is as though the painting has an intention – 'one of those works which draw heavily on your respect' – as though something apparently about the picture has made him invest attention in it. Just as something in any object of desire calls something up in us; indeed, that is how one recognizes an object of desire, it draws one out (even if one's response to being so drawn out is to draw in). James, involuntarily, is drawn on by the Velasquez. The patient's father, however, is involved in a quite different kind of exchange. He invites the analyst to draw on his fund of money. He believes that by investing more money in the situation he can get a more favourable (favourable to him) result. And this is what he intends to do. But he has to make the analyst the accomplice of his intention. And, by definition, she cannot be his accomplice.

This essay is about whether the fact that you cannot bribe an analyst tells us anything new about money, and anything new about psychoanalysis. Or, to put it more modestly, it is notes towards the definition of the word 'more'. Clearly the word 'money' has a complicated and a necessary relationship with the word 'more'. Money can give us more only of certain things, while wanting to persuade us that it can give us more of everything. The analyst with whom I started – the analyst who, of necessity, refuses her patient's father's bribe – is setting a limit. The more of something the father wants to buy is not available, is not commensurate with more money. The treatment may not be available for less money, but it is not more available, more effective, for more money. So what does the analyst have to sell that more money won't buy? Given the culture that the analyst and her client – as they are sometimes called – live in, the father's bribe, and his exasperation at its refusal, are entirely understandable. Is this some kind of joke?

It is in talking about jokes that Freud talks about bribery. Although he never wrote about bribery as a topic in its own right, six of his eleven references to it appear in his *Jokes and Their Relation to the Unconscious*. The joke, which, he says, 'the major purposes and instincts of mental life employ . . . for their own ends', is itself a kind of bribe. Indeed, we are bribable, Freud believes, because we are ineluctably in search of pleasure, however self-compromising and compromised our quests for pleasure are. The joke acts as a double bribe by offering us an initial pleasure in order to allow us to experience a further pleasure that is impermissible. So, for example, jokes free us, in Freud's view, to enjoy what he (or, rather, Strachey) calls, in an odd phrase, 'our hostile aggressiveness'. 'A joke will allow us,' Freud writes,

to exploit something ridiculous in our enemy which we could not, on account of obstacles in the way, bring forward openly or consciously; once again then the joke will evade restrictions and open sources of pleasure that have become inaccessible. It will further bribe the hearer with its yield of pleasure into taking sides with us without any very close investigation, just as on other occasions we ourselves have often been bribed by an innocent joke into overestimating the substance of a statement expressed jokingly.

Jokes are the black market of pleasure. They seduce us through pleasure into taking pleasures which would be otherwise forbidden us. The paradox that Freud adds to our moral life is that the sanctioned good is never sufficiently desirable because it is not forbidden. So we have to be very clever animals in desiring what we must not have; or in pursuing what we must not be seen – by ourselves or others – to be pursuing. (We dress to hide our motives from ourselves.) The joke bribes us, in part, by saying it's only a joke, when in fact we are indulging our most transgressive desires. Without what Freud calls 'any very close investigation', we get something we are not supposed to want. The joke disarms criticism; and the implication is that what we might once have called our critical faculties, or even our minds, are by definition the enemies of the forbidden pleasures we seek, the furtive sovereign good that is our secret heart's desire.

But the important point here is that Freud begins to realize in the Jokes book that in so far as desire is forbidden we have to be bribed into taking pleasure. And the only bribery that works is pleasure itself. This 'wrapping' that the joke does, and which Freud says 'bribes our powers of criticism', is essential to Freud's picture of the way the mind works. We have to bribe ourselves, we have to be bribed into pleasure, by pleasure. Jokes, like dreams, wrap our pleasures up – wrap our desires up, as though they were presents – so we can acknowledge them without having knowledge of them. Desire is bearable only in disguise; and for disguise to be effective it has to take on the nature of a bribe. We steal our pleasure rather than take it. We dress it up; and dress for it.

For 'bribe' the *OED* has: 'ɪ. to take dishonestly; to extort. 2. to influence corruptly, by a consideration, the action of . . . 4. to gain over by some influence . . . a thing stolen, robbery, plunder.' A bribe, in short, is a way of getting what one wants despite moral principle, not because of it. What Freud refers to as 'powers of criticism' or 'close investigation'; or in other contexts as the censor, the super-ego, the conscience; all these seats of virtue and discrimination have to be lured or persuaded or seduced or cajoled into blindness or surrender or merely consent. The joke is exemplary because it appears to be that impossible thing: an innocent bribe. But if it works it gets you to abrogate your principles, to see, without seeing, that your preferences do not always accord with your standards. That the racist or the sexist joke amuses you despite yourself. That you have been tricked into a pleasure that you would rather not be having. It is only through bribery, Freud is saying, that unconscious desire and forbidden pleasures are at all possible for us. Pleasure requires permission, for Freud, from the requisite internal agencies; and because the pleasures are forbidden the permission is immoral. In Freud's view we cannot agree, we have to be bribed.

'The writer,' Freud himself writes in 'Creative Writers and Daydreaming',

softens the character of his egoistic daydreams by altering and disguising it, and he bribes us by the purely formal – that is, aesthetic – yield of pleasure which he offers us in the presentation of his fantasies. We give the name of an incentive bonus or a fore-pleasure to a yield of pleasure such as this, which is offered to us so as to make possible the release of still greater pleasure arising from deeper psychical sources. In my opinion all the aesthetic pleasure which a creative writer affords us has the character of a fore-pleasure of this kind, and our actual enjoyment of an imaginative work proceeds from a liberation of tensions in our minds . . . It may even be that not a little of this effect is due to the writer's enabling us thenceforward to enjoy our own daydreams without self-reproach or shame.

What Freud calls the 'formal', the 'aesthetic pleasure', of a piece of writing, is a bribe – what he calls tellingly 'an incentive bonus' – that is synonymous with fore-pleasure; we are deceived into a relatively shameless enjoyment of the 'still greater pleasure arising from deeper psychical sources'. But without the bribe – which in the analogy with the incentive bonus is explicitly linked to money – this greater pleasure would be neither available nor possible. Unconscious desire is that which requires a bribe in order to be gratified. The bribe is the wrapping the joke does, the bizarre representational form the dream takes, or the aesthetic form the writer uses to make known what Freud calls his egotistical daydreams. And all these things, Freud suggests, as bribes are like incentive bonuses; money given to improve performance; money as a lure.

But in what sense does money work like a joke, or indeed like the aesthetic formalism of the writer? And the answer here might be: by giving you one seemingly innocent good, it gratifies something in oneself less innocent but more desired. It is, at least in following the logic of the link Freud makes, a cover story. It offers you one thing, a banknote, a joke, a piece of writing, but it promises you another. And yet a bribe is also different from an incentive bonus because a bribe, in the words of the *OED*, corrupts you, it compromises you morally. It is more about getting away with something than getting something. It speaks of the illicit, the underhand and the unofficial. It privileges, explicitly and implicitly, desire over scruple. Whatever it conceals it makes it clear that what someone wants is more important to them than the reasons they can't or shouldn't have it. Bribery, one might say as a crude Freudian, is the financial form incestuous desire takes. You bribe somebody for something only when you know that there is a reason – which you may not know – why you shouldn't have it. Or, which perhaps comes to the same thing, when you want more of something you have already got. Enough is morally acceptable; more than enough is too much. It is the difference between being dressed and undressed.

Writing to his friend and collaborator Fleiss in 1898 Freud made a startling, albeit Freudian, point, which I referred to earlier: 'Happiness,' he wrote, 'is the belated fulfilment of a prehistoric wish. For this reason wealth brings so little happiness. Money was not a childhood wish.' Freud seems to be saying something simple here, whether or not we believe it to be true. We are only really happy when we satisfy a childhood wish. No child has ever wanted money; therefore money doesn't really satisfy adults when they acquire it. But despite the obvious interest of Freud's point here it is also as though, at this moment, Freud has either forgotten himself (or, rather, his ideas); or it is too early in his project for him to quite see what he might be saying. What always was and will be, for Freud, *the* childhood wish is the incestuous one (or ones). And because these are forbidden, the child can develop only by finding disguised alternatives or substitutes for or sublimations of these desires. Any object of desire, by virtue of being one, for Freud has an echo of the forbidden, and so links us with our losses and our most fervent anticipations. In the Freudian schema it would be easy to see money as the ideal, that is to say, the perfectly disguised or displaced incestuous object. Everybody wants as much of it as they can get, and everyone feels profoundly ambivalent about this desire. It is called greed, which is perhaps a more manageable word than violation or transgression. Everyone organizes themselves around money; its acquisition, its distribution, its repudiation. It is that which can never be ignored, either positively or negatively. And it is therefore ripe for metaphorical elaboration; without the money economy James lived in he would not have been able – like Freud – to write in those terms about his aesthetic experience. So talking about money in this quasi-Freudian romance – talking in terms of money, of profit and loss, of wealth and poverty – is the best way modern people have of talking about incest. And it may be worth noting – in this context – that it is often far easier for people to talk about their sexuality now than about their money. When people come for psychoanalysis now their resistance to talking about money, their inability to speak freely about it, is patent. It is as though when people are talking (and not talking) about money they are always talking about or gesturing towards something else. Money buys you the clothes, and gets you the life dreamed up through the clothes. Talking about money is talking about the dressing-up box.

So there is something also poignant about the father trying to bribe his son's analyst; because if we don't bother to attribute a poor motive to the father we can see that at that moment he believes there is something – something in the culture – that can get him what he wants. Money can get him what he wants, and what he might want is his son's well-being. But if money can't get us what we want – and it can get us what we want only by telling us that what we want money can buy – how can we get what we want, or even discover what that might be? Whether or not what we want is for our childhood wishes to be fulfilled – whatever those might be or whatever we construe those as being – what is unavoidably true is that infancy and childhood are where wanting starts. And it is by linking the child with money as a way of linking the child with the adult he will become, and with the adults that look after him; and by linking money with wishing, that Freud gives us something to go on from. Money seen not as a material object the child may not want (the child would surely prefer affection), but as the hard currency of wishing – money as the wish given material form – would surely be something irresistible, once it was intelligible. Money becomes the adult medium for wishing; money is good to wish with. And part of the pleasure of its acquisition is its promise of further pleasure to come (as though one could buy the body, the soulmate, one desires). Like the wish it is promising, by formulating a future it makes a future. So one of the aims of psychoanalysis might be to make wishing itself pleasurable again, rather than merely persecutory or suggestive of disappointment.

A person bribing an analyst is someone willing what cannot be willed; arranging something that cannot be arranged. The analyst clearly wants to earn her living – and may even really like money – but more money can't buy a better promise of cure. Nor, more absurdly, would the patient be more likely to get better if the analyst paid them. The patient and the analyst are assumed to want something other than, or as well as, money. The money buys the conditions for a possible cure, but not the cure itself (just as a luxurious hotel bedroom may provide the conditions for a wonderful erotic experience, but it couldn't guarantee it happening). But the initial money exchanged is like a legitimate bribe; it gives the pleasure that might make possible a further pleasure, the pleasure of alleviated suffering, of becoming more the subject (less the victimized victim) of one's own desire. The bribe of the agreed-upon fee might work, but more bribe won't make a difference. What is curbed by the analytic contract is the power of the bribe. As though the analyst says to the patient: your bribe here goes so far and no further; I will give you my time, my attention, the skill and the personal history I have, but more money, more bribery, won't get you more of these things, because these things are not like that. Money doesn't work on them, nor will it make them work (you can buy the analyst's bodily presence, but not her responsive receptivity).

Unsurprisingly perhaps, given his time and his place, Freud tends to describe attention, attraction, the influence people have over each other, as forms of investment. The pleasure-seeking self, the libidinal body, gets and spends. It manages through distribution the excesses it is heir to, transforming daunting quantities of desire into rather more reassuring pieces of meaning. In its push for language – its always ambivalent desire for the forbidden object of desire – the pleasure-seeking person Freud describes courts and confounds his own intelligibility. And like James in Rome, like a father with a chequebook, he is fabulously impressed – informed and overawed – by fantasies of wealth; by what money can be used to do and say, by the language of accumulation and purchase. But also, paradoxically, we use money as a way of talking about what can't be bought. More of the analyst's skill or more of the father's wishes cannot be bought with more money; the riches of Rome, the Velasquez, cannot be bought, and it is not exactly acquisition of a material object that James is after. And children don't buy their parents, and can't buy their parents' love. Using money as linguistic currency shows us what is unlike money (just as speaking about clothes is a way of endlessly rediscovering what our bodies are not like). We keep coming up against where the analogy breaks down, and are continually caught out. More money will not buy us more love (which makes us wonder what love or desire might be like if they can't be bought). I may describe my attention as invested, but the consequences of my investment are unpredictable in ways in which my financial investments are not (I may be uncertain what is profit and what is loss). My so-called dream-work rewards me with a dream, whether or not the dream is rewarding to the person I think of as myself.

Perhaps it is necessary – or at least useful – to have a group of people in a culture who, by virtue of their profession, but not of their moral rectitude, are not fashion victims. The psychoanalyst, like everyone else in the culture, can be bribed by pleasure; indeed, in Freud's terms, has to be bribed in order to get pleasure. But the psychoanalyst cannot be bribed with money. She cannot help practising something that more money cannot buy more of. But, of course, in a culture bewitched by the language of money she finds it very difficult to describe what she does. People tend, that is to say, to be suspicious about her motives.

Two Talks on Needing to Know When It's Over

I About Time

A complete mastery of existence achieved at one moment
gives no warrant that it will be sustained or achieved
again at the next.

George Santayana, *Reason in Art*

Psychoanalysis has always been about time, and what it is about time that matters to us. There is the more or less scientific time that development takes, and the more or less conjectural timelessness of the unconscious; there is the insistence of the repetition compulsion that is nominally beyond the pleasure principle; and there is the recurring question of when the pleasure will start and when the pain will stop. When André Green asks in his *Time in Psychoanalysis*, with its spaced-out subtitle, *Some Contradictory Aspects*, 'Was there ever a point in Freud's work when he was not concerned by the subject of time?' he makes us wonder how, from a psychoanalytic point of view, it would be possible not to be so concerned. We think because we are subject to time. But it is our subjection to time that psychoanalysis prefers to describe; the time we are given tends to be privileged over the time we make. So when psychoanalysts talk about the length of treatment, or indeed the timing of interpretations, they are caught between the determinisms they must abide by and the choices they think they can make. To believe in good (and bad) timing is either to depend upon luck, which is the kind of dependence that dare not speak its name, or it is to assume a knowledge of how time works, which tends to be the talent of a god. To write about timing in psychoanalysis is to write about omniscience. It is not accidental that the length of sessions and the length of treatments have been such contentious issues in the psychotherapies. There is the timelessness (or otherwise) of unconscious desire, and the timeliness of development. Everything depends upon why we take sides, or how we become double agents, paid on both sides.

All therapies are time-limited, but some therapies some people assume they can set a time to. Or they know how much time should be set aside to do them properly (talking about the time therapy takes is always a coded way of talking about competence, about fantasies of rigour). And all therapies are brief from an evolutionary point of view, and far too long from a financial one. But to get huffy about brief therapy, like getting huffy about long-term therapy, is to assume a knowledge of – or at least to make a case for – what people really need (and how it should be provided). It is also to assume that what people really need can be generalized, both the needs and the people. Everyone agrees that (modern) people have needs, and that needs take time. But not everyone agrees, nor are they ever going to, about what those needs are or about how we should time them. Because we all tell the time in the same way, because time is standardized, we sometimes think that timing can be too. Time is of the essence, but no one can agree what it is the essence of.

Romantics believe that time should have its way with us; that we need to stop managing our affairs, which are affairs of the heart, in order to live the best lives we are capable of. That we should stop anxiously measuring things – body parts, feelings, money, and so on – and entrust ourselves to the music (and the noise) of what happens. Therapists sometimes call this, in quasi-scientific jargon (that is, mystification), following or allowing the process. For the romantic there is actually no process, only the patterns we give, the descriptions we use, for the logics we find, for what's happening. For the romantic our lives have their own unfolding logics, whether or not we can discern them. Time is not ours, any more than the breath we breathe is ours.

Pragmatists believe that we have problems to solve, and that we need to get on. For the pragmatist a life is a series of tasks – call them developmental tasks or existential projects – and they need to be at least acknowledged if not actually met. Indeed, from the pragmatist's point of view we are suffering from failed tasks (from the romantic's point of view we are suffering from the idea that life is something that we can succeed or fail at). Because there are things in life that must be done – learning to talk, leaving home, having sex, etc. – pragmatists are people who are running out of time. And this, for them, is the thing about time: it doesn't last for ever (for the romantics time is the kind of thing that can't be quantified, so it can't run out or run on; we always have the same amount of it, but it doesn't actually come in amounts). Because time is always running out for pragmatists they are always a bit frantic; they fear doing things called wasting their lives or not using their time well (or properly). For the romantic time is for whatever happens to happen in it. It is a medium not an instrument. For them the idea of using their time makes about as much sense as the idea of using their love or of using their capacity for friendship. Time, for them, can be neither money nor achievement; 'it' is like something else. If we wanted to put this distinction in psychoanalytic language we might say that time, for the romantic, is not something with which they have a sadomasochistic relationship. For them, words like 'use', 'submission' or 'properly' don't make sense in relation to time.

Put like this it might seem as though the brief therapist is an out-and-out pragmatist; but whether one is a romantic or a pragmatist does not entirely depend upon one's sense of time. It is more to do with the presuppositions one works with, or against; and more exactly with one's unconscious presuppositions (it is the difference between explicitly believing something, and living as if something is true). The professional propaganda about time is all pragmatic – as I am using the term – in intent. One way or another it prescribes the best use of the therapist's and the so-called patient's time. It works with developmental, biological or sociobiological schedules, and/or more or less cognitive problem-acknowledging and problem-solving strategies. Whether or not it talks of the timing of interpretations, or the appropriateness or otherwise of therapeutic interventions, something is being practised that can supposedly be taught. And it can be taught because it is so much of a piece with the prevailing economic climate in which, as the sociologist Pierre Bourdieu writes in *Acts of Resistance*, 'A whole set of presuppositions is being imposed as self-evident: it is taken for granted that maximum growth, and therefore productivity and competitiveness, are the ultimate and sole goal of human actions; or that economic forces cannot be resisted.' It is not difficult to see the various aims of the various psychotherapies as being versions of, or cover stories for, maximum growth, productivity and competitiveness. This, we are being persuaded to believe, is what time is for. This is the best use of our time.

To be pragmatic in this way both the therapist and the so-called patient must know what they want; and then the question becomes: how, if at all, can I be or have what I want? For the romantic therapist knowing what one wants is the problem masquerading as the solution. All therapy trainings teach people what people supposedly want – to resolve their Oedipus complexes, to achieve the depressive position, to bear dependence, to play, and so on. For the romantic therapist this runs the risk of training people how to have different versions of the same problem. And this is where time comes in. The romantic therapist starts from the assumption that time is not the sort of thing that can be exploited (and this in itself sets time apart from virtually everything else in the culture). So the time given or set aside for something is not necessarily commensurate with its value (good things happen quickly, over long periods of time, and not at all). Are the ego, the super-ego and the id assumed to be working according to Greenwich Mean Time? Do good and bad objects – not to mention our so-called cognitive faculties – work chrono-metrically? Clearly we know how long some things take; but unfortunately these are not the things people come to therapy for (we have only to wonder how long it takes to grow up or how quick is sexual desire to see the absurdity of these summings-up). The romantic therapist doesn't know how long the kind of things people come to therapy for will take; and not because she hasn't learned, but because such things could never be learned. So she could never be for or against short-term therapies or for or against long-term therapies. She would just assume that different therapists prefer to spend different amounts of time with the people they see; and that they do so for reasons of which they are mostly unconscious (though they will sometimes be more than capable of giving theoretical justifications for their preferences, which often involve pathologizing the alternatives). What happens in a therapy always has more to do with the therapist's past than with the patient's. In brief, the romantic therapist works (or, rather, lives) as if time guarantees nothing. Which doesn't mean she can't use the tradition, the experience, of practitioners before her; it just means that the tradition is no more and no less than lots of people's impressions about the relationship between time and timing. The time of one's life is not a calculation.

Brief therapy is no better or worse than longer-term therapy, it is just shorter; there is no superordinate point of view from which they can be compared. Indeed, once we stop thinking about how much time to allot to things, how much time is the right time, we could start thinking about what else we can give to the things that matter to us, and let the time take care of itself.

II Making Ends Meet

. . . courting a dead end but discovering how not to die.

Hugh Kenner, *The Stoic Comedians*

Nietzsche famously said that every man was an artist in his dreams; but every person of course, as Nietzsche knew, is an unusual kind of artist in their dreams, at once exemplary and anomalous. The dreamer, in his shadiness, in the obscurity of his identity, and the enigma of his very real gifts and talents, both reinforces and waylays our post-romantic assumptions about the so-called artist. The dreamer is unusally solitary, absent even from himself; the audience for his dream, apart from the dreamer himself, who has no choice in the matter, is undeclared; and the dreamer, perhaps above all in terms of this essay, has an unusual sense of what was once called form. In one sense there is nothing less strange to us now – after romanticism, after Freud, after surrealism – than the strangeness of our dreams; that we see them but without looking, with our eyes closed; that they exist and have their being only in our so-called shared world through our reports of them, which can only ever be reconstructions, impressions in language; that we can never predict the evening before what they will be; that they can be at once so vivid and so difficult to remember and hold on to; that more often than not they are surprising or enigmatic in content but fail to make obvious sense (and of course there is nothing more misleading, more defensive, in Freud's view, than the obvious sense they might seem to make). And some of us believe that dreams, like valuable art works, can be meaningful, indeed unique, sources of meaning and evocation; that they are subject to interpretation of a peculiarly illuminating kind. Dreams seem to speak to us even when, or especially when, we are most confounded by them. The dream, as though the dreamer were a character in a novel – which is actually what I think he is for Freud – says unusual things; and people who write about dreams use them to say their own unusual things, on the dream's behalf, as it were. Dreams may be peculiar, but they license in their interpretations the saying of more and more peculiar things. *The Interpretation of Dreams* might be thought of as *The Confessions of a Dreamer*, or as an interpretation of a character called the Dreamer.

And the Dreamer, at least in Freud's version – and as Nietzsche himself intimates – has his own unique dream-work, his own artistic tricks and devices, what Freud calls his considerations of representability; of how the forbidden wish can be depicted without too much disturbance. Following on in this tradition, Freud's theory of dreams was referred to by the literary critic Lionel Trilling as a theory of poetry, of tropes. The dreamer, as Freud described him or her – and we have to imagine the dreamer paradoxically, if we can imagine her at all, as a figure known only by her product (she has no biography other than the biography of the person whose dreamer she is – is a kind of artist. But we have to reconstruct her skills; we can never see her at work; she will never tell us how she does what she does, or what she is in fact doing. The dreamer, we want to believe, is less opaque, more intelligible, than her dream. So some of us might treat Freud or Jung or whoever as though they can really speak on the dreamer's behalf, as though they were conversant with mysteries rather than just saying and writing whatever dreams make them think of. The dream interpreter, in other words, is a double agent; at once a dreamer and au fait with the dream-work. Of Freud's three great characters, the Dreamer, the Joker and the Sexual Quester, the Dreamer is by far the most obscure even if she is of a piece, perhaps even of the same mind, as the other two.

The dreamer is a very unusual kind of artist in what have become more or less obvious ways. And yet perhaps the most unusual thing about the dreamer as artist is the thing that is less frequently remarked upon; and that is that the dreamer seems to be an artist without a sense of an ending. Not only is she someone who has to re-create in a verbal medium something that exists in a visual medium; but she also has to be a teller, a narrator, who can never be sure whether she has got the whole story; or indeed how much of it she has got. Dreams end either when we wake up or when we find we have no more to say. But we are never quite sure whether the dream has ended (bits can come back to us later, or later in the actual telling). The dreamer, the fictive presence who made the dream, who did the dream-work, may have a sense of an ending (prior to waking up) but we cannot be sure that we, the wide-awake narrator, can discern it. The dream narrator, unlike the dreamer perhaps, is an artist whose work has an indeterminate, an indefinite end. The dreamer, although we can never know this, may or may not have a sense of an ending for his dream; but the narrator of the dream – the dreamer's accomplice or alter-ego or side-kick – can never be quite sure; can never really know whether he has got the ending of his story of the dream right. It is certainly true to say that very few dreams end with the kind of conclusion, the kind of artfulness, we associate with either more traditional nineteenth-century fiction or indeed with more experimental or avant-garde contemporary fiction. We associate the end of the telling of the dream with a forgetfulness or an apparently abrupt arbitrariness. We either say 'and that was the end of the dream'; or we simply can't recall any more; but either way we are reliant on our memory for the ending. The end of a dream can only be remembered. As readers of fiction we are more than capable of not remembering endings. But we do not expect writers of fiction to say that they cannot remember the ending of the fiction they are making. Very few novels or short stories, if any, break off at the point at which the author says words to the effect of 'that's all I can remember' or 'and then it ended'. We ask of the fiction writer that he works out an ending; we ask of the dream reporter that they tell us what they can of their dream. We can have quite literally no idea where the dream ends – or perhaps begins; we can have a formal sense of where a written or a spoken fiction ends. There are, at their most minimal, conventions to indicate the end. So what is the significance of the fictions that are reported dreams not exactly ending? Or, perhaps more interestingly, what is the significance for fiction of there being fictions that have no sure way of ending?

In Frank Kermode's Epilogue to *The Sense of an Ending* – the newest ending of the book so far – he says, reiterating some of his previous arguments:

. . . to make sense of our lives from where we are, as it were, stranded in the middle, we need fictions of beginnings and fictions of ends, fictions which unite beginning and end and endow the interval between them with meaning. I called these 'concord fictions', taking them to be like the plots of novels, which often end with an appearance of concord or, in modern fiction a denial of it.

We might also think of ourselves as stranded in the middle of dreaming (in an early version of his new translation of *The Interpretation of Dreams* Jim Underwood used the singular 'dream' rather than 'dreams' to convey a sense of a continuous medium out of which we pick out objects we call dreams). In the middle of dreaming we need fictions of beginnings and ends in so far as we have to start somewhere when we tell our dreams and, at a certain point, we will have to stop; usually when the recollection runs out. Kermode stresses in his book just how much we 'may call books fictive models of the temporal world' depending on their endings, on the always already known fact that they will end; which is itself concordant with the knowledge – if it can be called that – that we ourselves will, however we construe it, end. The books that 'continue to interest us', Kermode writes, 'move through time to an end, an end we must sense even if we cannot know it'. We may speculate about what happens to the unhappy couple after the end of *Portrait of a Lady*, about whether Darcy and Elizabeth will go on enjoying each other's company, but we know, in James's words from the Preface to *Roderick Hudson*, that 'Really, universally, relations stop nowhere, and the exquisite problem of the artist is eternally to draw, by a geometry of his own, the circle in which they shall happily appear to do so.' However provisional, however fanciful, however arbitrary a sense of an ending, a boundary, a limit, is drawn; our ends are part of our means. Even the teller of dreams stops somewhere; the dream-teller, unlike the dreamer himself, draws 'by a geometry of his own' the circle within which his dream will appear.

But then Freud, as psychoanalyst – as interpreter – will invite the dream-teller, who is assumed not to be identical to the dreamer, to extend the circle; to, as Freud would say, associate to the elements of the dream. And what this method reveals to Freud is that the dream is inexhaustible. It is as if the story of the dream only seemed to have finished; once the patient starts associating to it, it starts up again, revealing an indeterminate number of constitutive dream-thoughts. 'There is often a passage,' Freud writes in *The Interpretation of Dreams*,

in even the most thoroughly interpreted dream which has to be left obscure; this is because we become aware during the work of interpretation that at that point there is a tangle of dream-thoughts which cannot be unravelled and moreover which adds nothing to our knowledge of the content of the dream. This is the dream's navel, the spot where it reaches down into the unknown. The dream-thoughts to which we are led by interpretation cannot, from the nature of things, have any definite endings; they are bound to branch out in every direction into the intricate network of our world of thought.

It is as though the dream interpreter and the willingly free-associating patient are people who don't want the dream to end; just as some literary critics are the people who don't want the books they have read to end. Their reading is protracted by writing. What Freud introduces here is that the dream thoughts that make up the dream 'cannot, from the nature of things, have any definite endings'. Freud is saying here with a certain rhetorical insistence – he doesn't in fact know what the nature of things is – that it is integral to the dream that it has no definite ending. He is not saying, as a vaguely experimental writer might, that he can provide you with multiple endings; he is saying that a dream is a telling that can have no definitive ending. When it comes to the telling of dreams, at least, this is a narrative satisfaction that we have to renounce. The only sense of an ending we can have about a dream is that we can have no sense of it.

In a certain sense, at least from Freud's point of view, we are always in the middle of a dream. As in the actuality of lived life, we are unaware of the beginning and uncertain of the end. Why, we might wonder, are uncompleted novels more often than not published if the (always distinguished) writer has died just before finishing them? Or, to put it the other way round, is a worked-on and worked-out ending so essential to our satisfaction? Poems, as Valéry said, may never be finished but only abandoned; but if they are abandoned with too little finish we think of them as failed poems. Our paradigm, clearly, is of the completed – that is, the completable – process; a beginning, a middle and an end. Without the end there is nothing we can intelligibly call a beginning or a middle. If you give up on endings you lose heart about a lot of other things too. Frustration is what we feel when a wished-for process is not brought to conclusion; a sense of an ending is a sense of the possibility of satisfaction. What we want to end is the suffering, the frustration, the suspense, the not knowing how it ends. It is as though it would be against nature, or at least against physiology, to propose the abandonment of endings. We would rather discuss bad endings than not have them at all.

Fictions about incompletion – about what is now called, academically, closure or lack – are legion; but uncompleted fictions about incompletion, novels that stop but in no way end, do not seem to be wanted. We want to believe in fictions of process; we want to believe that it is possible to be too young to die; that people have potential; that there is a difference – that we can know the difference – between a good and a bad ending. Literature, unlike dreams, reassures us that we can believe in such concordances and that we can believe in denying or suspecting them. We can at least see the end of the poem on the page, if we cannot see the end of its effect on us. Indefinite endings, of which there are in actuality so many, are not so much to our taste. In literature, at least, formlessness always has its forms. An ending, if nothing else, can be expected, can be looked forward to.

So it was always going to be interesting when a novelist who one way or another is going to have to complete his novel is preoccupied within the novel itself with endings. In the same way perhaps that we have familiarized dreams, many people are inured or just mildly amused by the self-consciousness of many contemporary novels, by their need to draw attention to what Kermode calls 'the dissonances between fiction and reality'. Certain modern novels want to at once spellbind us and make us think about spells, to suspend belief and wonder what belief must be like if we can do this. In 1871 Dostoevsky published a novel called *The Devils* which is about believers – revolutionary activists – who, as revolutionaries, have an end in sight. The novel has a traditional Dostoevskyan plot, all over the place but with a propulsive demonic energy, which ends with the suicide of the enigmatic hero, Stavrogin. It would be glib to say that *The Devils*, like all novels, has a self-inflicted end; but it is true that in this novel Dostoevsky is more than ever exercised by endings. Indeed, if one was to put it schematically, one could say that the novel works itself out around two possibly contradictory basic assumptions. The first one is that there is no such thing as an ending; and the second one is that a commitment to endings – a belief in them – makes people callous and cruel. Like Freud when he writes about dreams and their indefinite endings, it is as if Dostoevsky wants to alert us – and himself – to what we might do in the name of endings; to what the sense of an ending can make us do (murder someone, say, for the sake of the revolution). What would a novel be like – a fiction which, in Kermode's term, has not degenerated into a myth – that was not tyrannized by the necessity of its forthcoming end? How would we read a novel we knew to be without an ending? What would our relationship to our dreams be if we acknowledged that we could only ever come to provisional conclusions about them?

In *The Devils* the scurrilous young revolutionary Pyotr Stepanovich returns to meet his father, Stepan, a member of the old and now seemingly redundant intelligentsia. He is greatly disturbed by his son's principled lack of principle and tells the novel's narrator about the meeting:

'Cher,' he suddenly concluded, rising quickly, 'do you know that this will most certainly end with something?'

'That it will,' I said.

'Vous ne comprenez pas. Passons. But . . . in this world things usually end with nothing, but here there will be an end, most certainly, most certainly.'

A little later in the novel there is a conversation between Stavrogin and his secret lover, Darya Pavlovna, about their affair and his mother Varvara's suspicions about it:

'I myself thought we should break it off,' Darya said. 'Varvara Petrovna is too suspicious of our relations.'

'Well, let her be.'

'No, she shouldn't worry. And so, that's it now, until the end?'

'You're still so certainly expecting an end?'

'Yes I'm sure of it.'

'Nothing in the world ever ends.'

'Here there will be an end . . .'

'And what sort of end will it be?'

'You're not wounded and haven't shed blood?' she asked without answering his question about the end.

When the writer in the novel, Karmazinov, ends his writing career with a final public recitation the narrator remarks wryly that 'of course, the end was none too good, but the bad thing was that everything started with it'. What Stavrogin and Stepan – who was once Karmazinov's tutor – share is a disturbance in their sense of an ending. They have to start thinking about it. They are being urged, by themselves and others, to believe in endings, to take endings seriously; or, rather, to take seriously the fact that other people believe in endings, and that they themselves will be endangered if they ignore this. They are under pressure from other people's sense of an ending. It is as though their freedom has resided in believing that 'in this world things usually end with nothing'; or, which is not quite the same thing, that 'nothing in the world ever ends'; or, as the narrator suggests, everything starts with the end. There are now people around – as there are in our contemporary political reality – who are saying endings are absolute; not provisional or tentative or fictive or illusory, but terminal. Stavrogin and Stepan – who both die by the end of the novel – are beginning to realize in the new world order that if you do not create your own sense of an ending you will be enslaved by another man's.

The characters who are not hardened revolutionaries in *The Devils* all play hide and seek with the idea of endings. They ignore them, they deny their existence, they trivialize them, and they are compelled to take them with the grimmest seriousness. 'Nations are formed,' the idealist Shatov says, 'and moved by another ruling and dominating force, whose origin is unknown and inexplicable. This force is the force of an unquenchable desire to get to the end, while at the same time denying the end.' 'Ladies and Gentlemen,' Karmazinov declares as he bows out of his writing career, 'I have ended. I omit the ending and I withdraw. But permit me to read just six concluding lines.' The question for Dostoevsky's characters is, what would it be to live without a sense of an ending? Not denying the ending – which supposes a prior acknowledgement; nor evading the ending – which supposes its prior existence; nor ironizing endings – which implies just how daunting they must be. But living as if a sense of an ending was no longer pertinent. Only in fiction, as Kermode intimates in his great book, can we experiment with our sense of endings, can we work out in which areas of our lives a sense of an ending does us good; and this partly because when we finish the book – if it is a good one – it will not have ended. And neither will we. We can at least read to no foreseeable end.

Acknowledgements

'The Master-Mind Lectures' was given as a lecture on Freud in the Master-Mind series at the British Academy and published in a slightly revised form in the *London Review of Books*. 'Talking Nonsense and Knowing When to Stop' was given as the Madeleine Davis Memorial Lecture at the Squiggle Foundation in London. 'Making the Case' was given as a talk on a panel at the Modern Languages Association in New York, organized by Stephen Greenblat, and subsequently published in revised form in *Raritan*. 'Doing It Alone' was published as 'Desiring by Myself' in *Raritan*. 'For the Family' was published in *Threepenny Review*. 'On Not Making It Up' was given as one in the series of Wolfson Lectures at Oxford entitled 'The Varieties of Creative Experience' and was published in *Salmagundi*. Both 'Time Pieces' were published in *Threepenny Review*. 'The Dream Horizon' was written for a conference on Dream Writing at the University of Kent and given in a slightly different version as the Freud Lecture at the University of Essex. 'The Forgetting Museum' was published in *Index on Censorship*. 'Learning to Live' was published as 'Psychoanalysis as Education' in *Psychoanalytic Enquiry*. 'Nuisance Value' was given at the Crash Conference at the University of Cambridge and published in *Threepenny Review*. 'Waiting for Returns' was given as a lecture to the English Department at the University of York and at a conference on Modernism at the University of Birmingham and was published in *Salmagundi*. The first of the 'Two Lectures on Expectations' was given as the Freud

Lecture at Yale and both were given as the Patten Lectures at the University of Indiana. 'Paranoid Moderns' was published in the *London Review of Books*. 'Making Ends Meet' was given as a talk at PEN, London. The rest of the pieces are previously unpublished.

I am very grateful, as ever, to my editors – Mary-Kay Wilmers at the *London Review of Books*, Wendy Lesser at *Threepenny Review*, Jackson Lears and Stephanie Volmer at *Raritan* and Robert Boyers at *Salmagundi* – who have done so much to support my work. Linda Charnes made my giving of the Patten Lectures both possible and a pleasure.

Judith Clark read everything in this book first, which has made all the difference to me. Conversations with Lisa Appignanesi, John Forrester, John Gray, Stephen Greenblat, Hugh Haughton and Joyce Lindenbaum have contributed more to this book than they may have realized. This book is dedicated to two people who for nearly thirty years have been more than colleagues and always friends, and on whom I have depended.